Interactions 1

GRAMMAR

Elaine Kirn
Darcy Jack

D1536422

McGraw Hill

Interactions 1 Grammar, Silver Edition

Published by McGraw-Hill ESL/ELT, a business unit of The McGraw-Hill Companies, Inc. 1221 Avenue of the Americas, New York, NY 10020. Copyright © 2007 by The McGraw-Hill Companies, Inc. All rights reserved. No part of this publication may be reproduced or distributed in any form or by any means, or stored in a database or retrieval system, without the prior written consent of The McGraw-Hill Companies, Inc., including, but not limited to, in any network or other electronic storage or transmission, or broadcast for distance learning.

ISBN 13: 978-0-07-340640-4
ISBN 10: 0-07-340640-6
1 2 3 4 5 6 7 8 9 10 VNH 11 10 09 08 07 06

Editorial director: Erik Gundersen
Series editor: Valerie Kelemen
Developmental editor: Susannah Mackay, Angela Castro
Production manager: Juanita Thompson
Production coordinator: Lakshmi Balasubramanian
Cover designer: Robin Locke Monda
Interior designer: Nesbitt Graphics, Inc.
Photo researcher: Photoquick Research

The credits section for this book begins on page 325 and is considered an extension of the copyright page.

Cover photo: Steve Allen/Creatasimages

The McGraw-Hill Companies

A Special Thank You

The Interactions/Mosaic Silver Edition team wishes to thank our extended team: teachers, students, administrators, and teacher trainers, all of whom contributed invaluably to the making of this edition.

Macarena Aguilar, **North Harris College**, Houston, Texas ■ Mohamad Al-Alam, **Imam Mohammad University**, Riyadh, Saudi Arabia ■ Faisal M. Al Mohanna Abaalkhail, **King Saud University**, Riyadh, Saudi Arabia; Amal Al-Toaimy, **Women's College, Prince Sultan University**, Riyadh, Saudi Arabia ■ Douglas Arroliga, **Ave Maria University**, Managua, Nicaragua ■ Fairlie Atkinson, **Sungkyunkwan University**, Seoul, Korea ■ Jose R. Bahamonde, **Miami-Dade Community College**, Miami, Florida ■ John Ball, **Universidad de las Americas**, Mexico City, Mexico ■ Steven Bell, **Universidad la Salle**, Mexico City, Mexico ■ Damian Benstead, **Sungkyunkwan University**, Seoul, Korea ■ Paul Cameron, **National Chengchi University**, Taipei, Taiwan R.O.C. ■ Sun Chang, **Soongsil University**, Seoul, Korea ■ Grace Chao, **Soochow University**, Taipei, Taiwan R.O.C. ■ Chien Ping Chen, **Hua Fan University**, Taipei, Taiwan R.O.C. ■ Selma Chen, **Chihlee Institute of Technology**, Taipei, Taiwan R.O.C. ■ Sylvia Chiu, **Soochow University**, Taipei, Taiwan R.O.C. ■ Mary Colonna, **Columbia University**, New York, New York ■ Lee Culver, **Miami-Dade Community College,** Miami, Florida ■ Joy Durighello, **City College of San Francisco**, San Francisco, California ■ Isabel Del Valle, **ULATINA**, San Jose, Costa Rica ■ Linda Emerson, **Sogang University**, Seoul, Korea ■ Esther Entin, **Miami-Dade Community College**, Miami, Florida ■ Glenn Farrier, **Gakushuin Women's College**, Tokyo, Japan ■ Su Wei Feng, Taipei, Taiwan R.O.C. ■ Judith Garcia, **Miami-Dade Community College**, Miami, Florida ■ Maxine Gillway, **United Arab Emirates University**, Al Ain, United Arab Emirates ■ Colin Gullberg, **Soochow University**, Taipei, Taiwan R.O.C. ■ Natasha Haugnes, **Academy of Art University**, San Francisco, California ■ Barbara Hockman, **City College of San Francisco**, San Francisco, California ■ Jinyoung Hong, **Sogang University**, Seoul, Korea ■ Sherry Hsieh, **Christ's College**, Taipei, Taiwan R.O.C. ■ Yu-shen Hsu, **Soochow University**, Taipei, Taiwan R.O.C. ■ Cheung Kai-Chong, **Shih-Shin University**, Taipei, Taiwan R.O.C. ■ Leslie Kanberg, **City College of San Francisco**, San Francisco, California ■ Gregory Keech, **City College of San Francisco**, San Francisco, California ■ Susan Kelly, **Sogang University**, Seoul, Korea ■ Myoungsuk Kim, **Soongsil University**, Seoul, Korea ■ Youngsuk Kim, **Soongsil University**, Seoul, Korea ■ Roy Langdon, **Sungkyunkwan University**, Seoul, Korea ■ Rocio Lara, **University of Costa Rica**, San Jose, Costa Rica ■ Insung Lee, **Soongsil University**, Seoul, Korea ■ Andy Leung, **National Tsing Hua University**, Taipei, Taiwan R.O.C. ■ Elisa Li Chan, **University of Costa Rica**, San Jose, Costa Rica ■ Elizabeth Lorenzo, **Universidad Internacional de las Americas**, San Jose, Costa Rica ■

Cheryl Magnant, **Sungkyunkwan University**, Seoul, Korea ■ Narciso Maldonado Iuit, **Escuela Tecnica Electricista**, Mexico City, Mexico ■ Shaun Manning, **Hankuk University of Foreign Studies**, Seoul, Korea ■ Yoshiko Matsubayashi, **Tokyo International University**, Saitama, Japan ■ Scott Miles, **Sogang University**, Seoul, Korea ■ William Mooney, **Chinese Culture University**, Taipei, Taiwan R.O.C. ■ Jeff Moore, **Sungkyunkwan University**, Seoul, Korea ■ Mavelin de Moreno, **Lehnsen Roosevelt School**, Guatemala City, Guatemala ■ Ahmed Motala, **University of Sharjah**, Sharjah, United Arab Emirates ■ Carlos Navarro, **University of Costa Rica**, San Jose, Costa Rica ■ Dan Neal, **Chih Chien University**, Taipei, Taiwan R.O.C. ■ Margarita Novo, **University of Costa Rica**, San Jose, Costa Rica ■ Karen O'Neill, **San Jose State University**, San Jose, California ■ Linda O'Roke, **City College of San Francisco**, San Francisco, California ■ Martha Padilla, **Colegio de Bachilleres de Sinaloa,** Culiacan, Mexico ■ Allen Quesada, **University of Costa Rica**, San Jose, Costa Rica ■ Jim Rogge, **Broward Community College**, Ft. Lauderdale, Florida ■ Marge Ryder, **City College of San Francisco**, San Francisco, California ■ Gerardo Salas, **University of Costa Rica**, San Jose, Costa Rica ■ Shigeo Sato, **Tamagawa University**, Tokyo, Japan ■ Lynn Schneider, **City College of San Francisco**, San Francisco, California ■ Devan Scoble, **Sungkyunkwan University**, Seoul, Korea ■ Maryjane Scott, **Soongsil University**, Seoul, Korea ■ Ghaida Shaban, **Makassed Philanthropic School**, Beirut, Lebanon ■ Maha Shalok, **Makassed Philanthropic School**, Beirut, Lebanon ■ John Shannon, **University of Sharjah**, Sharjah, United Arab Emirates ■ Elsa Sheng, **National Technology College of Taipei**, Taipei, Taiwan R.O.C. ■ Ye-Wei Sheng, **National Taipei College of Business**, Taipei, Taiwan R.O.C. ■ Emilia Sobaja, **University of Costa Rica**, San Jose, Costa Rica ■ You-Souk Yoon, **Sungkyunkwan University**, Seoul, Korea ■ Shanda Stromfield, **San Jose State University**, San Jose, California ■ Richard Swingle, **Kansai Gaidai College**, Osaka, Japan ■ Carol Sung, **Christ's College**, Taipei, Taiwan R.O.C. ■ Jeng-Yih Tim Hsu, **National Kaohsiung First University of Science and Technology**, Kaohsiung, Taiwan R.O.C. ■ Shinichiro Torikai, **Rikkyo University**, Tokyo, Japan ■ Sungsoon Wang, **Sogang University**, Seoul, Korea ■ Kathleen Wolf, **City College of San Francisco**, San Francisco, California ■ Sean Wray, **Waseda University International**, Tokyo, Japan ■ Belinda Yanda, **Academy of Art University**, San Francisco, California ■ Su Huei Yang, **National Taipei College of Business**, Taipei, Taiwan R.O.C. ■ Tzu Yun Yu, **Chungyu Institute of Technology**, Taipei, Taiwan R.O.C.

Table of Contents

Chapter 1   Academic Life Around the World   2

BE; THE SIMPLE PRESENT TENSE; PRONOUNS AND ADJECTIVES

Chapter 2   Experiencing Nature   32

THERE IS / THERE ARE; POSSESSIVE NOUNS; THE PRESENT
CONTINUOUS TENSE; AND MODALS

Chapter **3** Living to Eat or Eating to Live? 62

QUANTITY; COMPARISONS AND MODAL VERBS

Chapter **4** In the Community 92

THE FUTURE; MORE ABOUT VERBS, PREPOSITIONS, AND ARTICLES

Chapter 5 Home   132

THE PAST TENSE; CONNECTING WORDS

Chapter 6 Cultures of the World   160

THE PRESENT PERFECT TENSE; SUPERLATIVES AND OTHER COMPARATIVES

Chapter 7 Health 194

KINDS OF VERBS, PRONOUNS, PHRASES, AND CLAUSES

Chapter 8 Entertainment and the Media 222

THE PAST, INFINITIVES, MODAL VERBS, AND PRONOUNS

Chapter 9 Social Life 254

THE PRESENT PERFECT TENSES; ADVERBS OF DEGREE

Chapter 10 Customs, Celebrations, and Holidays 288

MORE ABOUT VERB FORMS: GERUNDS, INFINITIVES,
AND VERB COMPLEMENTS

Welcome to Interactions/Mosaic Silver Edition

Interactions/Mosaic **Silver Edition** is a fully-integrated, 18-book academic skills series. Language proficiencies are articulated from the beginning through advanced levels <u>within</u> each of the four language skill strands. Chapter themes articulate <u>across</u> the four skill strands to systematically recycle content, vocabulary, and grammar.

NEW to the Silver Edition of Interactions/Mosaic Grammar:

- **World's most popular and comprehensive academic skills series**—thoroughly updated for today's global learners
- **Redesigned Grammar Charts**—numbered sequentially, formatted consistently, and indexed systematically—provide lifelong reference value
- **Carefully refined scope and sequence** responds to teacher recommendations for building the most logical continuum of grammar topics within and across books
- **Enhanced focus on global content** honors the diversity of *Interactions/Mosaic* students from each region of the world
- **New Self-Assessment Logs** encourage students to evaluate their learning
- **New "Best Practices" approach** promotes excellence in language teaching

Interactions/Mosaic
Best Practices

Our Interactions/Mosaic Silver Edition team has produced an edition that focuses on Best Practices, principles that contribute to excellent language teaching and learning. Our team of writers, editors, and teacher consultants has identified the following six interconnected Best Practices:

Making Use of Academic Content

Materials and tasks based on academic content and experiences give learning real purpose. Students explore real world issues, discuss academic topics, and study content-based and thematic materials.

Organizing Information

Students learn to organize thoughts and notes through a variety of graphic organizers that accommodate diverse learning and thinking styles.

Scaffolding Instruction

A scaffold is a physical structure that facilitates construction of a building. Similarly, scaffolding instruction is a tool used to facilitate language learning in the form of predictable and flexible tasks. Some examples include oral or written modeling by the teacher or students, placing information in a larger framework, and reinterpretation.

Activating Prior Knowledge

Students can better understand new spoken or written material when they connect to the content. Activating prior knowledge allows students to tap into what they already know, building on this knowledge, and stirring a curiosity for more knowledge.

Interacting with Others

Activities that promote human interaction in pair work, small group work, and whole class activities present opportunities for real world contact and real world use of language.

Cultivating Critical Thinking

Strategies for critical thinking are taught explicitly. Students learn tools that promote critical thinking skills crucial to success in the academic world.

Highlights of Interactions 1 Grammar

Compelling instructional photos strengthen the educational experience.

Activating Prior Knowledge
Questions and topical quotes stimulate interest, activate prior knowledge, and launch the topic of the unit.

Chapter

8

Entertainment and the Media

Connecting to the Topic

1. How often do you watch movies or television?
2. What types of movies do you enjoy?
3. What are your favorite television shows?

In This Chapter

The Past, Infinitives, Modal Verbs, and Pronouns

Part 1 The Past Continuous Tense; The Simple Past Tense Versus the Past Continuous Tense

Part 2 Infinitives

Part 3 Summary of Modal Verbs; Summary of Pronouns; Indefinite Pronouns

❝Nothing is so intolerable to man as being fully at rest, without a passion, without business, without entertainment, without care.❞
—Blaise Pascal
French mathematician, physicist, and philosopher (1623–1662)

Part 3 Prepositions of Place and Time

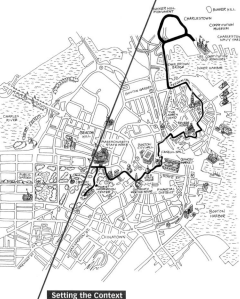

Setting the Context

Prereading Questions Discuss these questions with a small group.

Would you like to visit a city with many historical places? Why or why not?

Reading Read the passage.

Boston's Historic Freedom Trail

A great way to see old downtown Boston, Massachusetts, **during** the day is to walk the Freedom Trail. The trail is three miles long, and it takes you by many famous, historic places **from** the time of the American Revolution (1775–1783). The trail starts **at** an information booth **on** Boston Common, a large park **next to** Boston's Public Gardens. The booth is **on** Tremont Street **between** the Park Street and Tremont Street subway stations. You can get tour information and a trail map **at** the booth. There are many interesting stops **on** the trail.

One important stop is the Old State House **at** Washington and State Streets. Built **in** 1712, it now has a museum with exhibits about Boston's history. **From** the Old State House, you can walk **through** Faneuil Hall and Quincy Market. These old, historic buildings are now a busy center for shopping, dining, and entertainment. Many stores **in** Quincy Market stay open **until** 9:00 P.M., making them a perfect place to come back **to in** the evening, **after** dinner.

After Quincy Market, you can walk **toward** the North End. This part of Boston has many wonderful Italian shops, cafés, and restaurants. Also **in** the North End is Revere House, another important stop **on** the Freedom Trail. It is the home of Paul Revere (1735–1818), patriot **during** the American Revolution. Built **in** 1676, it is the oldest standing building **in** Boston.

The *U.S.S. Constitution*, a famous warship built **in** 1797, is **across** the Inner Harbor **in** the Charlestown Navy Yard. You can walk **over** the Charlestown Bridge to get there. The *U.S.S. Constitution* is the oldest American warship afloat today. The *U.S.S. Constitution* Museum is **near** the ship. You can visit the ship for free, but you have to pay to visit the museum.

Near the Charlestown Navy Yard is the Bunker Hill Monument, the last stop **on** the Freedom Trail. The monument commemorates the Battle of Bunker Hill, an important battle of the American Revolution, fought **on** June 17, 1775. **After** you finish the trail, you will probably be ready for a rest. You may wish to relax **in** one of Boston's beautiful parks, or get a coffee **at** one of the many cafés **in** the North End.

Discussion Questions Discuss these questions with a partner.

1. What kinds of places can you visit along the Freedom Trail?
2. Where is the information booth on Boston Common?
3. How can you get from Quincy Market to the North End?
4. What can you do in the North End?

2.11 Statements with Modals

	Explanations	Examples
Affirmative	In statements, modals come before the simple form of a verb. * Don't use *to* before the second verb. * *Will* can appear in short forms. The contractions with *will* are: *I will* = *I'll* *we will* = *we'll* *he will* = *he'll* *you will* = *you'll* *she will* = *she'll* *they will* = *they'll*	I **can** swim. The rain **may** stop soon. The tents **might** fall down. We **will** call you tonight.
Negative	*May not* and *might not* cannot appear in contractions.	I **can't** find my watch. He **won't** go with us. We **may not** need the compass. I **might not** come back.

2.12 Yes/No Questions with Modals

	Explanations	Examples	Possible Answers	
			Affirmative	Negative
Affirmative	In yes/no questions, modals come before the sentence subject.	**Can** you go with us? **Might** it rain tonight? **Will** we get there late?	Yes, I **can**. Yes, it **might**. Yes, we **will**.	No, I **can't**. No, it **won't**. No, we **won't**.
Negative	For negative questions, insert *not* after the modal.	**Can't** the children swim? **Won't** it be hot in August?	Yes, they **can**. Yes, it **will**.	No, they **can't**. No, it **won't**.

2.13 Information Questions with Modals

	Explanations	Examples	Possible Answers
Affirmative	In information questions, modals come after the question word.	What **can** we do? Who **may** visit us? What **might** happen? Where **will** they go?	We **can** run to that tree. Carlos **may** visit us. You **might** get sick. They**'ll** stay home.
Negative	For negative questions, insert *not* after the modal.	What **can't** Farshad eat with us? Who **may not** stay? Who **might not** go? Why **won't** Anita visit?	He **can't** eat meat. Hiroshi **may not** stay. Alma and Sapir **might not** go. (She **won't** visit) because she's at school.

B. Meanings

Each modal has more than one meaning or use. This chart gives examples of the meanings of *can, may, might,* and *will* in this chapter.

2.14 Meanings of Modals

Modals	Meanings	Examples
Can	ability or inability	I **can** speak English. (I am able to speak English.) He **can't** swim. (He isn't able to swim.) **Can** you dance? (Are you able to dance?)
May Might	future possibility	It **may** rain. (Maybe it will rain; maybe it won't.) I **might** not go. (Maybe I won't go; maybe I will.)
Will	future plans predictions	I**'ll** see you tomorrow. (I plan to see you tomorrow.) The movie **won't** be crowded. (I predict the movie won't be crowded.) **Will** you buy a tent? (Do you plan to buy a tent?)

1 Practice Underline the modals and following simple verbs in the conversation on pages 55 and 56. Does the modal in each statement or question mean *ability, future possibility, future plans,* or *prediction?*

Example I can't believe it's already time to go home. = *ability*

2 Practice Put these words into the correct order for statements or questions. Pay attention to the capital letter and the end-of-sentence punctuation.

Example with his friend / may / tonight / go / to a movie / He
       He may go to a movie with his friend tonight.

1. You / without matches / a fire / can't start

   _____

2. stay / at a campsite / You / all week long / can't

   _____

3. Who / take down / the tents / can

   _____?

4. with the extra food / you / will / What / do

   _____?

5. might / in an hour or so / be / home / We

   _____

6. we / Where / can / order / a pizza

   _____?

3. The Old State House is open _____ 9:30 A.M. _____ 5:00 P.M. _____ the summer. It was built _____ 1712.

4. Harvard University, _____ Cambridge, Massachusetts, is the oldest university _____ the United States. Many visitors like to walk _____ its campus.

5. The Bunker Hill Monument is _____ the Charlestown Navy Yard. You can easily get _____ the Monument _____ the Navy Yard.

6. Paul Revere House is located _____ 19 North Street _____ the North End. Paul Revere was a patriot _____ the American Revolution.

7. The Boston Children's Museum is _____ Congress Street. _____ Friday evenings, it's open _____ 9:00 P.M.

8. Many fine stores _____ Boston are _____ Newbury Street. The street stretches _____ the Public Garden _____ Massachusetts Avenue.

9. Quincy Market is open _____ 9:00 P.M. _____ night. It's a good place to shop _____ dinner _____ the evening.

10. _____ summer there are many fireworks displays in Boston. The biggest one is _____ the 4th of July.

3 Practice Look at the picture of a city street on page 122. Answer these questions with the prepositions of place: *in, on, at, between, near, next to, across from, under, over, to, toward, through, down, up,* and *across.* Can you answer each question in more than one way? You may add your own prepositions and other vocabulary.

Michael: (to himself) Red roses! They're beautiful! I bet they're from Janet. It's so nice of her to think ___of sending___ me flowers on Valentine's Day. I'll call her. (He dials Janet's number. The phone rings.)

Janet: Hello?

Michael: Hi, Janet. It's Mike. I just wanted to thank you _____ so romantic. I've often dreamed _____ roses from a woman.

Janet: Roses? I . . . uh . . . didn't send you roses. Anyway, haven't you heard? Phil and I are dating.

Michael: Sorry, Janet! I didn't know! I apologize _____ .

Janet: Why don't you try calling Sarah?

Michael: Sarah?

Janet: She told me that she was thinking _____ you flowers. The last time I spoke with her, she was trying to choose _____ you a card or flowers.

Michael: Really? I didn't even know that she liked me.

Janet: She's been planning _____ you, but she's so shy!

Michael: Wow. Thanks _____ me know. I've always had a crush on her, too! I'm going to call her right now.

Using What You've Learned

10 Doing Research About a Holiday As a group, use the internet or resource books in the library to find out about a holiday from another culture. Prepare a description of the holiday for the class, using as many gerunds as you can.

Example *Germans look forward to celebrating Fasching (Carnival) near the end of every winter. Dancing and participating in parades are common activities, and it's traditional to wear costumes. People look forward to having a great time at Fasching.*

Scope and Sequence

Chapter	Grammar Structures	Grammar in Context
1 Academic Life Around the World	**Be, The Simple Present Tense, Pronouns and Adjectives** **Part 1** The Verb *Be* **Part 2** The Simple Present Tense **Part 3** Personal Pronouns, Possessive Adjectives, and Pronouns	Meeting other new students Talking about classes Discussing textbooks
2 Experiencing Nature	***There Is / There Are*, Possessive Nouns, The Present Continuous Tense, and Modals** **Part 1** *There is / There are* **Part 2** Questions with *Whose*; Possessive Nouns **Part 3** The Present Continuous Tense; Nonaction Verbs **Part 4** Modal Verbs: *Can, May, Might, Will*	Deciding on a hiking route Setting up a picnic Making plans to go to the campground
3 Living to Eat or Eating to Live?	**Quantity, Comparisons, and Modal Verbs** **Part 1** Nouns and Expressions of Quantity **Part 2** Comparisons **Part 3** Modal Verbs: Requests, Offers, and Permission	The changing American diet Discussing products and prices in the supermarket Ordering food in a restaurant

Scope and Sequence

Chapter	Grammar Structures	Grammar in Context
4 In the Community	**The Future; More About Verbs, Prepositions, and Articles** **Part 1** Future Verb Forms **Part 2** Phrasal Verbs **Part 3** Prepositions of Place and Time **Part 4** Articles	Another busy day in town Waking up to face a full schedule Going on a walking tour
5 Home	**The Past Tense; Connecting Words** **Part 1** The Simple Past Tense (Regular Verbs); *Used to* **Part 2** The Simple Past Tense (Irregular Verbs); The Past Tense of the Verb *Be* **Part 3** Connecting Words	Talking about the good old days Moving into a new apartment Dividing the chores among roommates
6 Cultures of the World	**The Present Perfect Tense; Superlatives and Other Comparatives** **Part 1** The Present Perfect Tense (1) **Part 2** Superlatives **Part 3** Comparisons with *So, Too, Either*, and *Neither; But*	Meeting other travelers and sharing experiences Writing home while traveling Talking about favorite places

Chapter	Grammar Structures	Grammar in Context
7 Health	**Kinds of Verbs, Pronouns, Phrases, and Clauses** **Part 1** Verb + Object + Infinitive; Modal Verbs: *Should, Had better, Have to*, and *Must* **Part 2** Reflexive Pronouns; Tag Questions **Part 3** Relative Clauses	Getting health advice Working out at the gym Writing home from the hospital
8 Entertainment and the Media	**The Past, Infinitives, Modal Verbs, and Pronouns** **Part 1** The Past Continuous Tense; The Simple Past Tense Versus the Past Continuous Tense **Part 2** Infinitives **Part 3** Summary of Modal Verbs; Summary of Pronouns; Indefinite Pronouns	A news broadcast A commercial Going to the movies
9 Social Life	**The Present Perfect Tenses; Adverbs of Degree** **Part 1** The Present Perfect Tense (2) **Part 2** The Present Perfect Continuous Tense; The Present Perfect Continuous Tense Versus the Present Perfect Tense **Part 3** Adverbs of Degree: *So, Such, Enough,* and *Too*	Discussing the social scene Sharing pastimes and interests Talking about dating
10 Customs, Celebrations, and Holidays	**More About Verb Forms: Gerunds, Infinitives, and Verb Complements** **Part 1** Gerunds and Infinitives as Subjects **Part 2** Gerunds and Prepositions **Part 3** Verbs and Gerunds; Verbs Before Objects and Simple Verb Forms	Celebrating birthdays New Year's celebrations around the world Body language across cultures

Author Acknowledgements

To my father Isadore Fendelman

1917–2004

— Elaine Kirn

Academic Life Around the World

❝He who learns but does not think, is lost. He who thinks but does not learn, is in great danger.**❞**

—Confucius
Chinese philosopher (551–479 B.C.)

Connecting to the Topic

1 Do you enjoy going to school?

2 What is difficult about school?

3 What is enjoyable about school?

Setting the Context

Prereading Questions Discuss these questions with a small group.

How do you feel on your first day of school? Is it difficult to find your classes?

Reading Read the conversation.

Carlos: Excuse me. **Is** this seat free?

Imad: Yes, it **is**.

Carlos: Thanks. (*Carlos sits down.*) I'**m** Carlos.

Imad: Hi, Carlos. I'**m** Imad. **Are** you a new student here?

Carlos: Yes, I **am**. This **is** my first day at this school. How **is** this class?

Imad: It'**s** great! The students **are** very nice, and the professor **is** a fantastic teacher.

Carlos: Wow! The professor **is** that good?

Imad: Yes, he **is**. Professor Jimenez **is** one of my favorite teachers.

Carlos: Umm . . . **Isn't** this professor Kazahri's class?

Imad: No, it **isn't**.

Carlos: **Isn't** this room 409?

Imad: No, it'**s not**. This **is** room 406. Room 409 **is** across the hall.

Carlos: Oops. I'**m** in the wrong class!

Discussion Questions Discuss these questions with a partner.

1. Is Imad a new student?

2. Is Imad happy with his class? Why or why not?

3. Is Carlos's class in room 406?

4. Is Carlos in the wrong class? How does he know?

5. How does Carlos feel? Why do you think so?

Grammar Structures and Practice

A. Affirmative and Negative Statements; Contractions

The verb *be* has different forms after different subjects.

1.1	**Affirmative and Negative Statements**	
	Explanations	**Examples**
Affirmative Statements	Use *am* with the pronoun *I*. Use *are* with plural nouns and *we, you, they, these,* or *those*. Use *is* with singular nouns and *he, she, it, this,* or *that*.	I **am** from Japan. The students **are** late. You **are** twins! The teacher **is** over there.
Negative Statements	Use *not* after a form of *be* in negative sentences.	I **am not** late. She **is not** in this class.

Contractions are short forms. Use them in conversation and informal writing. Use full forms in more formal writing.

1.2	**Contractions**		
	Full Forms	**Contractions**	
Affirmative	I am Mexican. He is a new student. She is a professor. It is Tuesday. We are sisters. You are very smart. They are in class.	I**'m** Mexican. He**'s** a new student. She**'s** a professor. It**'s** Tuesday. We**'re** sisters. You**'re** very smart. They**'re** in class.	
Negative	I am not interested. He is not in the office. She is not happy. It is not here. We are not students. You are not married. They are not friendly.	I**'m not** interested. He**'s not** in the office. She**'s not** happy. It**'s not** here. We**'re not** students. You**'re not** married. They**'re not** friendly.	(no contraction) He **isn't** in the office. She **isn't** happy. It **isn't** here. We **aren't** students. You **aren't** married. They **aren't** friendly.

1 **Practice** Underline forms of the verb *be* in statements in the conversation between Carlos and Imad on page 4. How many examples are singular? How many are plural?

Example I'm Carlos.

2 **Practice** Circle the correct words or word parts in each set of parentheses.

Kaveh: Hi. I (('m)/'s) Kaveh.

Maria: Hello. We ('s/'re) Maria and Ellen Johnson.
  1

Kaveh: Oh, you ('re / aren't) twins!
  2

Maria: No, we (aren't / isn't) twins. But we (am / are) sisters.
  3   4

Kaveh: But you ('s / 're) exactly alike!
  5

Ellen: No, I ('m / 's) nineteen years old, but Maria (isn't / aren't) even eighteen
  6   7
yet.

Kaveh: I see now. Ellen, you ('re / 's) a little taller, and Maria's eyes (is / are) a little
  8   9
darker. (*Jim enters.*) Hi, Jim. Jim, this (is / are) Maria Johnson and her
  10
sister Ellen.

Jim: Hello. Oh! You ('m / 're) twins!
  11

3 **Practice** Complete the sentences with the correct forms of the verb *be*. Use contractions when possible.

Kami: The instructor _____isn't_____ (not) here yet. She

_____ late.
1

Yumiko: No, she _____ (not). It _____
2   3

early. It _____ (not) even 9:45. A lot of students
4

_____ (not) here yet either.
5

Kami: Well then, let's get a cup of coffee. The snack bar _____
6

open.

Yumiko: No, thanks. I _____ (not) ready for class yet. I have
7

to do the homework.

Kami: The homework _____ difficult! The exercises
8

_____ too hard! Fifteen minutes
9

_____ (not) enough time for them.
10

Yumiko: Ssshhh! You _____ making me nervous.
11

Kami: I _____ sorry. But it really _____
12   13

too late for the homework now.

Yumiko: You _____ probably right.
14

---

4 **Practice** Use the prompts below and write present tense statements about the
people in the pictures. *A* in parentheses means "affirmative." *N* means "negative." After
the first sentence in each group, use *he, she,* or *they*.

Example   Professor Winters
                tall (A)   *Professor Winters is tall.*
                an old man (N)   *He is not an old man.*

Professor Winters

1. a good teacher (A) _____

2. a boring speaker (N) _____

3. very funny (N) _____

4. in the English department (A) _____

5. married (A) _____

Doctor Silbert

6. a scientist (A) _____

7. bored (N) _____

8. in the English department (N) _____

9. friendly (A) _____

10. busy (A) _____

These students

11. in their chairs (A) _____

12. tired (A) _____

13. serious students (N) _____

14. interested in the lesson (N) _____

15. prepared for the next exam (N) _____

B. Yes/No Questions and Short Answers

Yes/No questions are questions with *yes* or *no* answers.

1.3 Yes/No Questions and Short Answers

	Explanations	Examples	Affirmative	Negative	
Affirmative Questions	In a yes/no question, put the verb before the subject.	**Am** I early? **Are** you from Japan? **Is** this your class? **Are** you students?	Yes, you are. Yes, I am. Yes, it is. Yes, we are.	No, you're not. No, I'm not. No, it's not. No, we're not.	No, you aren't. —— No, it isn't. No, we aren't.
Negative Questions	Use negative questions to show your expectation.	**Aren't** you early? **Isn't** that woman a professor? **Aren't** they twins?	Yes, I am. Yes, she is. Yes, they are.	No, I'm not. No, she's not. No, they're not.	—— No, she isn't. No, they aren't

Note: Don't use contractions in affirmative short answers. Use the contractions *isn't* and *aren't* in negative short answers.

5 **Practice** Put two lines under the verb *be* in the yes/no questions and short answers in the conversation between Carlos and Imad on page 4.

Example Excuse me. <u>Is</u> this seat free?

6 Practice Put affirmative or negative forms of *be* on the lines. Use contractions when possible.

Chen: _____ *Are* _____ you in Professor Ali's class?

Estella: Yes, I _____.
                        1

Chen: _____ it a beginning level class?
            2

Estella: No, it _____. It _____ an
                    3   4

advanced class.

Chen: _____ she a good teacher?
            5

Estella: Yes, she _____, but she's very strict.
                        6

Chen: _____ she patient with the students?
            7

Estella: Actually, no, she _____.
                                8

Chen: _____ the exams difficult?
            9

Estella: Yes, they _____!
                        10

Chen: _____ the homework difficult, too?
            11

Estella: Yes, it _____! _____ you
                    12   13

interested in the class?

Chen: Umm. I _____ not sure anymore.
                    14

7 Practice Write questions for these answers. Many different questions are possible.

Example A: *Is Marco a good student?*
                B: Oh, yes. He's the best student in the class.

1. A: _____
        B: No, he isn't. He's in the English department.

2. A: _____
   B: No, she isn't. She's from New York.

3. A: _____
   B: Yes, we are.

4. A: _____
   B: Yes, they are.

5. A: _____
   B: No, I'm not.

8 **Practice** Read the questions and answers. Are there any mistakes in the underlined words? Rewrite the sentence correctly. If there are no mistakes, write *Correct*.

Example *Are you from Osaka? Correct*

1. A: <u>Is</u> you from Osaka?
   B: No, <u>I'm</u> not. <u>I'm</u> from Kobe.

2. A: <u>Is</u> your brother a student here also?
   B: Yes, he <u>'s</u>.

3. A: <u>Are</u> I the only woman in this class?
   B: No, you <u>aren't</u>.

4. A: <u>Aren't</u> you in my history class?
   B: No, I <u>aren't</u>.

5. A: <u>Is</u> Carlos and Coletta business majors?
   B: Yes, they <u>is</u>.

6. A: <u>Is</u> the history department in this building?
   B: No, <u>it's</u> isn't.

7. A: <u>Am</u> I early?
   B: Yes, <u>you're</u>.

8. A: <u>Are</u> we in the right place?
   B: Yes, we <u>is</u>.

Using What You've Learned

 9 **Making Introductions** Introduce yourself to a classmate. Talk about your classes and your teachers. Use sentences with *be*.

Example A: *Hi, I'm Juan. I'm new here. Are you in this class?*
   B: *Yes, I am.*

   A: *Is the professor good?*
   B: *I'm not sure. She's new here, too.*

10 **Describing Yourself** Sit in a circle with your class. Make two sentences about yourself with the verb *be* in the present tense. The next student repeats your information and then makes two statements about himself or herself. The third student repeats the first and second students' information, then makes two statements, and so on. If someone forgets any information, group members can help. *Note:* If you are a large class, you can divide into groups of six to eight.

Example A: **I'm** Maria. **I'm** from Barcelona.

B: **She's** Maria. **She's** from Barcelona. **I'm** Eduardo. **I'm** a business major.

C: **She's** Maria. **She's** from Barcelona. **He's** Eduardo. **He's** a business major. **I'm** . . .

11 **Making Questions and Answers** There are many ways to answer yes/no questions without the words *yes* and *no*. Here are some examples of other affirmative and negative answers.

	Formal	Informal
Affirmative	Certainly.	Sure.
	Of course.	Yeah.
	I think so.	Uh-huh.
	Indeed.	Right.
Negative	Certainly not.	Nope.
	Of course not.	No way.
	I don't think so.	Uh-uh.
	I'm afraid not.	Nah.

Play this question-and-answer game quickly. One student goes to the front of the room. That student answers the other students' yes/no questions. He or she tries to answer all the questions without the words *yes* or *no*. What if that person accidentally says *yes* or *no*? Then another student goes to the front and continues the game.

Example A: *Are you a student in this class?*

B: *Of course.*

C: *Is this your favorite class?*

B: *I think so.*

D: *Is it cold today?*

B: *It is.*

A: *Is it raining?*

B: *No, it . . . Ooops!*

(Another student continues.)

Setting the Context

Prereading Questions Discuss these questions with a small group.

Who is your favorite teacher? Why is that teacher good?

Reading Read the conversation.

Alana:	Hi, Margo. I'm free for a while before my next class. Are you?
Margo:	Yeah, I am.
Alana:	**Let's** get a cup of coffee.
Margo:	Great. **Get** a table, and I'll get the coffee. What **do** you **take** in your coffee?
Alana:	Cream and sugar. **Get** a cookie too, please. (*Alana **sits** at a table, and Margo **returns** with the coffee.*)
Margo:	So, how **do** you **like** your classes this semester?
Alana:	I **like** them all, except for math. I **don't like** the instructor at all!
Margo:	Why not?
Alana:	Well, he **talks** too quickly, he rarely **explains** things clearly, and he isn't very patient. Also, he never **takes** breaks!
Margo:	**Does** he **give** exams often?

Alana:	He sure **does.** He **gives** quizzes once a week! And he **doesn't prepare** us for them. I am completely confused in class.
Margo:	Maybe you **need** extra help. **Get** a tutor.
Alana:	That's a good idea. **Do** you **know** any math tutors?
Margo:	Actually, yes, I **do.** I **know** a math teacher and tutor who always **explains** things slowly and carefully. He's also very patient and kind.
Alana:	I **like** him already. What's his name?
Margo:	Mr. Michaels. He's my advisor.
Alana:	Mr. Michaels? He's my math teacher!

 Discussion Questions Discuss these questions with a partner.

1. Why are Alana and Margo having coffee?
2. How does Alana feel about her math teacher? Why?
3. What is Margo's suggestion?
4. What jobs does Mr. Michaels have?
5. What advice would you give Alana?

Grammar Structures and Practice

A. The Imperative Form: Instructions, Orders, and Suggestions

The imperative form uses the simple form of the verb. It doesn't have endings.

1.4 The Imperative Form		
	Explanations	**Examples**
Affirmative Statements	To give instructions or orders, begin with a verb. The subject *you* is not included.	**Come** in.
	The word *please* makes the instruction more polite.	**Sit** down, please. Please **sit** down.
Negative Statements	In negative imperatives, *don't* comes before the verb.	**Don't talk.** Please **don't come** in.

An imperative statement can be formed for the first-person plural subject (*we*) with *let's* + the simple form of a verb.

1.5 *Let's*		
	Explanations	**Examples**
Affirmative Statements	*Let's* = *let us*. *Let's* means "I suggest we . . ."	**Let's** have coffee.
Negative Statements	Use *let's* + *not* to talk about what you do not want to do.	**Let's** not wait.

---

1 **Practice** Circle the imperative verbs in the conversation between Alana and Margo on pages 12 and 13.

Example (Let's get) a cup of coffee. (Get) a table.

2 **Practice** Imagine you are a teacher. What instructions would you give your students on the first day of class? Use the following phrases to form affirmative and negative imperative sentences.

Example be late to class

Please don't be late to class.

1. bring your textbooks to class

2. come in quietly

3. eat in class

4. drink coffee in class

5. sleep in class

6. cheat on tests

7. speak your native language in class

8. take notes in class

9. ask questions in class

10. talk loudly and clearly

 3 **Practice** Work with a partner. Take turns. Make suggestions for each of these situations with *let's*.

Example You are hungry. *Let's get a slice of pizza.*

1. You are tired of studying.

2. You need to get some cash.

3. You need to send an email message.

4. You want to get some fresh air.

5. You want to dance or hear some music.

6. You need some physical exercise.

7. You want to do something new and different.

8. You need to relax (reduce your stress level).

9. You want to be creative.

10. You want to improve your English.

B. Affirmative and Negative Statements of the Simple Present Tense

The simple present tense is used for everyday activities and habits, general statements of fact, and opinions. With some verbs, the simple present shows an existing condition (something happening now).

1.6	The Simple Present Tense	
	Explanations	**Examples**
Everyday Activities and Habits	An object sometimes follows the verb.	Karim and Ricardo often **study** math together. I **drink** three cups of tea a day.
Statements of Fact	With third-person singular subjects, the verb ends in -s.	Lu **speaks** three languages. Mr. Michaels **teaches** math and **advises** students.
Opinions	In negative statements, *do* or *does* comes before *not*. The contractions are *don't* and *doesn't*. The main verb is always in the simple form.	I **don't like** the instructor. He **doesn't teach** math very well.
Existing Conditions	Other verbs for existing conditions are *like, need, want, seem, know, hear, understand,* and *believe*.	I **hear** music. Lorenzo **doesn't understand** your question.

Spelling Rules for -s Endings

For the third-person singular verb form, follow these spelling rules:

1. If the simple form of a verb ends in -*y* after a consonant, change the *y* to *i* and add -*es*.
   Examples carry/carries   try/tries

2. If the simple form of a verb ends in -*s*, -*z*, -*sh*, -*ch*, -*x*, or -*o* (after a consonant), add -*es*.
   Examples teach/teaches   pass/passes   go/goes

3. There are two irregular verb forms.   be/is   have/has

4. In all other cases, add -*s* to the simple form.
   Examples wear/wears   work/works   pay/pays

4 Practice Underline the simple present tense verbs in statements in the conversation between Alana and Margo on pages 12 and 13.

Example I <u>like</u> them all, except for math.

5 Practice Use the prompts below and make present tense statements about the people in the pictures. *A* in parentheses means "affirmative." *N* means "negative." After the first sentence in each group, use *he, she,* or *they*.

Examples Mr. Shida

be 32 years old (A)   *Mr. Shida is 32 years old.*

have a beard (A)   *He has a beard.*

Mr. Shida

1. be a teaching assistant (A)
2. be a professor (N)
3. help Mr. Michaels (A)
4. teach three days a week (A)
5. give lectures (N)
6. work with students in small groups (A)
7. wear a suit and a tie (N)
8. like to wear jeans every day (A)
9. carry a briefcase (N)
10. have a board in his classroom (N)

Ms. Wong and Mr. Garcia

11. he: be a student advisor (A)

12. she: be a college administrator (A)

13. they: teach classes (N)

14. they: give grades (N)

15. he: advise students on their classes (A)

16. she: often go to meetings (A)

17. she: have an easy job (N)

18. he: help students with their problems (A)

19. they: have enough time for all their work (N)

20. they: make a lot of money (N)

C. Yes/No Questions and Short Answers

In simple present yes/no questions without a form of *be*, a form of *do* comes before the subject.

- Use *does* with *he, she*, and *it*.
- Use *do* with *I, you, we*, and *they*.
- Use the simple form of the main verb.
- Use the appropriate form of *do* in short answers.

1.7	**Yes/No Questions and Short Answers in the Present Tense**		
	Examples	**Affirmative Answers**	**Negative Answers**
Affirmative Questions	**Do I look** like my mother? **Does he do** good work? **Does she study** a lot? **Does it work?** **Do we need** our umbrellas? **Do you have** change for a dollar? **Do they know** the address?	Yes, you **do.** Yes, he **does.** Yes, she **does.** Yes, it **does.** Yes, you **do.** Yes, I **do.** Yes, they **do.**	No, you **don't.** No, he **doesn't.** No, she **doesn't.** No, it **doesn't.** No, you **don't.** No, I **don't.** No, they **don't.**
Negative Questions	**Don't I need** a ticket? **Doesn't he teach** English? **Doesn't she play** the piano? **Doesn't it bite?** **Don't we leave** tonight? **Don't you do** the homework? **Don't they like** pizza?	Yes, you **do.** Yes, he **does.** Yes, she **does.** Yes, it **does.** Yes, we **do.** Yes, I **do.** Yes, they **do.**	No, you **don't.** No, he **doesn't.** No, she **doesn't.** No, it **doesn't.** No, we **don't.** No, I **don't.** No, they **don't.**

6 Practice Ask yes/no questions with these words. Your partner can answer your questions with short answers. Can you add more questions of your own?

Examples A: *Does this school have a cafeteria?*
B: *Yes, it does. (or: No, it doesn't. It only has a snack bar.)*
A: *Is the food good?*
B: *No, it isn't. It's terrible.*

1. this school have a cafeteria

2. the food good

3. the place clean

4. it have comfortable chairs

5. students study there

6. it open late

7. any students work there

8. the place serve hamburgers

9. it have coffee

10. the prices high

7 Practice Change roles. Your partner asks you yes/no questions with these words. Give short answers. Can your partner add more questions?

1. your English class difficult

2. you like your English class homework

3. the classroom big

4. the instructor give many exams

5. you have homework every day

6. you often late to class

7. you sometimes need help with your

8. the teacher check your homework

9. you have a textbook

10. you study enough

8 Practice Change partners. Write some yes/no questions about other people, places, or activities at your school (examples: the dean of students, the library, the drama club). Ask your new partner your questions. Listen to the answers. Answer your partner's questions, too. What did you learn from this conversation? Tell the class.

D. Information Questions and Answers

An information question begins with a question word. Its answer is not *yes* or *no*.

- Usually, a form of *do* separates a question word from the subject. Then the main verb is in its simple form.
- Use *do* or *does* only in sentences with a main verb. Otherwise, use a form of *be*.

1.8 Information Questions in the Simple Present Tense

Question Words	Explanations	Examples	
		Questions	**Possible Answers**
Who	*Who* is for people. *Who* can be the subject of a question. *Who* usually comes before a singular verb.	**Who are** your teachers? **Who is** your advisor? **Who helps** you?	(My teachers are) Mr. Yoshida and Ms. Lee. Mr. Michaels (is my advisor). Mei Ling and Ignacio (help me).
Whom	*Who* (or *Whom*) can be an object of a verb. *Whom* is only for formal questions. *Who* is for informal speech.	**Who/Whom do** you **ask** for help?	(I ask) my tutor.
What	*What* is for things. *What* can be the subject of a question. *What* can also be an object of a verb.	**What interests** you? **What is** in the bag? **What do** you **want**? **What does** she **teach**?	Books and movies (interest me). My lunch (is in the bag). I want some money. She teaches history.
Where	*Where* is for questions about places.	**Where is** the snack bar? **Where are** your classes? **Where does** the class **meet**? **Where do** we **go** now?	(It's) in the student center. (They're) in the new science building. (It meets) in Moore Hall. (We go) to English class.

(continued)

Question Words	Explanations	Examples	
		Questions	**Possible Answers**
When	*When* is for questions about time.	**When is** the final exam?	(It's) next week.
		When are our papers due?	(They're due) on Wednesday.
		When does class **begin**?	(It begins) in five minutes.
		When do you **work**?	(I work) on Mondays and Fridays.
Why	*Why* is for questions about reasons.	**Why is** the building closed?	(It's closed) because it's a holiday.
		Why aren't they home?	They're on vacation.
		Why does Alex **come** home so late?	He has a job after school.
		Why isn't he in class today?	(He isn't in class) because he's sick.
How	*How* can be for a degree (of something). *How* can be for a state or condition (for example, health). *How* can be for a way or a method (of doing something).	**How is** your math class? **How are** you? **How do** you **get** to school?	(It's) very hard. I'm OK. (I get here) by bus and subway.

Note: Contractions for question words + *be* in informal speech are: *who + is = who's; what + is = what's; where + is = where's; when + is = when's; why + is = why's; how + is = how's.*

---

9 **Practice** Put two lines under the question words in the conversation between Alana and Margo on pages 12 and 13.

Example So, <u>how</u> do you like your classes this semester?

10 **Practice** Make information questions for these answers. Use the simple present tense and the question words *who, what, where, when, why,* or *how.*

Example *How are you?*
          I'm very well, thanks.

1. ?
   She's my English teacher.

2. ?
   I walk to school.

3. ?

He teaches math.

4. ?

It will be on Friday.

5. ?

I can't because it's too expensive.

6. ?

It's in the refrigerator.

7. ?

It's blue.

8. ?

He's my father.

9. ?

It's on the first floor.

10. ?

It's horrible!

 11 **Practice** Make information questions with these words. Your partner answers your questions. You can add some questions of your own. Use *do* or *does* only in sentences with a main verb. Otherwise, use a form of *be*.

Examples   How . . . your classes this term?
A: *How are your classes this term?*
B: *They're boring.*

Why . . . you like them?
A: *Why don't you like them?*
B: *The courses are too easy.*

1. Who . . . your English teacher?

2. How . . . you like him or her?

3. Why . . . you like him or her?

4. Where . . . your teacher from?

5. When . . . your English class?

6. Where . . . your English class meet?

7. What . . . you bring to class?

8. What textbook . . . you use?

9. How . . . you like the textbook?

10. Who . . . you study with?

12 Practice Change roles. Now your partner asks information questions with these words. Answer the questions. Can your partner add real questions of his or her own?

1. What . . . you do first in the morning?
2. How . . . you get to school?
3. Who . . . you usually come to school with?
4. When . . . your first class begin?
5. What . . . your first class?
6. When . . . your first class end?
7. Where . . . you go between classes?
8. How . . . you like the food in the cafeteria?
9. What . . . your favorite food in the cafeteria?
10. When . . . you usually go home?

E. Frequency Adverbs

Frequency adverbs go with verbs or adjectives. They answer the question *How often?* Here are the meanings of some frequency adverbs in approximate percentages of time:

> always = 100%
> usually = 90%
> often = 70%
> sometimes = 50%
> occasionally = 20%
> rarely = 10%
> never = 0%

These charts give some examples of frequency adverbs in affirmative and negative statements and questions.

1.9 Frequency Adverbs

Explanation		Examples
In statements, one-word frequency adverbs usually come after the verb *be* but before other verbs.	**Affirmative Statements**	Students are **always** busy. He's **often** hungry. She **sometimes** gets sick. Students **occasionally** meet. They **rarely** sit together.
	Negative Statements	I'm not **often** tired. Kim isn't **always** here. Tony is **never** late. She doesn't **often** rest. We don't **ever** want to go there again. They don't **usually** study.

1.10 Questions with Frequency Adverbs

Explanations		Examples	Possible Answers	
			Affirmative	**Negative**
In questions, one-word frequency adverbs usually come after the subject.	**Affirmative Questions**	Are you **often** homesick? Does the teacher **ever** give quizzes? Do they **always** eat pizza for lunch?	Always. Often.	Not often. Rarely.
Use *ever* in questions and *never* in negative answers.	**Negative Questions**	Don't you **ever** get homesick? Doesn't he **often** come to class late? Don't we **always** enjoy the weekend?	Yes, sometimes. Occasionally.	No, rarely. Never.

1.11 Frequency Phrases

Explanations	Examples
A frequency phrase usually follows the verb phrase. Some frequency phrases are: *every day, every other week, every two hours, once a year*, and *now and then*.	He teaches **three times a week.** We have a test **every month.** Do you relax **now and then?**

---

13 Practice Put a box around the frequency adverbs and phrases in the conversation between Alana and Margo on pages 12 and 13.

Example Well, he talks too quickly, he rarely explains things clearly, and he isn't very patient.

 14 Practice Put the words in parentheses in the correct order for statements or questions. Pay attention to the punctuation. Then practice the conversation with a partner.

Galina: _____You often look tired_____ (tired / look / You / often), Alek.

_____ (get / eight hours of sleep each night /

1

you / usually / Don't)?

Alek: No. _____ (I / five days a week / eight o'clock
classes / have). Also, _____ (rarely / before 2:00
A.M. / get to bed / I).

Galina: Why do you go to bed so late? _____ (Do / go
out / every night / you)?

Alek: Oh, no. _____ (never / during the week / I / go
out). _____ (My roommate and I / every night /
study together). _____ (until 1:00 in the
morning / usually / don't / finish / We). In fact, _____
(rarely / goes to bed / my roommate / before 3:00).

Galina: That's terrible. _____ (work so hard / always /
you / Do)?

Alek: Yes, because _____ (always / worried about
grades / we're).

Galina: Well, you graduate soon, right? What do you plan to do then?

Alek: Sleep!

 15 Practice Use these phrases for present tense questions. Answer your partner's
questions. Add frequency adverbs to your questions and answers.

Examples A: Do you **often** bring your lunch to school?
B: No, not **often.** I **occasionally** bring my lunch to school.
(Change roles.)
B: Are you **ever** tired in class?
A: Yes, I'm **sometimes** tired in class.

1. stay up all night

2. cram for a test

3. get eight hours of sleep

4. ask questions in class

5. be worried about school

6. speak with your advisor

7. be satisfied with your grades

8. study with friends

9. get help from a tutor

10. ask for advice

11. not do your homework

12. be finished with classes by 3:00

Using What You've Learned

 16 Interviewing Classmates Interview three classmates. Prepare ten questions for them on your own paper. In a chart like this, write some:

- yes/no questions with *do/does* before a verb
- information questions with question words
- questions with frequency adverbs

Examples	STUDENT 1	STUDENT 2	STUDENT 3
1. What's your name?			
2. Do you live on campus?			
3. Do you ever walk to school?			
4. Do you belong to any clubs?			

Listen carefully to your classmates' answers. Take notes. Keep your notes for Activity 17.

 17 Describing Classmates Tell the class about one of your classmates. Use the notes from your interview in Activity 16. Make both affirmative and negative statements about the person.

Example *This is Sam Chen. He doesn't live on campus. He never walks to school. He takes the bus to school. He belongs to the debating club.*

 18 Asking Questions Follow the directions below.

1. Cut a piece of paper into six or more pieces.
2. Write one noun, adjective, or adverb on each piece. Turn your pieces of paper over so no one can see your words.
3. Choose a partner.
4. Your partner turns over one of your pieces of paper. He or she makes a question for that answer (the word on the paper).
5. Answer your partner's question with a statement.
6. Now turn over one of your partner's pieces of paper. Make a question for that answer (the word on the paper).
7. Your partner answers your question.
8. Play until there are no more pieces of paper left.

Example

A: (Turns over a piece of paper with the word black.)
What color is my hair?

B: *It's <u>black</u>.*
(Turns over a piece of paper with the word Wednesday.)
When do we have English class?

A: *We have English class on <u>Wednesday</u>.*
(Turns over a piece of paper with the word quickly.)
How does our teacher speak?

B: *He speaks <u>quickly</u>.*

Part 3 | Personal Pronouns, Possessive Adjectives, and Pronouns

Setting the Context

Prereading Questions Discuss these questions in a small group.

Do you have a dictionary? How often do you use it? Is it helpful to you?

Reading Read the conversation.

Leon: Hi, Anita. What's up?

Anita: Hi, Leon. **I** need a dictionary for **our** ESL class. **I** can't decide. . . which dictionary do **I** buy? What dictionary do **you** have?

Leon: **I** don't think **mine** is good for **you**. **It**'s very basic. But **my** roommate, Mario, has a great dictionary. **He** lets **me** use **it** all the time. Actually, **I** probably use **it** more than **he** does.

Anita: Does **his** dictionary include idioms?

Leon: No, **I** don't think **it** does. But **Aleme's** dictionary has idioms.

Anita: **I** know. **I** like **hers** a lot, but the bookstore doesn't have **it.**

Leon: What bookstore is **it** from? Why don't **you** ask **her?**

Anita: **She** says **she** doesn't remember.

Leon: Hmm. Hey, why don't **you** get an electronic dictionary?

Anita: Don't **you** remember? **Our** teacher won't let **us** use **them.**

Leon: Oh, yeah.

Anita: **I** don't know what to do! **All** of these dictionaries look the same to **me** right now.

Leon: **I** have a suggestion. Go home, relax, and come back to-morrow. Then **you** can look at **them** again.

Anita: Good idea, Leon.

 Discussion Questions Discuss these questions with a partner.

1. How do Leon and Anita know each other?

2. Whose dictionary does Leon use?

3. Why does Anita like Aleme's dictionary?

4. Why can't Anita use an electronic dictionary in her ESL class?

5. Describe your own dictionary. Why did you choose it?

Grammar Structures and Practice

A. Personal Pronouns

A pronoun replaces a noun. In the chart on page 28, the nouns in the examples are underlined. The pronouns are in bold type. They are used in place of the nouns.

1.12 Personal Pronouns

Explanations	Subject Pronouns	Object Pronouns	Examples
A pronoun can be the subject or object of a sentence. An object pronoun comes after a verb or a preposition.	I	me	"This is <u>Akiko Kameda</u> speaking. **I** am lost. Can you help **me**?"
	you	you	"<u>Farshad</u>, **you** look different in a suit. I hardly recognize **you**."
	he	him	<u>Carlos</u> is from Mexico. **He** is a new student. I want to talk to **him**.
	she	her	<u>Ms. Sanchez</u> is the teacher. **She** teaches Spanish. My brother is in **her** class.
	it	it	I just bought <u>a computer</u>. **It** is heavy. I had to carry **it** home.
	we	us	"It's <u>Rosa and Laura</u>. **We** are downstairs. Please let **us** in."
	you	you	"<u>Yuriko and Hiroshi</u>, **you** look tired. Can I take **you** home?"
	they	them	"<u>Alma and Hasnaa</u> are here. **They** want to come in Please let **them** in."

1 **Practice** In the conversation between Anita and Leon on pages 26 and 27, underline the subject pronouns. Put a double underline under the object pronouns.

Example <u>He</u> lets <u><u>me</u></u> use <u><u>it</u></u> all the time.

2 **Practice** Finish the following sentences with the appropriate subject and object pronouns.

Example I love her, but _____ *she* _____ doesn't love _____ *me* _____.

1. You want to speak to him, but _____ doesn't want to speak to

   _____ .

2. My sister wants to work with them, but _____ don't want to

   work with _____ .

3. We visit them, but _____ don't visit _____ .

4. She sends letters to Rosa and José, but _____ don't send

   letters to _____ .

5. I am worried about her, but _____ isn't worried about

   _____ .

6. My mother cooks for my father, but _____ doesn't cook for

_____.

7. He takes photos of us, but _____ don't take photos of

_____.

8. That woman knows you, but _____ don't know

_____.

9. The students ask him for advice, but _____ doesn't ask

_____ for advice.

10. We understand them, but _____ don't understand

_____.

B. Possessive Adjectives and Pronouns

Possessive adjectives come before nouns. Possessive pronouns are not followed by nouns; they stand alone.

1.13	Possessive Adjectives and Pronouns	
	Forms	**Examples**
Possessive Adjectives	my your his her its ours yours their	That isn't **my** pen. These are **your** shoes. It's **his** problem. Those are **her** flowers. **Its** tail is brown. **Our** seats are here. I am **your** teacher. This is **their** car.
Possessive Pronouns	mine yours his hers ours yours theirs	That pen isn't **mine**. Those shoes are **yours**. The problem is **his**. The flowers are **hers**. The seats are **ours**. I am **yours**. The car is **theirs**.

3 Practice Circle the possessive adjectives and put a box around the possessive pronouns in the conversation between Anita and Leon on page 27.

Example I need to buy a dictionary for (our) ESL class.

I don't think [mine] is good for you.

4 Practice Choose the correct word in each set of parentheses.

Example (I / me /(my)) pencil is broken. Can I borrow (you / your /(yours))?

1. Professor Smith is (me / my / mine) biology teacher.

2. (They / Their / Theirs) books are here. Where are (us / our / ours)?

3. (She / Her / Hers) studies with (she / her / hers) roommate.

4. (We / Us / Our) work on (we / us / our) project every Monday.

5. She has (she / her / hers) coffee with cream. I have (me / my / mine) coffee black.

6. I spend two hours a night on (me / my / mine) homework. How long do you spend on (you / your / yours)?

7. (You / Your / Yours) apartment is closer to school than (I / my / mine).

8. (Me / My / Mine) brother is on the debating team with (they / them / their).

9. (He / Him / His) works as a teaching assistant. (He / Him / His) job is very satisfying.

10. A tutor comes to (us / our / ours) house once a week. (She / Her / Hers) helps (we / us / our) with our schoolwork.

Using What You've Learned

5 Describing a Person or Place Choose one school-related person or place (Examples: an advisor, a professor, the school library, the cafeteria). Write one or two paragraphs about the person or place. How many personal pronouns, possessive adjectives, and possessive pronouns can you use? Finish your writing. Then underline and count the number of personal pronouns and possessive adjectives and pronouns. Which student used the most? That person can read his or her paragraphs to the class.

Example _I like our school library. It is in a beautiful building. It has thousands of books. Students can check them out for up to a week, or they can just read them in the library. The librarian is a very nice woman. Her name is Ms. Freed. She is helpful and kind. She tells me how to find the information I need. If I don't have a pen, she lets me use hers._

 6 Describing a Mystery Person Think of a person in your school. (All your classmates should know this person.) It can be a student, a teacher, or an administrator. Don't tell the identity of the person (who it is). Instead, write ten sentences about the person (clues to his or her identity). Use personal pronouns, possessive adjectives, and possessive pronouns. Read your clues to the class. How fast can someone correctly guess the person's identity? The person with the correct guess then reads his or her clues to the class.

Example   A: *She often comes to class late.*
She is a good athlete.
(pointing to a jacket) *That jacket is hers.*
Her name rhymes with "fancy."
B: *Is the person "Nancy"?*
A: *Yes! Your turn.*

Self-Assessment Log

Each of the following sentences describes the grammar you learned in this chapter. Read the sentences and then check the best box for how well you understand each structure.

	Needs Improvement	Good	Great
I can use the verb *to be* to make statements and ask questions.	❑	❑	❑
I can use the simple present tense to interview and talk about my classmates.	❑	❑	❑
I can use personal pronouns to talk about people and things.	❑	❑	❑
I can use possessive adjectives to talk about people and things.	❑	❑	❑

Experiencing Nature

"Joy in looking and comprehending is nature's most beautiful gift.**"**

—Albert Einstein
German physicist (1879–1955)

Connecting to the Topic

1. What is this family doing?

2. Do you like to spend time outside?

3. What activities do you enjoy in nature?

Setting the Context

Prereading Questions Discuss these questions with a small group.

Do you like to go hiking? If so, where do you hike?

Reading Read the conversation.

Rafael: (*Looking at a map*) **There are** about five miles to go to Emerald Lake.

Gil: Five miles?! **There are** blisters on my feet. I can't walk anymore.

Rafael: **There are** bandages in my backpack. Do you need them? Now let's see . . . **there are** two different paths on the map. **There is** one path along the river, and **there's** another through the forest.

Susana: Let's take the forest path! **There are** beautiful trees and interesting animals in the forest.

Gil:	**There are** also bugs in the forest.	
Susana:	Oh, Gil! This is a wonderful hike. Why are you so un-happy?	
Gil:	I guess I'm just hungry and tired.	
Susana:	**Is there** a good place for us to stop and have our lunch?	
Marta:	Why don't we take the path along the river and stop for lunch on the way? **There isn't** any water in our canteens, so we can fill them up at the river.	
Rafael:	That sounds like a good plan.	
Gil:	Look! **There's** a deer!	
Susana:	Where?	
Gil:	Behind that tree! And look! **There are** two more over there!	
Marta:	Gil! I don't believe it. **Is there** a smile on your face?	
Gil:	Maybe just a small one.	

 Discussion Questions Discuss these questions with a partner.

1. Where are Rafael, Gil, Susana, and Marta?

2. What decision do they need to make?

3. Why is Gil unhappy?

4. Why does he finally smile?

5. Does a hike like this interest you? Why or why not?

A. *There is / There are*

Some statements and questions can include *there is / there are*. *There* means that the sentence subject exists or is in a place.

- *There is* is for a singular noun subject.
- *There are* is for a plural noun subject.

2.1 Statements with *There is / There are*

	Explanations	Examples
Affirmative Statements	The contraction for *there is* is *there's*. There is no contraction for *there are*.	**There is** a bee on the flower. **There's** a bee on the flower. **There are** meadows on the way.
Negative Statements	The contraction for *there is no* is *there isn't any*. The contraction for *there are no* is *there aren't any*.	**There is no** water in my canteen. **There isn't any** water in my canteen. **There are no** rocks on the trail. **There aren't any** rocks on the trail.

2.2 Questions with *There is / There are*

	Examples	Affirmative Answers	Negative Answers
Affirmative Questions	**Is there** a river near the trail?	Yes, there is.	No, there's not. No, there isn't.
	Are there any sleeping bags?	Yes, there are.	No, there aren't.
Negative Questions	**Isn't there** a map of the park?	Yes, there is.	No, there's not. No, there isn't.
	Aren't there hills on the hike?	Yes, there are.	No, there aren't.

1 **Practice** Underline the verb phrases *there is / there are* in the conversation between the hikers on pages 34 and 35. Circle the sentence subjects (singular and plural nouns).

Example There are about five miles to go until we reach Emerald Lake.

2 **Practice** Make sentences for the picture on page 34. Use *there is / there are* and the words below.

Example   two dogs / in the park *There are two dogs in the park.*

1. four hikers in the nature scene
2. backpacks on their backs
3. blisters on their feet?
4. a trail sign with three place names on it
5. pine trees on the hill
6. no birds in the trees
7. three tents in the meadow below
8. no people at the campsite
9. no ponds or rivers in the scene
10. no water at all in the picture

3 **Practice** Fill in the blanks with one or more of these words: *there, there's, is, isn't, are, aren't.* These can be statements or questions.

Augustin: Andrea, _____*there's*_____ nothing to do in the city. Let's go

camping!

Andrea: Camping? But _____ any people our age in the
                                               1

mountains.

Augustin: Sure _____. And _____ camping
                                  2   3

equipment in our garage. Let's see . . . I think _____
                                                                         4

a tent and _____ two sleeping bags.
                           5

Andrea: But _____ a camp stove?
                              6

Augustin: Yes, _____. But _____ no
                                  7   8

backpacks, and _____ any hiking boots.
                                 9

Andrea: That's fine with me. I don't want to hike anyway. _____
                                                                                      10

bathrooms and showers at the campground?

Augustin: Of course _____.
                                     11

Andrea: _____ a hotel nearby? Just in case it rains . . .
                     12

Augustin: I think _____. Come on! Let's go hiking!
                                 13

_____ nothing to lose.
            14

4 **Practice** Describe the picture below. Use sentences beginning with *there is /*
there are.

Examples There is a deer in the meadow.
There are two people by the river.

Using What You've Learned

 5 **Describing a Picture from Memory** Student A studies the picture on page
39 for one minute and then closes the book. Student B looks at the picture. Using *is
there / are there*, Student B asks Student A questions about the picture, and Student A
tries to answer the questions from memory.

Example B: *Is there a river?*
   A: *No, there's not. But there's a lake.*
   B: *Is there anything on the lake?*
   A: *Yes. There are two sailboats on the lake.*

Now change roles. Student B studies the picture for one minute and then closes the book. Student A looks at the picture. Using *is there / are there*, Student A asks Student B questions about the picture. Student B tries to answer the questions from memory.

 6 Describing Nature Scenes Repeat Activity 5 with a nature picture from a magazine or calendar. This time, you can write down your questions about the scene. You can give your partner the questions to answer from memory.

 7 Describing Places in Nature Close your eyes and relax. Think about your favorite park, garden, or other place in nature. Choose a partner. In sentences with *there is / there are* (when possible), Student A describes the place in his or her mind. Student B listens and draws a simple picture from the description. Then Student A looks at the picture and makes corrections and changes, if necessary. Then change roles. Repeat the activity with another scene description. This time, Student B talks, and Student A draws.

Setting the Context

Prereading Questions Discuss these questions with a small group.

Do you get hungry when you exercise? What do you like to eat?

Reading Read the conversation.

Marta:	The sandwiches are all mixed up. This one is mine, but **whose** ham and cheese sandwich is this?
Rafael:	That's mine.
Marta:	**Whose** egg sandwich is this?
Rafael:	I think it's **Gil's**.
Marta:	No, Gil doesn't like eggs. So it's probably **Susana's**. Is there any fruit?
Rafael:	Yeah. There are apples from **Susana's grandparents'** farm.

Marta: Great. And I have candy bars from the **school's** vending machine. So there's plenty of food. But do we have anything to sit down on?

Rafael: Here—this is my **parents'** picnic blanket.

Marta: Perfect. So where are Gil and Susana with our water? When do we eat?

Rafael: I can't wait. I'm so hungry from the hike, I could eat my backpack!

 Discussion Questions Discuss these questions with a partner.

1. Whose picnic blanket does Rafael have?

2. Where is Marta's candy from?

3. Where's the group's water?

4. Why is Rafael so hungry?

5. Do you enjoy picnic lunches? Why or why not?

Grammar Structures and Practice

A. Questions with *Whose*

Whose is used in questions about possession.

2.3 Questions with *Whose*		
Explanations	**Examples**	**Possible Answers**
To form a question with *whose*, put the word *whose* at the beginning of the question, followed by the noun for the item of possession.	**Whose tent** is this? **Whose canteen** is this? **Whose farm** is it? **Whose canteens** are these? **Whose backpacks** are those?	It's Hiroshi's. It's Miguel's. It's Yuri's parents' farm. They're Tomoko's. They're Jila's and Majin's.

Note: Use *this* for an item close to you. Use *that* for an object not close to you. Use *these* for things close to you and *those* for objects further away.

B. Possessive Nouns

Possessive nouns can be people, places, or things that have possession of something.

2.4 Possessive Nouns

	Explanations	Nouns	Possessive Forms
Singular Nouns	If a name or singular noun ends in *-s*, add ' or *'s* for the possessive form. If a name or singular noun does not end in *-s*, add *'s* for the possessive.	Carlos Hiroshi tomorrow the boy the student the lady the child the man	Carlos' or Carlos's Horoshi's tomorrow's the boy's the student's the lady's the child's the man's
Plural Nouns	If a plural noun ends in *-s*, add ' for the possessive form. If a plural noun does not end in *-s*, add *'s*.	the boys the students the ladies the Smiths the men the children the people	the boys' the students' the ladies' the Smiths' the men's the children's the people's

1 Circle the possessive nouns in the conversation between Marta and Rafael on pages 40 and 41.

Example I think it's (Gil's).

2 Write questions and answers about these pictures. Use the words below. Include *whose* in the questions and possessive nouns in the answers.

1. book / Ellen

Q: _____ Whose book is this? _____

A: _____ It's Ellen's. _____

2. clothes / those girls

Q: _____

A: _____

3. sandwich / Azis

Q: _____

A: _____

4. garbage / other people

Q: _____

A: _____

5. sailboat / my brother

Q: _____

A: _____

6. backpacks / some children

Q: _____

A: _____

7. bicycles / those boys

Q: _____

A: _____

8. sleeping bags / my parents

Q: _____

A: _____

3 **Practice** Complete the sentences below. Use the possessive forms of the nouns in parentheses.

1. (Mr. Estrada) That's _____ canteen by the tent.

2. (today) _____ weather is going to be hot and sunny.

3. (Sarah / parents) _____ house is on a farm in the country.

4. (women) The _____ showers are over there.

5. (boyfriend) I don't have a backpack, but you can use my _____.

6. (brothers) His _____ names are Roberto and Victor.

7. (campers) The _____ tents aren't very strong.

8. (wife) My _____ brother is a forest ranger.

9. (birds) The _____ nest is high up in the tree.

10. (fishermen) The _____ boat is in the harbor.

Using What You've Learned

4 **Asking and Telling about Possession of Real Objects** Each student takes out an object (such as a watch, a book, some lipstick, etc.). In turn, they show the object to the class. They then place it in a box or on a desk at the front of the room. Next, the instructor picks up each object. The class identifies the owner in a two-line conversation: first a question with *whose* and then an answer with a possessive noun. Each object is identified and then given back to its owner.

Example   (Instructor picks up a ski jacket.)
           A: *Whose ski jacket is this?*
           B: *It's Dennis's. (It's his jacket.)*

Setting the Context

Prereading Questions Discuss these questions with a small group.

Do you like being outside in the rain? Why or why not?

Reading Read the converstaion.

Susana: This **is** a perfect spot. The birds **are singing**. **Do** you **hear** them? A gentle breeze **is blowing**. It all **seems** so peaceful.

Marta: I **know** what you **mean**. I **feel** so relaxed. I**'m** not **thinking** about any of my problems. But the sky **is turning** black. I **suppose** we should get back to the campground.

Susana: I **guess** you**'re** right. Ooh—I **hate** rainstorms! What **are** Gil and Rafael **doing**?

Marta: Gil **is taking** a nap over by that tree. Listen—**he's snoring**! And Rafael **is collecting** rocks.

Susana: Why **is** he **doing** that?

Marta: He**'s taking** a geology class. He**'s learning** about different kinds of rocks. I **think** rocks **are becoming** one of his hobbies.

Susana: Oh! I **believe** it**'s beginning** to rain.

Marta:	That**'s** OK. We **have** raincoats and we**'re** all **wearing** heavy, waterproof hiking boots.(*Rafael appears.*) Look, there**'s** Rafael. Hi, Rafael. Perfect timing. Let's get ready to leave.
Susana:	What **are** you **looking** for, Rafael?
Rafael:	My backpack.
Marta:	Gil **is using** it as a pillow.
Rafael:	**Is** he still **sleeping**? Let's wake him up and head back to the campgrounds.

 Discussion Questions Discuss these questions with a partner.

1. What are Susana and Marta doing?

2. What is Gil doing?

3. What is Rafael doing? Why?

4. Imagine you are on this hike. What are you doing at the present moment? Why?

5. Why are the hikers leaving Emerald Lake?

Grammar Structures and Practice

A. The Present Continuous Tense

The present continuous tense consists of the verb *be* + the *-ing* form of a verb. This tense is for an action happening at the moment of speaking. It's also for an action currently in progress.

2.5 Statements with the Present Continuous Tense		
	Explanations	**Examples**
Affirmative Statements	In these examples, the action is happening right now—at the moment of speaking.	Marta **is carrying** a heavy bag. They**'re relaxing** by the lake.
	In these examples, the action is currently in progress—*today, this term*, etc.	We**'re learning** Italian this semester. She**'s majoring** in biology.
Negative Statements	For the negative, put *not* between the form of *be* and the verb in the *-ing* form.	Hiroshi **isn't wearing** boots. They **aren't going** on the hike. She **isn't keeping** a journal.

2.6 Yes/No Questions with the Present Continuous Tense

	Explanations	Examples	Possible Answers	
			Affirmative	**Negative**
Affirmative Questions	To form a question, place the form of *be* in front of the subject. The *-ing* form of the verb comes after the subject.	**Is** Carlos **carrying** Susana's backpack? **Are** the guys **picking** flowers?	Yes, he is. Yes, they are.	No, he isn't. No, they aren't.
Negative Questions	For negative questions, insert *not* after the form of *be*.	**Isn't** Rafael **walking** on the trail? **Aren't** you **getting** tired?	Yes, he is. Yes, I am.	No, he isn't. No, I'm not.

2.7 Information Questions with the Present Continuous Tense

	Explanations	Examples	Possible Answers
Affirmative Questions	For information questions, put the *wh-* word first, followed by the form of *be*.	**When are** we **leaving?** **Why are** you **sneezing?**	(We're leaving) at noon. I'm getting a cold.
Negative Questions	For negative information questions, insert *not* after the form of *be*.	**Who isn't carrying** a canteen? **Why aren't** they **wearing** shoes?	Anita and Paul aren't. (Not Anita or Paul.) Their feet are hurting them.

Spelling Rules for *-ing* Verbs

The Simple Form of the Verb	Rule	Examples	
1. Ends in a silent *-e* after a consonant	Drop the *-e* and add *-ing*.	have sneeze	having sneezing
2. Ends in *-ie*	Change the *-ie* to *y* and add *-ing*.	die untie	dying untying
3. Has one syllable and ends in one consonant after one vowel	Double the last consonant and add *-ing*. **Exception:** If the last consonant is an *x* or a *w*, do not double the consonant.	get run box row play*	getting running boxing rowing playing*
4. Ends in an accented (stressed) syllable**	Follow Rule 3 for one final consonant after one vowel.	begin	beginning
5. All other verbs	Add *-ing* to the simple form.	walk eat carry	walking eating carrying

Note: *The letter *y* at the end of a word is a vowel, therefore just add *-ing*.

** If the last syllable is not accented, just add *-ing*. Example: háppen/happening

1 Practice Underline the present continuous verb phrases in the conversation between Marta, Susana, and Rafael on pages 45 and 46.

Example The birds <u>are singing</u>.

2 Practice Fill in the blanks with the present continuous forms of the verbs in parentheses.

Paul: Ah-choo! Ah-choo!

Anita: Paul! Why _____*are*_____ you _____*sneezing*_____? _____ you
                                          (sneeze)

_____ sick?
              1 (get)

Paul: Maybe. The water in the river is really cold.

Anita: You _____ _____! Why _____ you
                                    2 (shiver)

_____ a shirt and hat?
              3 (not wear)

Paul: You're right. I _____ _____.
                                          4 (freeze)

Anita: Where's my book? Oh no! Is that it there in the water? It _____

_____ down the river.
              5 (float)

Paul: Ow! (*He hits his back.*)

Anita: What's the matter?

Paul: I think something _____ _____ me.
                                                6 (bite)

Anita: Let me see. Oh, Paul! There are huge ants all over your back!

Paul: Anita, look. The hikers _____ _____ back.
                                                    7 (come)

Anita: Where? I don't see them.

Paul: They _____ _____ down the trail.

8 (walk)

Anita: Oh, yeah. Now I see them. But they _____ _____.

9 (not walk)

They _____ _____. I wonder why.

10 (run)

Paul: I don't know.

Anita: There _____ something _____ them. What is

11 (chase)

that? Is that a deer?

Paul: No, it's a *bear*! They _____ _____ away from a

12 (run)

bear!

3 **Practice** What is happening in each picture? With the words below, write two sentences in the present continuous tense.

1. Susana / give / her backpack / to Rafael
   Her back / hurt
   Susana is giving her backpack to Rafael.
   Her back is hurting.

2. Paul / get dressed
   Ants / bite him
   _____
   _____

3. The tents / fall down
Anita / fix them

_____

_____

4. Susana / make lunch
The hamburgers / burn

_____

_____

5. Marta / sit on a rock
A snake / come toward her

_____

_____

6. Gil / throw his boots in the river
They / float away

_____

_____

7. Rafael / make noise
The bear / run away

_____

_____

8. Marta and Rafael / have lunch
They / eat apples

_____

_____

4 **Practice** Look at these pictures with a partner. Student A asks eight present continuous questions with these words. Student B answers the questions.

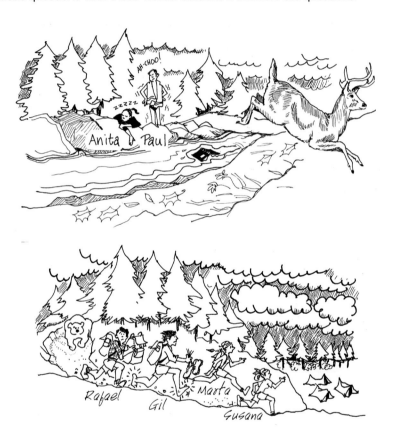

Example Who / run / with no backpack?
A: *Who is running with no backpack?*
B: *Susana (is running with no backpack).*

1. the sky / get cloudy?

2. Who / sleep? Where / she / sleep?

3. What / the bear / do?

4. What / Paul / wear? Why / he / not wearing a shirt?

5. the hikers / have trouble?

6. What / the deer / do?

7. What / happen / to the tents? Where / it / happen?

8. What / Gil / do? Why / he / do that?

Change roles. Now Student B asks present continuous questions with these words, and Student A answers.

9. How / the weather / change?

10. What / the hikers / do? Where / they / do it?

11. Who / carry / an extra backpack?

12. What / Paul / do? Why / he / freeze?

13. anyone / swim? Why / not anyone / swim?

14. What / happen / to Anita's book? Where / it / float?

15. Why / Gil / carry / the boots?

16. What / Anita / do? Why / she / not wake up?

B. Nonaction Verbs

Some verbs do not appear very often in the continuous tense. In their nonaction meanings, these verbs have only one present tense form—the simple present. These verbs have the following meanings:

- feeling and thought
- possession
- sensory perception

2.8	**Verbs for Feeling or Thought**		
	Verbs		**Examples**
appear	know	recognize	I **know** his telephone number. (NOT: I am knowing his telephone number.)
appreciate	like	remember	
be	love	seem	Anita **needs** a new jacket. (NOT: She is needing a new jacket.)
believe	mean	suppose	**Do** you **recognize** me? (NOT: Are you recognizing me?)
dislike	need	understand	
hate	prefer	want	**What do** you **mean**? (NOT: What are you meaning?)

2.9 Verbs for Possession

Verbs	Examples
belong to have owe own possess	Akeno **owns** a camping stove. (NOT: Akeno is owning a camping stove.) **Do** you **have** a car? (NOT: Are you having a car?) Who **does** this rock **belong** to? (NOT: Who is this rock belonging to?)

2.10 Verbs for Sensory Perception

Verbs	Examples
feel see hear smell look taste	The pizza **smells** good. (NOT: The pizza is smelling good.) Do you **hear** that noise? (NOT: Are you hearing that noise?) The campers **see** a deer outside their tent. (NOT: They are seeing a deer outside their tent.)

Note: There are some very specific cases in which some of these verbs can be used in the continuous form. Example: *I am not feeling well = I am sick.*

---

5 **Practice** Circle the correct verb or verb phrase in each set of parentheses.

Susana: There (are / are being) so many stars out!

(Are you recognizing / Do you recognize) any constellations?

                                  1

Marta: Well, I (am supposing / suppose) that ('s / 's being) the Big Dipper.

                           2   3

Susana: Hey, I (think / 'm thinking) I (am seeing / see) a shooting star!

                     4   5

Marta: Oh yes! I (am seeing / see) it too!

                     6

Susana: What's that noise?

Marta: I (am not hearing / don't hear) anything.

               7

Susana: You (aren't listening / don't listen) closely.

               8

Marta: Oh, that noise. That's just Gil. He's (snoring / snore).

               9

Susana: No, that's not what I (am meaning / mean). There's another noise. It

               10

(is sounding / sounds) like someone speaking.

       11

Marta: You're right. I (am thinking / think) Rafael (is talking / talks) in his

               12   13

sleep.

Susana: I (am wondering / wonder) what he (is dreaming / dreams) about.

             14   15

Marta: Probably about being home in his own bed! I (get / 'm getting) tired.

                                  16

And we ('re having / have) a big day tomorrow. Let's go to sleep.

       17

Susana: OK. Good night!

Using What You've Learned

6 Describing an Activity Scene There are many activity scenes in this chapter. Choose one picture, but don't tell its page number. With *there is / there are* and simple and continuous present verb forms when appropriate, give a short description of it. Can your listeners find the picture? Can they add more information to your description?

Example A: *There are two people in this scene. They're kneeling on a picnic blanket. The woman is putting cups on the blanket, and the guy is taking a sandwich out of a backpack.*

B: *It's the "Setting the Context" picture on page 40. Is there anything else on the blanket? Yes, there is. There's a thermos. There's also a canteen. But there are no other picnickers doing anything.*

7 **Describing a Chosen Place at a Chosen Time** Take turns and choose one item from each list. Pretend you are in that place at that time. Imagine the activities of the people there. Tell about them with the present continuous tense when possible. How quickly can your listener(s) guess the place and the time? Can they add more details?

Example A: *There are many people here. People are swimming. One man is fishing. Children are playing in the sand.*

B: *You're at the beach in summer. One kid is building a sand castle. Many people are sunbathing.*

Places	Times
in the mountains	in winter
in the desert	in summer
on a river	in spring
at the beach	in fall
at a lake	in the early morning
at a park	at sunset
in a forest	in the middle of the night

8 **Adding Sensory Details to a Place Description** Take turns and choose one item from each list in Activity 7. This time, use as many nonaction verbs as possible (*be, appear, know, need, have, see, smell, taste, feel, hear,* etc.) to describe the place to your listeners. How fast can they guess the scene?

Example A: *I hear seagulls. They sound funny. I taste salt air. I feel a strong wind. It feels cold.*

B: *You're on the beach in the winter. The sky is already dark, but more clouds are forming. There aren't many people there because a storm is coming.*

Part 4 Modal Verbs: *Can, May, Might, Will*

Setting the Context

Prereading Questions Discuss these questions with a small group.

Do you have memories of a favorite trip? Why will you always remember that trip?

Reading Read the conversation.

Susana: I **can't believe** it's already time to go home. I**'ll have** great memories of this trip. How **will** you **remember** it?

Rafael:	Well, I hope I **won't remember** my dreams—or the bear!
Marta:	That **might be** a good idea.
Susana:	We **will be** home in an hour or so. What **will** you **do** first?
Rafael:	**I'll take** a good, long, hot shower.
Marta:	I **might take** a nap.
Gil:	I **may order** a pizza.
Marta:	Don't you want a huge homemade meal?
Gil:	Sure I do, but I **can't cook**.
Marta:	I **can**. I think **I'll make** a huge pasta dinner tonight.
Gil:	Sounds delicious. And big. **Can** you **eat** it all on your own?
Marta:	Probably. But you **can come** over and **join** me if you want.
Gil:	I think I **may do** that!
Rafael:	Uh-oh. It looks like it **might rain** again.
Gil:	I **can't believe** it.
Rafael:	**It'll stop** soon.
Susana:	Oh, I love this place! **Can** we **do** this again next weekend?
Gil:	*You* **can**. Next weekend **I'll be** home on my couch. I **will watch** TV and **eat** junk food!

 Discussion Questions Discuss these questions with a partner.

1. What will Rafael do first at home?

2. What might Marta do?

3. What might Gil do?

4. Who wants to go hiking next weekend?

5. How might each person feel about the hiking trip? Explain your answers.

Grammar Structures and Practice

A. Forms and Patterns of Modal Verbs

Can, may, might, and *will* are examples of modal auxiliaries.

■ Modals never change form or end in *-s* or *-ed*.

■ The simple form of another verb comes after a modal in a full sentence.

■ These charts show the position of modals and the verbs that follow in statements and questions.

2.11 Statements with Modals

	Explanations	Examples

Affirmative	In statements, modals come before the simple form of a verb.
	  * Don't use *to* before the second verb.
	  * *Will* can appear in short forms.
	The contractions with *will* are:
	I will = I'll *we will = we'll*
	he will = he'll *you will = you'll*
	she will = she'll *they will = they'll*
		I **can** swim.
		
		The rain **may** stop soon.
		
		The tents **might** fall down.
		
		We **will** call you tonight.

Negative	*May not* and *might not* cannot appear in contractions.	I **can't** find my watch. He **won't** go with us. We **may not** need the compass. I **might not** come back.

2.12 Yes/No Questions with Modals

	Explanations	Examples	Possible Answers	
			Affirmative	**Negative**
Affirmative	In yes/no questions, modals come before the sentence subject.	**Can** you go with us? **Might** it rain tonight? **Will** we get there late?	Yes, I **can**. Yes, it **might**. Yes, we **will**.	No, I **can't**. No, it **won't**. No, we **won't**.
Negative	For negative questions, insert *not* after the modal.	**Can't** the children swim? **Won't** it be hot in August?	Yes, they **can**. Yes, it **will**.	No, they **can't**. No, it **won't**.

2.13 Information Questions with Modals

	Explanations	Examples	Possible Answers
Affirmative	In information questions, modals come after the question word.	What **can** we do? Who **may** visit us? What **might** happen? Where **will** they go?	We **can** run to that tree. Carlos **may** visit us. You **might** get sick. They**'ll** stay home.
Negative	For negative questions, insert *not* after the modal.	What **can't** Farshad eat with us? Who **may not** stay? Who **might not** go? Why **won't** Anita visit?	He **can't** eat meat. Hiroshi **may not** stay. Alma and Sapir **might not** go. (She **won't** visit) because she's at school.

B. Meanings

Each modal has more than one meaning or use. This chart gives examples of the meanings of *can, may, might,* and *will* in this chapter.

2.14 Meanings of Modals

Modals	Meanings	Examples
Can	ability or inability	I **can** speak English. (I am able to speak English.) He **can't** swim. (He isn't able to swim.) **Can** you dance? (Are you able to dance?)
May **Might**	future possibility	It **may** rain. (Maybe it will rain; maybe it won't.) I **might** not go. (Maybe I won't go; maybe I will.)
Will	future plans predictions	**I'll** see you tomorrow. (I plan to see you tomorrow.) The movie **won't** be crowded. (I predict the movie won't be crowded.) **Will** you buy a tent? (Do you plan to buy a tent?)

1 Practice Underline the modals and following simple verbs in the conversation on pages 55 and 56. Does the modal in each statement or question mean *ability, future possibility, future plans,* or *prediction?*

Example I can't believe it's already time to go home. = *ability*

2 Practice Put these words into the correct order for statements or questions. Pay attention to the capital letter and the end-of-sentence punctuation.

Example with his friend / may / tonight / go / to a movie / He
He may go to a movie with his friend tonight.

1. You / without matches / a fire / can't start

_____.

2. stay / at a campsite / You / all week long / can't

_____.

3. Who / take down / the tents / can

_____?

4. with the extra food / you / will / What / do

_____?

5. might / in an hour or so / be / home / We

_____.

6. we / Where / can / order / a pizza

_____?

7. I / take / a nap / or watch TV / may

_____.

8. a good, long, hot shower / take / I'll

_____.

9. your mother / tomorrow / Will / make / a fantastic meal

_____?

10. eat / on your own / a big pasta dinner / you / Can

_____?

11. When / we / to this beautiful area / will / again / come

_____?

12. won't / all the backpacks / next time / carry / I

_____.

3 **Practice** Circle the correct words in each set of parentheses.

There are some clouds, but it (willn't rain / (won't rain)) today. At least I don't think

it (will / will rains). It (can be / will be) a beautiful day. I (might to catch / might catch)
      1   2   3

some fish. They (can might be / might be) big fish. Uh-oh. There's water coming
                4

into the boat. There (might be / will to be) a leak. I (not / can't) (see / to see) the
                 5   6   7

bottom of the boat under the water. Help! Help! What might that noise (be / to be)?
                                              8

It ('ll / might) (is / be) a waterfall. Oh, no! It is a waterfall! Well, I (mayn't / may not)
 9   10   11
(will save / save) the boat, but I (mayn't / 'll) be able to save my life. I (can / can't to)
 12   13   14
(swim / to swim)! And the water (may / have) not (be / being) too deep—I hope!
 15   16   17

Using What You've Learned

4 **Telling About Abilities and Inabilities** What *can* and *can't* you do? Have a
conversation with a partner about these and other activities.

swim	read maps
ride a horse	use a compass
sail a boat	set up a tent
hike ten miles	plan and make a picnic lunch

Example   A: *I can swim. Can you?*
                  B: *Yes, I can. But I can't swim very well. How long can you tread
                      water?*
                  A: *I can stay afloat about 15 minutes.*

5 **Telling About Weekend Plans** What *will* or *might* you do next weekend?
Have a conversation with a partner about these and other activities.

go to the park	sleep late
cook	read the paper
study	rent a movie
take a short trip	visit friends or relatives

Example   A: *Will you go to the park next weekend?*
                  B: *I may.*
                  A: *Who might you go with?*
                  B: *I may go with my sister. But if it rains, I'll do my laundry
                      instead.*

6 **Discussing the Possibilities of Situations** Work in small groups. Take turns
and make statements with modals about each of the following situations. What *may,
may not, might, might not, can, can't, will,* or *will not happen* in each situation? Come up
with as many ideas as possible.

Example   *You are driving on an icy mountain road. You go around a curve
                  in the road. A deer suddenly jumps out in front of your car. What
                  might happen?*

A: *I will hit the deer.*

B: *I might have an accident.*

C: *The car might slide on the ice.*

D: *I will try to stop.*

1. You are standing under a big tree. It's raining hard, and there is thunder and lightning.

2. You and your friends return to your campground late in the evening after a long hike. There is a bear eating your food.

3. Some campers want to start a fire for dinner. Their matches are wet from the rain last night.

4. Some students are hiking on a new trail. It's almost dark, and they're lost.

Self-Assessment Log

Each of the following sentences describes the grammar you learned in this chapter. Read the sentences and then check the best box for how well you understand each structure.

	Needs Improvement	Good	Great
I can use *there is / there are* to talk about things in nature.	❑	❑	❑
I can use *whose* in questions to ask about possession.	❑	❑	❑
I can use possessive nouns to describe people and things they own.	❑	❑	❑
I can use the present continuous tense to talk about activities in progress.	❑	❑	❑
I can use nonaction verbs to talk about feelings, thoughts, possession, and perception.	❑	❑	❑
I can use modals to express ability, possibility, and predictions.	❑	❑	❑

Living to Eat or Eating to Live?

"Food is our common ground, a universal experience.**"**

—James Beard
American chef (1903–1985)

Connecting to the Topic

1. What kind of food do you enjoy eating?

2. Do you like to eat at home or in restaurants?

Setting the Context

Prereading Questions Discuss these questions with a small group.

What do you usually eat on a typical day or during a typical week? Are your diet choices changing? If so, why?

Reading Read the passage.

The Changing American Diet

What are **some examples** of "typical" American **meals**? On the **weekend, a** typical **breakfast** may consist of **two or three eggs, some pancakes** with **butter** and **syrup,** and **a few pieces of bacon.** During the **week, some people** have only **toast** or **a sweet roll** and **some juice** or **coffee** for **breakfast.** Or they might eat **a bowl of** sweet **cereal** with **some milk.** For **lunch, many people** eat **junk food** or just **a few snacks.** For example, they may stop at **a** fast-food **place** for **a cheeseburger** or **a hot dog** with **a little ketchup** or **mustard** and **some relish, some French fries, a milkshake** or **a soft drink,** and **a few cookies.** A typical American **dinner** consists of **meat, a baked potato,** and **some bread** and **butter. Dinner** often ends with **a dessert**—typically, **cake** or **pie** and **ice cream.**

Nutritionists don't believe that the typical American **diet** is very healthy. **Many kinds of** American **food** are high in **sugar** or artificial **sweetener, salt, fat, caffeine,** or unhealthy **cholesterol.** These food **substances** may cause **disease.** In general, **Americans** don't eat **many** whole-grain **items** or **vegetables.** They don't consume **much fish,** which contains healthful **protein** and fish **oils.** They eat only **a little** fresh **fruit,** which contains important **vitamins, minerals,** and **fiber.** For **weight loss, many Americans** read best-selling **diet books** and follow their

advice. Then they consume only one **food**—like **grapefruit** or **mushrooms** or **soybeans**—for **a few weeks**. Or they eat only **meals** with **a lot of protein** and very **few carbohydrates**—or vice versa.

Even so, some **Americans** are becoming much more interested in scientific **research** about good **health.** Because of this, they're changing their eating **habits.** For example, they're eating more whole grain **bread** and **cereal** and **less** white **bread** and sugared **cereal**. They're substituting **chicken** and **fish** for **red meat. A lot of people** are eating **more** fresh **vegetables** in **salads** and **fewer** canned or overcooked **vegetables**. They are drinking **less coffee** and **soda**, and more decaffeinated **coffee**, herbal **tea**, and fruit **juice**.

 Discussion Questions Discuss these questions with a partner.

1. What does a "typical" American breakfast consist of during the week? On the weekend?

2. What might an American have for lunch at a fast-food place?

3. Describe a "typical" American dinner.

4. How are some Americans changing their eating habits? What kinds of food are they eating more of? Less of?

5. How does your diet compare with the "typical" American diet? What's the most healthful eating plan, in your opinion?

Grammar Structures and Practice

A. Count and Noncount Nouns

There are two basic types of nouns: count nouns and noncount nouns.

- Speakers of English use count nouns for things with numbers like *one egg, five cups,* or *three meals*.
- For noncount nouns, speakers may talk about amounts of these items but not numbers. Some examples are *a lot of food, a little water,* and *some advice.*

3.1 Count and Noncount Nouns

	Explanations	Singular	Plural
Count Nouns	Count nouns have both singular and plural forms. Singular count nouns can have *a/an* before them; most plural count nouns have an *-s/-es* ending.	a meal an egg one waiter a chair one restaurant	three meals some eggs waiters some chairs restaurants
Noncount Nouns	Noncount nouns are always singular. They have no plural form (no *-s/-es* endings). Most noncount nouns name an item made up of smaller or different parts. Some noncount nouns name abstract things, such as ideas, feelings, and concepts.	butter some juice electricity salt some jewelry traffic freedom anger some luck	

Notes: The word *a* means "one." Use *a* before a consonant sound, such as *a <u>b</u>ig breakfast, a <u>w</u>eek, a <u>E</u>uropean meal.* Use *an* before a vowel sound—like *an <u>A</u>merican diet plan, an egg, an <u>h</u>our.* In some special expressions, there may not be *a* or *an* before a singular noun; for example: *for lunch, for instance, have dessert.*

---

1 **Practice** Underline the singular count nouns in the reading on pages 65 and 66. Put two lines under the plural nouns. Circle the noncount nouns.

Example What are some <u>examples</u> of "typical" American <u>meals</u>? On the <u>weekend</u>, a typical <u>breakfast</u> may consist of two or three <u>eggs</u>, some <u>pancakes</u> with (butter) and (syrup), and a few <u>pieces</u> of (bacon.)

2 **Practice** Take turns describing the pictures on pages 64 and 65. Your sentences might include *there is / there are*. Use as many count and noncount nouns as possible.

Example Student A: *There are two big plates in the first picture. On one plate, there are two eggs and some bacon.*

3 **Practice** Look around the classroom. What objects and items do you see? For five minutes, write sentences with as many count and noncount nouns as possible.

Example *There's a clock on the wall. There are books on the shelf. There's some paper on the teacher's desk.*

Now compare your sentences with a classmate's. How many similar things did you and your classmate notice? How many different things did you see?

B. *Some* and *Any*

Some and *any* are used to describe "an unspecified number or amount." *Some* and *any* can appear before both count and noncount nouns.

3.2 *Some* and *Any*		
	Explanations	**Examples**
Some	Use *some* in affirmative statements and questions.	Please buy **some** napkins. There's **some** milk in that cup. Do you have **some** shopping bags? Would you like **some** spaghetti?
Any	Use *any* in negative statements and in affirmative and negative questions.	There aren't **any** plates on the table. I don't use **any** salt at all. Do you have **any** pots in your kitchen? Isn't there **any** fish?

Note: Not any before noncount and plural count nouns means *no.* For example: *There aren't any hot dogs.= There are no hot dogs.*

---

4 **Practice** Put *some* or *any* on each line. In some cases, both may be correct.

1. I always eat _____*some*_____ fruit for breakfast—maybe

   _____ grapefruit or _____ mango.

2. I'm going to the supermarket. Do you want _____ white

   bread, or would you prefer _____ whole grain bread?

3. We need _____ food for a salad; we don't have

   _____ fruit or vegetables.

4. I want _____ coffee, but there isn't

   _____ decaffeinated coffee on the shelf.

5. Are there _____ health food markets near your apartment?

6. Do you have _____ experience as a cook?

7. Would you like _____ ketchup or _____
   mustard for your hamburger?

8. Is there _____ tofu (soy protein) in the typical American
   diet?

9. I'd like _____ onions and _____ mushrooms
   on my pizza.

10. My family doesn't eat _____ red meat, but we occasionally

    eat _____ chicken or _____ fish.

11. There are _____ great Italian restaurants near here, but

there aren't _____ good Chinese places.

12. You can't have _____ ice cream, but you may try

_____ frozen yogurt.

13. Are there _____ waiters in this restaurant? There doesn't

seem to be _____ service.

14. I'd like _____ eggs, but I don't want _____
bacon.

15. I'm full. I can't eat _____ more food.

 5 Practice Take turns. Ask and answer questions about the food in the pictures on pages 64 and 65. Use *some* or *any* in your sentences.

Example A: *Is there any juice in the breakfast picture?*
B: *There isn't any juice, but there is some coffee.*

6 Practice Describe your favorite ice-cream sundae. You can include the ice-cream flavors and toppings in the picture. Use *some* or *any* in your sentences.

Example *My sundae has some vanilla and chocolate ice cream, but it doesn't have any strawberry ice cream. It has some nuts and some whipped cream.*

C. *A lot of / Many / Much*

A lot of, many, and *much* mean "a large quantity of something."
■ *A lot of* may appear before both noncount and plural count nouns.
■ *Many* may appear only before plural count nouns.
■ *Much* may appear only before noncount nouns.

3.3 A lot of, Many, and Much

	Explanations	Examples
A lot of	*A lot of* is for affirmative and negative statements and questions.	My roommate doesn't eat **a lot of** hamburgers. There is **a lot of** salt in this soup. Is there **a lot of** fresh bread at the bakery? Don't you eat **a lot of** apples?
Many	*Many* is for plural nouns in affirmative and negative statements and questions.	**Many** fast-food restaurants serve hamburgers. I don't like **many** kinds of vegetables. Do **many** people have poor diets? Aren't there **many** eggs in the refrigerator?
Much	*Much* is for noncount nouns only—mainly in negative statements and affirmative and negative questions. *Much* doesn't usually appear in affirmative statements.	The Japanese don't eat **much** red meat. We don't drink **much** tea or coffee. Does chicken have **much** cholesterol? Don't they eat **much** fish?

7 **Practice** Make one question and one answer about each picture. Use *a lot of, many,* or *much.*

1. _____ Is there a lot of ice cream in the bowl? _____?
Yes, there's a lot.

ICE CREAM

2. _____?

COOKIES

3. _____?

MILK

APPLES

4. _____
   _____ ?
   _____
   _____

PIZZA

5. _____
   _____ ?
   _____
   _____

RICE

6. _____
   _____ ?
   _____
   _____

PANCAKES

7. _____
   _____ ?
   _____
   _____

SPAGHETTI

8. _____
   _____ ?
   _____
   _____

WATER

9. _____
   _____ ?
   _____
   _____

EGGS

10. _____
    _____ ?
    _____
    _____

11. _____

_____?

_____

_____

12. _____

_____?

_____

_____

D. Common Units of Measure

Units of measure give amounts of either count or noncount nouns. These units make noncount nouns into countable noun phrases.

■ *Of* follows all of these expressions, except *dozen*.

3.4 Units of Measure	
Unit terms	**Noncount nouns**
bag	sugar, potatoes, flour
bar	chocolate, hand soap
bottle	detergent, ketchup, soda
box	cereal, detergent, tissues
bunch	bananas, grapes, flowers
can	soup, beans, soda
carton	eggs, milk
cup, tablespoon, teaspoon	all liquid and dry recipe ingredients
dozen	eggs, bakery products, fruit and vegetables
gallon, quart, pint	all liquids, ice cream
head	cabbage, cauliflower, lettuce
jar	mayonnaise, jam, peanut butter
loaf	bread
package	cookies, potato chips, spaghetti
piece	cake, bread, meat
pound, ounce	meat, fruit and vegetables, cheese
roll	paper towels, toilet paper
stick	butter, gum
tube	toothpaste

8 **Practice** Put a unit of measure before each item in the list below the pictures.

1. _____two bottles_____ of soda

2. _____ of milk

3. _____ of toothpaste

4. _____ of butter

5. _____ of lettuce

6. _____ of peanut butter

7. _____ of jam

8. _____ of hand soap

9. _____ of flour

10. _____ of flowers

9 **Practice** What grocery items do you need on your next shopping trip? Make a shopping list. Include a unit of measurement for each item.

Example *a pound of ham*
a bottle of olive oil
two bottles of soda
a dozen eggs
two bags of onions

E. Asking Questions with *How Many* and *How Much*

How many is for questions with plural count nouns. *How much* is for questions with noncount nouns.

3.5	*How Many* and *How Much*		
	Explanations	**Examples**	**Possible Answers**
How many	*How many* begins a question about a number, so it appears only before a plural noun—or if the noun is understood.	**How many** eggs do you want? **How many** cakes are you making? **How many** different vegetables do you have? **How many** do you have?	two only one three
How much	*How much* begins a question about an amount, so it appears only before a noncount noun—or if the noun is understood.	**How much** coffee does he drink? **How much** rice do we need? **How much** pizza can you eat? **How much** can you eat?	three cups ten pounds two slices

Note: Use *how many* with a unit of measure before a noncount noun. For example: *How many cups of coffee does he drink?* means *How much coffee does he drink?*

10 **Practice** Take turns. Ask and answer questions about the pictures on pages 70–72. Use *how many* or *how much* in your questions.

Example A: *How much ice cream is in the bowl?*
B: *There's a lot of ice cream. How many cookies are on the plate?*
A: *There are two cookies on the plate. (or There aren't many.)*

F. *A few / A little*

A few and *a little* are for a small number or quantity of something.

- *A few* appears only before plural count nouns.
- *A little* appears only before noncount nouns.

3.6	*A Few / A Little*	
	Explanations	**Examples**
A few	*A few* is used with count nouns in affirmative statements and affirmative and negative questions.	There are **a few** olives in the jar. Would you like **a few** potatoes? Aren't there **a few** cookies in the box?
A little	*A little* is used with noncount nouns in affirmative statements and affirmative and negative questions.	I'd like **a little** tomato sauce on my pasta. Is there **a little** sugar in that bowl? Don't you want **a little** milk in your tea?

11 **Practice** Put *a few* or *a little* on each line.

Example Do you have time for _____*a little*_____ coffee and
_____*a few*_____ cookies?

1. I usually put _____ sugar in my tea.

2. Cooks need _____ pots and pans to make dinner.

3. Can you get me _____ apples and _____
orange juice from the refrigerator?

4. I'd like _____ napkins, please.

5. Does your brother want _____ pieces of bacon with his eggs?

6. Would you like _____ soup?

7. There are _____ forks, but there aren't any spoons.

8. We're having _____ cake for dessert and
_____ cups of coffee.

9. I like to eat lunch with _____ friends.

10. My husband needs _____ ice cubes for his soda.

Using What You've Learned

12 **Matching Units of Measure with Nouns** The class divides into two
groups: Group A and Group B. Each member of each group writes a unit of measure on
one piece of paper and a noun for this unit of measure on another piece of paper.
Group A and Group B exchange their pieces of paper. Group members work together.

As quickly as possible, try to put all the nouns with appropriate units of measurement. Who can finish the task correctly first? They are the winners.

 13 Telling About Your Favorite Eating Place What is your favorite or least favorite restaurant, café, or eating place? Write a paragraph about the kinds of food there. (A menu from the place can give you ideas.) Use count and noncount nouns and expressions of quantity.

Example *Pongsri is a good Thai restaurant. You can order a lot of delicious Thai food there. They have many chicken, beef, and pork dishes. Many dishes come with rice or noodles. They also serve a lot of fish and other seafood. They have a few salads and some interesting kinds of soup.*

Now work with a classmate. Read and talk about each other's descriptions. Do the count and noncount nouns follow correct quantity expressions? Do you want to go to your partner's eating place? Why or why not? How can the class make a restaurant guide? Class members can collect, copy, and put together all students' paragraphs.

 14 Interviewing In pairs, interview each other about food habits and diets. The interviewer should ask questions with *how many* and *how much*. The other person should use count and noncount nouns and expressions of quantity. Take notes on your partner's information.

Example A: *How many meals do you eat in a typical day?*
B: *I usually eat three meals a day. I also usually have a little snack between lunch and dinner. Maybe just a few nuts or a little yogurt.*

Now use your interview notes to tell the class about your partner's eating habits.

Setting the Context

Prereading Questions Discuss these questions with a small group.

Who usually does the grocery shopping in your household? How does that person decide what to buy?

Reading Read the conversation.

Dolores:	Felicia! Hello, there!
Felicia:	Oh, hello, Dolores.
Dolores:	My goodness! You certainly have a lot of things in your cart! You're getting **a lot more than** I am.
Felicia:	Yes, well, you know we have five children.
Dolores:	Are you buying Pearly White Dishwashing Liquid? There are **cheaper** brands, you know.
Felicia:	It's **more expensive than** other brands, but I think it lasts **longer.**
Dolores:	Why are you buying that huge package of spaghetti? There are **smaller** sizes . . .

Felicia:	The **larger** size is always **cheaper**. And the pasta cooks just **as well**. Well, nice seeing you again . . .
Dolores:	Those cherries look **nicer than** the strawberries in my cart! May I taste one? *(She takes a cherry.)* Oh, my. They're **much tastier than** the cherries last year.
Felicia:	Dolores, I have to get home **as soon as** possible.
Dolores:	Do you really like brown rice **better than** white rice? It cooks **more slowly**.
Felicia:	Brown rice tastes just **as good as** white rice, and it's **more nutritious**.
Dolores:	You know, the sign says this market has **lower** prices, but I think it's just **as expensive as** the others. It's **farther** from home, too. What do you think?
Felicia:	I think one market is **as good as** any other. Well, I'll let you go now, Dolores. I know you're **as busy as** I am.

 Discussion Questions Discuss these questions with a partner.

1. What is Dolores asking Felicia questions about?

2. Why does Felicia buy Pearly White Dishwashing Liquid?

3. Why does Felicia buy the larger size package of spaghetti?

4. What does Dolores think about the cherries in Felicia's cart?

5. Why does Felicia buy brown rice?

6. What do Dolores and Felicia think about Save-A-Lot Market?

7. Is Felicia enjoying the conversation? How do you know?

Grammar Structures and Practice

A. Comparisons with *As . . . as* and *Less . . . than*

Use the phrase *as* + adjective / adverb + *as* to compare two or more people or things in affirmative and negative statements and questions. You can also use the pattern *less* + adjective / adverb + *than* in some negative comparisons.

3.7 As . . . as, Less . . . than

	Explanations	Examples
As . . . as **Affirmative Statements and Questions**	Affirmative sentences compare things that are the same in some way.	This market is **as expensive as** the others. You're **as busy as** I am. Are the cherries **as nice as** the strawberries?
As . . . as **Negative Statements and Questions**	Negative sentences compare things that are different in some way. You can leave out the words in parentheses if they are understood.	White rice **isn't as nutritious** (as brown rice). Brown rice **doesn't cook as quickly** (as white rice). Aren't the cherries **as good as** (the cherries) last year?
Less . . . than **Negative Statements**	You can use *less* with many adjectives of two or more syllables; *less* is usually not used with one-syllable adjectives.	White rice is **less nutritious** (**than** brown rice). Brown rice cooks **less quickly** (**than** white rice).

1 **Practice** Underline the phrases with *as . . . as* in the conversation between Felicia and Dolores on pages 77 and 78.

Example Dolores, I have to get home <u>as soon as</u> possible.

2 **Practice** Compare the items below. Write an affirmative or a negative sentence with *as . . . as* and the adjectives next to each picture. When possible, write a second sentence with *less . . . than*.

1. expensive ___*Pie is as expensive as cake.*___

2. cheap _____

3. delicious _____

4. sweet _____

5. nutritious _____

6. cook quickly _____

7. healthy _____

8. fresh _____

B. Comparisons with *-er than* and *More . . . than*

Use the pattern adjective or adverb + *-er than* or *more* + adjective or adverb + *than* to compare two or more people or things that are different.

3.8 Comparisons with *-er than* and *More . . . than*

	Explanations	Examples
One-Syllable Adjectives and Adverbs	Add *-er* to most one-syllable adjectives and adverbs. If a word ends in one vowel and one consonant, double the last consonant and add *-er*.	These cherries are **sweeter than** those. This market is **cheaper than** the others. Brown rice cooks **slower than** white rice. These eggs are **bigger than** those.
Two-Syllable Adjectives Ending in *-y*	If a word ends in *-y*, change the *y* to *i* and add *-er*.	This fish is **tastier than** that fish. Thai food is **spicier than** American food. Fruit is **healthier than** ice cream.
Adjectives and Adverbs with Two or More Syllables	Use *more* with most adjectives and adverbs that have two or more syllables.	It's **more expensive than** the other brands. It's **more nutritious than** white rice. Fresh vegetables are **more delicious than** frozen ones.
Irregular Forms	The comparative forms of *good*, *bad*, and *far* are irregular: *good/better* *bad/worse* *far/farther (further)*	Cream tastes **better than** milk. Coffee is **worse** for your health **than** tea. The health food store is **farther than** the supermarket.

3 Circle the comparisons with *-er than* and *more . . . than* and the irregular comparatives in the conversation between Felicia and Dolores on pages 77 and 78.

Example You're getting (a lot more than) I am.

 4 With a partner, take turns and compare the pairs of food items in each of the following pictures. You may want to use words from this list as well as words of your own. Make as many sentences as you can for each picture with *as . . . as, less . . . than, -er than,* or *more . . . than.*

expensive	tasty	spicy
healthy	(taste) good	easy (to make)
delicious	(taste) bad	(cook) fast
nutritious	sweet	fattening

Examples A: *Ice cream isn't as healthy as frozen yogurt.*
B: *Ice cream tastes better than frozen yogurt.*
A: *Ice cream is sweeter than frozen yogurt.*
B: *Ice cream is as expensive as frozen yogurt.*
A: *I don't think that's true. I think frozen yogurt is more expensive.*

1. _____
2. _____
3. _____
4. _____
5. _____
6. _____
7. _____
8. _____
9. _____
10. _____

C. More Comparisons: *As Much / As Many . . . as* and *More / Less / Fewer . . . than*

Use *as much / as many . . . as* and *more / less / fewer . . . than* to compare numbers or amounts of count or noncount nouns.

3.9	Comparison Phrases	
	Explanations	**Examples**
As much / as many . . . as	Use *as many . . . as* with plural count nouns. Use *as much . . . as* with noncount nouns.	Does frozen yogurt have **as many calories as** ice cream? Fruit juice doesn't have **as much sugar as** soda.
More / less / fewer . . . than	Use *more* before plural count and noncount nouns. Use *less* only before noncount nouns. Use *fewer* only before plural count nouns.	I eat **more apples than** oranges. She drinks **more tea than** coffee. There is **less sugar than** salt in this sauce. Canned food has **fewer vitamins than** frozen food.

5 **Practice** Compare the food items in the pictures. Use the words under the pictures to make sentences with *as much / as many . . . as* or *more / less / fewer . . . than*.

1.

steak / chicken / market

There's less chicken than steak at the market.

There's more steak than chicken at the market.

2.

a chocolate bar / an apple / calories

_____

_____

3.

peaches / bananas / basket

_____

_____

4.

fish / meat / fat

_____

_____

5.

milk / cream / refrigerator

_____

_____

6.

fresh carrots / frozen carrots / vitamins

_____

_____

6 Read the recipes for brownies from two different cookbooks. Write sentences comparing the ingredients in the two recipes.

Example *The first recipe uses more chocolate than the second. The first recipe uses as much butter as the second.*

Double Chocolate Brownies

Ingredients:

5 ounces chocolate

$1/2$ pound butter

$1^3/_4$ cups sugar

5 eggs

$1^1/_2$ teaspoons vanilla

1 cup flour

1 cup walnuts

The Fancy Farmer Cookbook   10

Brownie Delight

Ingredients:

4 ounces chocolate

$1/2$ pound butter

2 cups sugar

4 eggs

1 teaspoon vanilla

1 cup flour

1 cup peanuts

$1/2$ cup chocolate chips

The Creative Cook Cookbook   54

Using What You've Learned

7 **Telling About Eating Habits** For ten minutes, write about your eating habits. You can answer these questions: What kinds of food do you typically eat? Why? Where and with whom do you eat them? How do you cook them?

Example *I eat a lot of beef, chicken, beans, and rice. For religious reasons, I never eat pork or bacon or ham. I like a lot of spices in my food, so I often cook with spices like chili peppers, garlic, onions, and cilantro. Most of the time, I eat at home with my roommate. I'm a good cook, so I usually do the cooking. Occasionally, I go out to dinner with friends. But I never eat in expensive restaurants.*

Now exchange your work with a partner. Read about your partner's eating habits. How are they similar to yours? How are they different? With as many phrases of comparison as possible, compare your usual diet and food habits.

Example A: *You like spicier foods than I do. I eat foods with fewer hot ingredients.*

B: *But you are as good a cook as I am. You just cook with fewer spices.*

A: *I think you make more exotic dishes than I do. Do they have fewer calories?*

 8 **Writing Recipe Instructions** With your partner, choose one of the food dishes from the following list or another dish familiar to both of you. Separately, make a list of the ingredients and their amounts from your favorite recipe for that dish. You can also write the main preparation and cooking steps.

an omelette	cookies
a fish dish	a kind of soup
pancakes	another kind of dessert
a cake	a meat dish
spaghetti	a vegetable dish

When you finish, compare your lists of ingredients. Make sentences comparing your recipes.

Example recipes

Alfredo's omelette

1. 2 eggs

2. $^1/_2$ cup grated cheese

3. 1 chopped sausage

4. 1 small onion, chopped

5. 1 clove chopped garlic

6. 1 teaspoon chili sauce

Heat up an omelette pan with a little melted butter in it. Is the pan hot? Then put in the garlic, onion, and sausage for a minute or so. Beat the eggs and add them to the pan. After another minute, add the cheese and chili sauce. Put a lid on the pan, and cook for about two more minutes. Then serve the omelette.

Maria's omelette

1. 3 eggs

2. $^3/_4$ cup grated cheese

3. 6 sliced mushrooms

4. $^1/_2$ green pepper, chopped

Put a little olive oil in a heavy skillet. Let it heat up. Beat the three eggs, pour them into the skillet, and add the mushrooms and green pepper to the mixture. After a few minutes, sprinkle the grated cheese on the omelet. Then turn it. (Flip half of it onto the other half.) In another minute or so, you'll have a fancy, gourmet breakfast dish. Have fresh salsa on the table to put on it.

Examples **Maria:** *My recipe has more eggs than yours. Your omelette has more ingredients than mine.*

Alfredo: *My omelette is spicier than yours.*

Setting the Context

Prereading Questions Discuss these questions with a small group.

Do you ever go out to eat? If so, what kind of places do you go to? Describe a typical restaurant experience.

Reading Read the conversation.

Waiter: Good evening. **May** I **take** your order?

Woman: **Could** we **see** a menu first?

Waiter: Of course. (*The waiter gives them menus. Later, he returns.*)

Waiter: **Can** you **give** me your order *now*?

Man: I'd like the swordfish, please.

Waiter: *We* can't serve that anymore. It might not be good for you.

Man: All right, don't worry about it. I'll order the sea bass.

Waiter: Sorry, we just ran out of that.

Man: Well, **would** you **tell** us . . . what *do* you have?

Waiter: **May** I **suggest** the wild salmon? It's excellent.

Man: (*sighs*) But it's so expensive. I can't pay . . . . Oh, well, . . . all right.

Waiter: Madame?

Woman: Salmon is so high in fat, but . . . OK. **May** I **have** the salmon, too?

Waiter: Excellent!

Man: I don't have cash with me. **Can** we **pay** with a credit card?

Waiter: No, I'm sorry. You can't. We can only accept cash.

Man: Uh-oh. We may have to leave then.

Woman: Well, *I* have to get up now anyway. **Can** you **tell** me. . . Where's the ladies' room?

Waiter: Uh. . . I'm afraid you can't use it. It's out of order.

Woman: You know, I'm ready to go.

Man: Me, too. (*The man and woman get up to leave.*)

Waiter: It's a pleasure to serve you. Please come again soon!

Discussion Questions Discuss these questions with a partner.

1. Who makes the first request in this conversation? What is the request for?
2. What does the man try to order? What happens?
3. Why do the customers finally order the salmon?
4. Why do the man and woman leave the restaurant before dinner?
5. How do you think they feel when they leave? Explain your answer.

Grammar Structures and Practice

A. Modal Verbs: Requests, Offers, and Permission

In questions, the modals *may, can, could, will,* or *would* can be used for requests, offers, and requests for permission. The modal appears before the subject.

3.10 Making Requests		
Explanations	**Examples**	**Possible Answers**
Questions with *could, would, will, can +* *you* are requests. The speaker wants the listener to do something. *Could* and *would* are for both informal and formal situations. *Can* and *will* are informal.	**Could** you please **bring** a fork? **Would** you **suggest** a dessert? **Will** you **pass** the salt, please? **Can** we **have** a menu, please?	Of course. I'd be glad to. Certainly. Sure.

Note: Please makes any request more polite.

3.11 Making Offers		
Explanations	**Examples**	**Possible Answers**
Questions with *I* or *we* are offers. The speaker offers to do something for the listener. *May* sounds formal. *Can* is less formal.	**May** I **help** you? **Can** we **get** you something to drink?	Yes. Can I get a menu? I'd like an iced tea, please.

3.12 Requesting Permission		
Explanations	**Examples**	**Possible Answers**
Questions with *I* or *we* can also be requests for permission. The speaker wants consent for something. *May* sounds very formal. *Could* is for both formal and informal requests. *Can* is the least formal.	**May** we **join** you? **Could** I **borrow** some money? **Can** I **use** a credit card?	No, you may not. Yes, you can. No, you can't.

Note: Don't use *may* in questions with the subject *you.*

1 Practice Underline the modal verb phrases in the conversation on page 87. Is the phrase a request? Then put *R* next to it. Put *O* after the offer phrases and *P* after the requests for permission.

Example _____May_____ I take your order? *O*

2 Practice Imagine yourself in these situations. Make appropriate requests, offers, and/or requests for permission for each situation.

A. You are having dinner at your good friend's house.

1. You want to help your friend bring the food to the table.
_Can I help you bring the food to the table?_____

2. You want a second helping of rice.
_____

3. You want the last piece of bread.
_____

4. You want your friend to give you the recipe.
_____

5. You want to start clearing the table.
_____

B. You are having tea with a classmate in a café. Your teacher walks in.

1. You want your teacher to join you.

_____

2. You want the waiter to bring another cup.

_____

3. You want to pour the tea for your teacher.

_____

4. You want your friend to pass you the sugar.

_____

5. You want the waiter to bring the check.

_____

3 **Practice** Circle the correct words in each set of parentheses.

Luis: (May / (Would)) you please (pass / to pass) the hot sauce, Abdul?
1

Abdul: Sure. (Will / Can) I have the tartar sauce?
2

Luis: (Can / Will) I (ask / to ask) you something, Abdul? Why do you put tartar
3   4

sauce on your fish? Yuck!

Abdul: (_laughing_) (Will / Might) you (be / are) quiet, Luis?
5   6

Luis: Sorry.

Abdul: I need more butter. (Can / Are) you call the waiter, Luis?
7

Luis: (_snaps his fingers_) Waiter! (Can / May) you (bring / brings) us more
8   9

butter, please?

Abdul: Shh . . . (May / Could) you talk more softly? And (may / would) I
10   11

(make / to make) a suggestion? Please don't snap your fingers to get a
12

waiter's attention. It isn't polite.

Luis: Psssst! Waiter!

Abdul: (May / Would) I make another request? Please don't hiss at the waiter.
13

That's also rude.

Luis: Oh, I didn't know that. (Will / Can) I wave at him?
14

Abdul: Sure, that's fine.

Waiter: Yes, (can / would) I get you something else?
15

Abdul: (Could I / I could) have some more butter, please?
16

Waiter: Sure.

Abdul: (Can / Will) we also have the check, please?
17

Waiter: Of course.

Using What You've Learned

4 **Creating a Conversation** Write a conversation for one of the following situations or a situation of your own. Make sure to use modals for making requests, offers, and requesting permission. Practice your conversation and perform it for the class.

1. A mother and child are in a supermarket. The child wants candy and other sweet things, but the mother wants to buy healthy food.

    Example   A: *Can I have a candy bar?*
                       B: *How about some fruit? It's much better for you.*
                       A: *Noooo! I don't want fruit. Will you buy me a cookie?*

2. Two apartment mates are eating together. One feels cold, and the other is too warm.

    Example   A: *May I open the window?*
                       B: *I'm actually cold. Will you lend me your sweater?*
                       A: *Sure. Then can I turn on the air conditioner?*

3. Two friends are cooking together. One loves spicy food. The other only likes mild food.

    Example   A: *Would you chop up that chili pepper?*
                       B: *Can you leave the chili pepper out of the sauce?*
                       A: *But it will be so bland without it. Can I use garlic and ginger?*

Self-Assessment Log

Each of the following sentences describes the grammar you learned in this chapter. Read the sentences and then check the best box for how well you understand each structure.

	Needs Improvement	Good	Great
I can use count and noncount nouns to talk about food and other things.	❑	❑	❑
I can use *some, any, a lot of, many,* and *much* to describe quantity.	❑	❑	❑
I can use expressions for units of measure to describe quantity.	❑	❑	❑
I can use *how much / how many* and *a few / a little* to ask and answer questions about quantity.	❑	❑	❑
I can use expressions and phrases to compare two items.	❑	❑	❑
I can use modal verbs to make requests, make offers, and request permission.	❑	❑	❑

In the Community

"This city is what it is because our citizens are what they are.**"**

—Plato
Greek philosopher (427–347 B.C.)

Connecting to the Topic

1. Do you prefer to live in the city or the country?

2. What are the advantages and disadvantages of city life?

Setting the Context

 Prereading Questions Discuss these questions with a small group.

What kind of town or city do you live in? Is the pace of life there typically hectic or relaxed? Why do you think so?

Reading Read the passage.

Another Day in Rushville

It's the start of a new day in Rushville. And just like any other day in Rushville, it**'s going to be** busy. It's only 9:00 A.M. and already there's a lot of activity in the town square. Do you see the woman **about to cross** the street? That's Dr. Drill, the dentist. She's in a hurry because her office **opens** in 15 minutes. She**'s meeting** her first patient at 9:15, but she**'s going**   5

to try to get to the bank first. See the man at the public phone? He**'s going to make** a phone call. Who**'s** he **going to call**? Well, he's Dr. Drill's patient, and he's nervous because he**'s getting** a few teeth pulled. He**'s** probably **going to call** Dr. Drill's office to cancel the appointment at the last minute.

Look! There's Officer Nabbed. Uh-oh. What**'s going to** happen? He**'s going to write** a ticket! The owner of that car **will be** surprised when he **returns**.

Do you see the boy on the bicycle? Where **is** he **going to throw** that paper? He's the town's newspaper delivery boy. He**'ll** probably **break** at least one window today. He usually does, you know. **Is** his aim **going to improve**? If not, he**'s** probably **going to lose** his job. And what about that woman **about to get** on the bus? That's Mrs. Tardy, the paper boy's mother. Her work shift **starts** at 9:00, so she**'s going to be** late for work as usual. Why **will** she **be** late? She**'ll have** to explain that to her boss—again.

See the students behind her? They usually take a later bus, but they**'re taking** an exam at 9:30 and don't want to be late for class. They**'ll** probably **get** there a little early. Then they**'ll** probably **come** back later for some big events in town today. The mayor **is giving** a speech in the square at 11:00. The circus **is coming** to town this afternoon. The town council **is meeting** at 4:00 to discuss local issues. Tonight at the community center, there**'s going to be** a protest of their plans for a new shopping mall. Yes, it**'s going to be** another busy day in Rushville.

 Discussion Questions Discuss these questions with a partner.

1. Why is Dr. Drill in a hurry?

2. Who's nervous? Why?

3. What's the paperboy going to do? What will probably happen to him?

4. What time does Mrs. Tardy start work? Will she get there on time?

5. Why are the students taking an earlier bus than usual?

6. What's happening in Rushville later today?

7. When does the scheduled town council meeting begin?

8. How is Rushville like your town? How is it different?

Grammar Structures and Practice

A. *Be going to*

The phrase *be* + *going to* + the simple form of a verb is for predictions, plans, and intentions.

- It's common in conversation.
- In quick, informal speech, *going to* often sounds like *gonna*, but don't use *gonna* in writing.

4.1 Statements with *Be Going to*

Purpose	Explanations	Examples	
		Affirmative	**Negative**
Predictions	A phrase with *be going to* + a simple verb is the most common future form. Use it to make predictions about the future.	The sky looks gray. It**'s going to rain** soon. A policeman **is going to give** you a ticket if you park in a crosswalk.	Tomoko **isn't going to arrive** in time for tonight's movie. The cafe **isn't going to be** crowded this early.
Plans and Intentions	Use *be going to* + a simple verb to tell plans made in the past for future activity.	We**'re going to eat** at a new restaurant tonight. I**'m going to walk** to school more often in the future.	People **aren't going to go** to the post office today because it's closed. Sam Hill **isn't going to run** for mayor again.

4.2 Yes/No Questions with *Be Going to*

	Explanations	Examples	Possible Answers	
			Affirmative	**Negative**
Affirmative	In yes/no questions about the future, put the appropriate form of *be* before the sentence subject.	**Is** the doctor **going to be** in today? **Is** the post office **going to close** early tomorrow? **Are** we **going to meet** downtown?	Yes, she is. Yes, it is. Yes, we are.	No, she isn't. No, it isn't. No, we aren't.
Negative	In negative yes/no questions, the contractions *isn't* and *aren't* are much more common than the full forms *is not* or *are not*.	**Isn't** Noriyuki **going to get** to the park before we get there? **Isn't** it **going to rain** on Saturday? **Aren't** the council members **going to go** to the bank?	Yes, he is. Yes, it is. Yes, they are.	No, he isn't. No, it isn't. No, they aren't.

4.3 Information Questions with *Be Going to*

	Explanations	Examples	Possible Answers
Affirmative	Except when *who* or *what* is the sentence subject, a form of *be* separates the question word (*where, when, why, how*) from the subject.	Where **is** Yuko **going to go** this afternoon? Why **is** Carlos **going to catch** the bus? When **are** we **going to meet**?	(She's going to go) to the supermarket. (He's going to catch the bus) because his car isn't working. (We're going to meet) at seven o'clock this evening.
Negative	The most common question word in negative questions is *why*. The form in negative questions is the same as affirmative questions. Add *not* next to the form of *be*.	Why **aren't** you **going to come** with us to the theater tonight? Who else **isn't going to be** there?	(I'm not going to come) because I have to work. Ruben (isn't going to be there).

Note: About to means "going to in the very near future." For example: *Who's <u>about to</u> cross the street?* = *Who's going to cross the street right now or in a few seconds?*

Note: Is there a clause with *if, before, when, while, after,* or a similar connector in a future-time sentence? Usually, the verb in that clause is in a *present* tense. **Example:** *The owner of that car will be surprised when he <u>returns</u>.*

---

1 Practice Underline the verb phrases with *be going to* in the reading on pages 94 and 95. Identify the sentences as statements or questions, singular or plural, affirmative or negative.

Example And just like any other day in Rushville, <u>it's going to be</u> busy. (*singular affirmative statement*)

 2 Practice Look closely at the picture on page 94. With a partner, answer this question in as many ways as you can: *What's going to happen next in this scene?* Use the structure *be + going to +* the simple form of a verb.

Example *A woman is going to cross the street.*

3 Practice For each sentence from Activity 2, make one yes/no question and one information question. Answer the questions.

Example *A woman is going to (about to) cross the street.*
Is she going to cross the street at the corner?   No, she isn't.
Why is she going to cross the street?   She isn't carrying any letters or packages, so she's probably not going to go to the post office. Maybe she's going to stand in line at the telephone booth.

4 **Practice** These pictures show people's thoughts about future plans or intentions. For each item, make one or more sentences with *be going to*.

1. *Is this man going to join a gym? He probably is. Why is he going to become a gym member? Because he thinks he's going to lose weight with exercise. But he's probably not going to go there very often.*

2. _____
_____
_____
_____
_____

3. _____
_____
_____
_____
_____

4. _____
_____
_____
_____
_____

5. _____
   _____
   _____
   _____
   _____
   _____

6. _____
   _____
   _____
   _____
   _____

7. _____
   _____
   _____
   _____
   _____
   _____

8. _____
   _____
   _____
   _____
   _____
   _____

B. The Simple Future Tense

Like *be going to,* the simple future tense is for intentions.

- In some cases, *will* and *be going to* are interchangeable. However, *going to* might suggest some planning, but *will* may suggest a spontaneous, unplanned intention.
- Unlike *going to, will* is also for offers, promises, and requests. Only the simple form of the main verb can follow *will.*

4.4 Statements with the Simple Future Tense

Explanations	Purpose	Examples	
		Affirmative	**Negative**
For the simple future tense, *will* is followed by the simple form of the verb. These contractions are common after subject pronouns: *I'll, we'll, you'll, he'll, she'll, they'll.*	Intentions	We**'ll buy** a computer this semester.	My sister **won't shop** in that store anymore.
	Offers and Promises	I**'ll come** to the park with you this afternoon.	I **won't be** late.
	Predictions	It **will be** sunny today. You**'ll drive** me to the video store, I hope.	It **won't rain.** I **won't be** able to come with you.

4.5 Yes/No Questions with the Simple Future Tense

	Explanations	Examples	Possible Answers	
			Affirmative	**Negative**
Affirmative	Yes/No questions with *will* may be requests.	**Will** you **make** an appointment with the doctor for next week? **Will** it **rain** today?	Yes, I will. Yes, it will.	No, I won't. No, it won't.
Negative	Negative yes/no questions may suggest surprise.	**Won't** your family **go** shopping? **Won't** they **meet** us at the restaurant tomorrow?	Yes, we will. Yes, they will.	No, we won't. No, they won't.

4.6 Information Questions with the Simple Future Tense

Explanations		Examples	Possible Answers
Except when *who* or *what* is the sentence subject, *will* or *won't* separates the question word (*who[m], what, where, when, why, how*) from the subject.	Affirmative	What **will** you **do** on Saturday? When **will** you **go** to the bakery?	I'll go shopping. I'll go this afternoon.
	Negative	Why **won't** you **come** with us? Why **won't** your friend **buy** a hot dog from the street vendor?	I don't feel well. He's a vegetarian.

5 Practice Double underline the simple future tense verb phrases with *will* or *won't* in the reading on pages 94 and 95. Identify the sentences as statements or questions, singular or plural, affirmative or negative.

Example The owner of that car <u><u>will be</u></u> surprised when he returns. (*singular affirmative statement*)

6 Practice Shirley goes to a fortune teller to find out about her future and the future of her community. Match Shirley's questions with the fortune teller's predictions. Then make a full sentence with *will* for each answer.

Example *How old will I be when I get married? You'll be 29.*

Shirley:

_f_ **1.** How old will I be when I get married?

___ **2.** Will I marry someone from this town?

___ **3.** Where will I meet my future husband?

___ **4.** How many children will I have?

___ **5.** Will my children go to school here?

___ **6.** Will I open up a business in town?

___ **7.** Will I buy a house here in the next few years?

___ **8.** What new shops will open in town next year?

___ **9.** Will the town's traffic problem get better?

___**10.** Will I be happy in this town?

Fortune teller:

a. Yes, they will—at the local high school and community college.

b. No, but there's a nice condominium in your future.

c. Four kids—two sons and two daughters.

d. No. Worse.

e. Yes, you will—very happy.

f. 29

g. A pet store, a pharmacy, and a few cafés.

h. At the supermarket.

i. No, you won't. You're a teacher, not a businessperson.

j. Yes —Bob, the fireman.

7 Practice With a partner, ask and answer all of the questions in Activity 6 again. This time, use *be going to*.

Example A: *How old am I going to be when I get married?*
B: *You're going to be 29.*

8 Practice Circle the best word part or word(s) in each set of parentheses. In some cases, both answers may be correct.

Chiara: Hi, Angela.

Angela: Chiara!

Chiara: Those shopping bags look heavy. I (ʼll)/(ʼm going to) carry a few for you, OK?

Angela: Thanks. What are you doing in town?

Chiara: Just errands. Are there any good movies playing this week? I don't have a newspaper, so I (ʼll / ʼm going to) check at the Multiplex.
1

Angela: I'm free tonight. I (ʼll / ʼm going to) go with you if you want.
2

Chiara: That (ʼs going to / will) be great.
3

Angela: I just have to get these groceries home and have dinner first.

(Will you / Are you going to) meet me at the movie theater around 7:00?
4

Chiara: Sure. But I don't see your car. How (will you / are you going to) get
5
home?

Angela: I (ʼll / ʼm going to) take the bus.
6

Chiara: Don't be silly. I (ʼll / ʼm going to) drive you. My car is right here.
7

Angela: That (ʼs going to / ʼll) help me a lot. Thanks! Oh no, this bag is ripping.
8
The groceries (will / are going to) fall out. I (ʼll / ʼm going to) be right
9   10
back.

Chiara: Where are you going?

Angela: I (ʼll / ʼm going to) get another bag.
11

Chiara: I (ʼll / ʼm going to) wait for you here.
12

Angela: OK. I (ʼll / ʼm going to) be back in a minute! We need to decide which
13
movie to see.

C. The Present Continuous and the Simple Present to Express Future Time

In some situations, the present continuous and the simple present can express future time.

4.7 The Present Continuous for Future Time

	Explanations	Examples
Statements	For a planned event or for definite intention, the present continuous may indicate future time. This use of the present continuous is common with a future time expression, like *tonight*, *tomorrow, next week*, etc.	These stores **are moving** to Main Street next month. The town council **isn't meeting** next week.
Questions	The future meaning of the present continuous doesn't change its form. The *be* form of the verb still comes before the subject.	Where **are** we **getting** together tonight? **Aren't** you **going** downtown this weekend?

4.8 The Simple Present for Future Time

	Explanations	Examples
Statements	The simple present can express future time in sentences about scheduled events. A time expression or the context makes the future time clear. Only a few verbs are used this way. These include *open, close, begin, end, start, finish, arrive, leave, come,* and *return*.	The movie **begins** at 8:00. I **leave** town on Friday. His train **arrives** at 3:00. The museum **opens** at 9:00 tomorrow.
Questions	The future meaning of the simple present doesn't change its form. The *do* form of the verb still comes before the subject.	When **does** the movie **begin**? **Does** the museum **open** at the usual time tomorrow?

9 **Practice** Circle the simple present tense verbs with a future meaning in the reading on pages 94 and 95. Put a box around the present continuous verb phrases used with a future meaning.

Example She's in a hurry because her office (opens) in 15 minutes.
She's meeting her first patient at 9:15, but she's going to try to get to the bank first.

10 Practice Koto has a busy schedule this weekend. Answer these questions about his schedule. Use the present continuous or simple present for future time.

Saturday		Sunday	
8:00 A.M.		8:00 A.M.	
9:00	do laundry	9:00	sleep
10:00	↓	10:00	↓
11:00	work at café	11:00	work out at gym
12:00 P.M.		12:00 P.M.	↓
1:00		1:00	lunch with sister in park
2:00		2:00	watch baseball game with sister
3:00		3:00	swim at community pool
4:00		4:00	↓
5:00	↓	5:00	community meeting at Town Hall
6:00	dinner at China Palace with Reiko	6:00	↓
7:00	↓	7:00	work at café
8:00	movie with Reiko	8:00	
9:00		9:00	↓
10:00	↓	10:00	pick up roommate at airport

1. What is Koto doing first on Saturday morning? *He's doing his laundry first on Saturday morning.*

2. Is he working out at the gym on Saturday morning?

3. When is he going to his job on Saturday? Where is he working?

4. What's he doing at 6:00 on Saturday evening? Where is he having dinner?

5. Who's he seeing a movie with on Saturday night? When does the movie start? When does it end? (When is it over?)

6. Is he sleeping late on Sunday morning?

7. Is Koto seeing his sister this weekend? What are they doing together?

8. Where is he having lunch on Sunday?

9. Is he playing baseball this weekend or is he going to a baseball game? Where's the game? When is it?

10. What is he doing at 5:00 on Sunday?

11. When does he start work that day?

12. When does his shift probably end?

13. Why is Koto going to the airport late Sunday night?

14. When does his roommate's plane arrive?

11 Practice On each line, write the simple present or the present continuous form of the verb in parentheses. Choose the better form.

1. My housemate's bus (arrive) _____ _arrives_ _____ at 9:00 tonight.

2. Reiko can't come to the park with us this afternoon. She (work) _____ then.

3. (go) _____ you _____ to a concert or a play this weekend?

4. Koto (leave) _____ in a few minutes. Do you want to go with him?

5. The train (leave) _____ Bedford at 3:00 and (arrive) _____ in Ashland at 4:00.

6. The town museum (open) _____ at 10:00 A.M. on Sunday. It (close) _____ at 5:00 P.M.

7. What time (meet) _____ you _____ your mother tomorrow? Where (get) _____ you _____ together?

8. What (do) _____ you _____ this weekend? (What are your plans?)

9. I (take) _____ a train to Ciudad Juarez.

10. What time (begin) _____ the film _____ at the Tivoli?

11. Excuse me. What time (arrive) _____ this train _____ in Ankara?

12. I (go) _____ not _____ out this evening. I (stay) _____ home and (do) _____ work.

Using What You've Learned

12 Making Future Plans What are some ways to help out in your community? In a group, list possible kinds of volunteer work or other helpful activities. Which idea sounds the most interesting to you? Tell your intention. Then list the intended steps (your plans) for that activity. Use verb phrases with future meaning.

Example *I'm going to help at the local soup kitchen. First, I'll find the number of the soup kitchen in the phone book or from the* *community center. (It opens at 9:00 A.M.) Then I'll call up the kitchen. I'll find out about volunteering. I think I'll either sign up to cook food or to serve it. That will depend, of course. (What are they going to need in the near future?)*

Try to follow through with your plans. Tell the class about your experiences.

 13 **Planning a Weekend Schedule** Make a calendar for this weekend. (Follow the model on page 104.) Put in your real and/or imaginary plans for Saturday and Sunday. Leave only two or three time slots empty. Then work with two other students. Don't look at one another's schedules. Try to find a time during the weekend to get together to study. Write your plan in your calendar.

Example A: *What are you doing on Saturday at 11:00?*
B: *I'm babysitting for my aunt's twins. What's going on Saturday at 1:00?*
A: *I'm not doing anything then.*
C: *But I am! I'm playing softball in the park with some friends.*

Part 2   Phrasal Verbs

Setting the Context

 Prereading Questions Discuss these questions with a small group.

Do you have a lot to do every day? Do you make a lot of plans? If so, do you complete your plans on time? Why or why not?

Reading Read the conversation.

Mikki: Erika, **wake up!** Why didn't your alarm **go off? Get up** and get dressed!

Erika: Please **go away.**

Mikki: But there's so much to do today. You can't **sleep in.**

Erika: What are you **talking about?**

Mikki: Don't you remember? We're **speaking out** at the community center tonight.

Erika: Huh?

Mikki: Your speech! The town council wants to **tear down** the old museum. They're going to **put up** a shopping mall, they say. We're **speaking up** against it.

Erika: Oh, right.

Mikki: A few neighbors are **coming over** for dinner before the meeting. I'm doing the cooking, but you'll need to **pick** some things **up** at the supermarket.

Erika: **Calm down.** There's plenty of time.

Mikki: Not if we want to **work out** at the gym this afternoon. Also, we need to **stop off** at the bank to **take** some cash **out**. On the way there, we can **drop off** this overdue video. And we'll need to **fill** the car **up** with gas on our way home.

Erika: **Slow down!**

Mikki: And of course, we have to **get back** in time to **clean up** the house. Then we'll **go over** our notes before the meeting. *(Erika **pulls** the sheet **up** over her head.)* What are you doing?

Erika: **Going back** to sleep. All your talk is **wearing** me **out**.

Mikki: I **give up!**

Erika: Mikki?

Mikki: Yes?

Erika: **Turn** the light **off** on your way out, would you? And please don't **come back** for a couple of hours.

 Discussion Questions Discuss these questions with a partner.

1. Why does Mikki want Erika to get up?

2. What does Erika have to do today? (Tell some of the things.)

3. Why is Erika giving a speech at the community center?

4. What does Erika do at the end of the conversation?

5. Do you have trouble waking up in the morning? What helps you wake up?

Grammar Structures and Practice

A. Phrasal Verbs: Forms

A phrasal verb is a verb + a preposition or an adverb. Together, these two or three words have a special meaning—different from the meanings of the individual words.

- The preposition or adverb part of the phrasal verb is called a *particle*.
- Some phrasal verbs are *inseparable*: no word may separate the verb and its particle.
- A *separable* phrasal verb may have a noun object before the particle.

4.9 Inseparable Phrasal Verbs

Explanations	Phrasal Verbs	Examples	
		With Nouns	**With Pronouns**
The direct object can be a noun or a pronoun. It comes after an inseparable phrasal verb.	**ran into**	I **ran into** my biology teacher at the library.	I **ran into** her at the library.
	get on	**Get on** the train before it leaves!	**Get on** it before it leaves!
	get along with	Do you **get along with** your neighbors?	Do you **get along with** them?

4.10 Separable Phrasal Verbs

Explanations	Phrasal Verbs	Examples	
		With Nouns	**With Pronouns**
With a separable phrasal verb, a noun direct object can go after the particle (as in the *a* examples) or between the verb and the particle (as in the *b* examples). A pronoun goes between the verb and particle (as in the *c* examples).	**make up**	(a) He may **make up** the lost time. (b) He may **make** the lost time **up**.	(c) He may **make** it **up**.
	fill out	(a) Please **fill out** this form. (b) Please **fill** this form **out**.	(c) Please **fill** it **out**.
	clean off	(a) **Clean off** your shoes. (b) **Clean** your shoes **off**.	(c) **Clean** them **off**.

1 **Practice** Underline the phrasal verbs in the conversation between Mikki and Erika on pages 106 and 107. Identify them as separable or inseparable.

Example Erika, wake up! Why didn't your alarm go off?
            (separable)   *(inseparable)*

2 Practice In each of the following groups of sentences, one of the sentences is incorrect. Put a check by all the correct sentences. Cross out the incorrect sentence.

Example   **drop off** (separable)

✔ You need to drop off this video.

✔ You need to drop this video off.

~~You need to drop off it.~~

✔ You need to drop it off.

1. **run into** (inseparable)

I frequently run into your sister in town.

I frequently run into her in town.

I frequently run her into in town.

2. **wake up** (separable)

Don't wake up the children.

Don't wake up them.

Don't wake the children up.

Don't wake them up.

3. **pick up** (separable)

Will you pick up my mail at the post office?

Will you pick up it at the post office?

Will you pick it up at the post office?

Will you pick my mail up at the post office?

4. **call up** (separable)

She calls her father up every week.

She calls up her father every week.

She calls up him every week.

She calls him up every week.

5. **look after** (inseparable)

Please look after my plants while I'm gone.

Please look after them while I'm gone.

Please look them after while I'm gone.

3 Practice Su-Yen is sick. She needs help from her friend Juan. Fill in Juan's part of the conversation. Answer all of Su's requests with full, affirmative statements. Remember: With a separable phrasal verb, you may put a pronoun between the verb and the particle. Put a pronoun object after the particle for an inseparable phrasal verb.

1. Su-Yen: Juan, will you please fill up my juice glass for me?

    Juan: _____ *Sure, I'll fill it up for you, Su. No problem.* _____

2. Su-Yen: Thank you so much. And can you look after my cat? She shouldn't be any trouble.

    Juan: _____

3. Su-Yen: Thanks. And will you call up the doctor and set up an appointment? Her name is in my address book.

    Juan: _____

4. Su-Yen: Great! I'd appreciate that. And could you also take out my roommate's dog? He's making me sneeze.

    Juan: _____

5. Su-Yen: Thanks so much! And when you leave, would you drop off my library books on your way home?

    Juan: _____

6. Su-Yen: Oh! But what about my medicine? Could you get to the drug store? Can you pick up my prescription at the pharmacy?

    Juan: _____

7. Su-Yen: Ooh. And I'd really like some chicken soup. They have it with noodles at the delicatessen next to the drug store. Will you pick up an order for dinner?

    Juan: _____

8. Su-Yen: You know, my relatives don't even know I'm sick. Would you please call up my mother to tell her?

    Juan: _____

9. Su-Yen: Oh, that's so nice of you, Juan! And will you also drop by later?

    Juan: _____

10. Su-Yen: Oh—and just one more thing! Will you turn the light off?

    Juan: _____

B. Phrasal Verbs: Meanings

The following are some examples of inseparable phrasal verbs and their meanings.

4.11 Inseparable Phrasal Verbs: Examples		
Phrasal Verbs	**Meanings**	**Examples**
come back	return to a place	We will **come back** later.
drop by	visit informally	I often **drop by** my aunt's house.
get along (with)	be on good terms with	They **get along with** their neighbors well.
get off*	come out or off of a form of transportation	Driver, I want to **get off** here.
get on	board a kind of transportation	Do you want to **get on** the bus with me?
get up*	arise from bed after sleeping	I hate to **get up** early.
go away	leave	**Go away!** You're bothering me.
go back	return to a place	My father wants to **go back** to school for a degree.
go off	ring (for an alarm) or explode (for a gun)	A gun will **go off** at the beginning of the race.
go over	review	Let's **go over** the rules of the game one more time.
grow up	become an adult	I want my children to **grow up** in this town.
look after	take care of	Please **look after** my plants while I'm gone.
move out (of)	leave	Do you want to **move out of** this neighborhood?
run into	meet accidentally	We always **run into** each other here!
sleep in	sleep late	My roommate loves to **sleep in** on the weekends.
speak out	talk freely in public	We need to **speak out** about public issues.
speak up	speak loudly and without fear	Do you **speak up** for your rights?
stop off	make a short stop	Let's **stop off** at the drug store on our way.
work out	exercise (usually in a gym)	I'm always tired after I **work out.**

Note: * Get something off means "remove a stain or mark." Get someone up means "wake someone up." In these examples the object cannot move. It must appear between the verb and the particle.

The following are some examples of separable phrasal verbs and their meanings.

4.12	Separable Phrasal Verbs: Examples	
Phrasal Verbs	**Meanings**	**Examples**
bring up	raise (children), introduce (an idea)	My sister is **bringing up** her kids by herself.
call up	telephone (verb)	I'll **call** you **up** tonight.
calm down	(help someone) relax	**Calm** the kids **down.** They're getting too excited.
clean up	make neat and orderly	We're going to help **clean** the park **up** this weekend.
drop off	leave something/someone at a place	Could you **drop** me **off** downtown?
fill out	write the necessary information on (a form)	You need to **fill** this form **out** for your license.
fill up	make or become full	**Fill** the gas tank **up**.
find out	get information	What's playing at the movie theater? I don't know, but I'll **find out**.
get back	return	We have to **get** the books **back** to the library.
give up	surrender, let go of, stop trying	I often **give** my seat **up** on the bus.
help out	assist	We need you to **help** us **out** with some arrangements.
look up	search for (information in a reference book)	I often **look up** words in the dictionary.
make up	compensate for	I have to **make up** an exam.
pick up	go to get someone/something	I have to **pick** my kids **up** from school.
put up	construct, raise	They want to **put up** a wall between buildings.
slow down	go less quickly	**Slow** the car **down.** Don't drive so fast.
take out	remove, bring outside	I'm going to **take out** the garbage.
tear down	pull down, demolish	The city is going to **tear down** that building.
tire out	exhaust	City politics **tire** me **out.** I don't like to argue.
turn off	stop a machine, light, or faucet	The streetlights **turn** themselves **off** automatically at 6:00 A.M.
turn up / turn down	increase / decrease	Can you **turn up** the radio? I can't hear it.
wake up	stop sleeping	I **wake** the kids **up** when the alarm rings.
work out	find a solution for	The city is trying to **work out** the traffic problem.

4 Practice On each of these lines, put one of the inseparable phrasal verbs from the list on page 111. You may need to change the form of the phrasal verb.

1. The mail carrier is so friendly and easygoing. He ___gets along with___ everybody.

2. How do I get to the football stadium? _____ the Number 10 bus here at the bus stop. After about two miles, _____ at Clark Street and you're there!

3. My literature professor often _____ her students in town. Then she always stops to talk with us.

4. I want to _____ of my tiny apartment and move into a bigger place.

5. Do you express your views on important local issues? Do you _____ at town meetings?

6. Feel free to _____ my place any time. I'm always happy to see you.

7. Maria is _____ my cat while I'm out of town.

8. You're leaving town? Are you _____ for a long time? I hope you _____ soon. I miss you already!

9. What time do you usually _____ in the morning? When does your alarm clock _____?

10. I don't like to _____ because the morning is my favorite time of day—except on cold, rainy days.

11. Construction begins tomorrow. The construction workers need to _____ the plans for the house very carefully first.

12. Your son is _____ so quickly. I still think of him as a little boy!

13. At the gym, do you usually _____ on the treadmill and the stationary bicycle or do you lift weights?

14. When is the race going to begin? When will the gun _____?

5 **Practice** On each of the lines, put one of the separable phrasal verbs from the list on page 112. You may need to change the form of the phrasal verb.

1. My brother is _____*bringing up*_____ his children very well. They are smart, happy, and kind because he _____*brings*_____ them _____*up*_____ effectively.

2. Can you please _____ my dress at the dry cleaner's? Please _____ my jacket _____, too. They need cleaning.

3. My clock is broken. I can't _____ the alarm when it rings. Now it's unplugged.

4. Why is the city going to _____ those old buildings? It's _____ them _____ to make room for a new clinic.

5. The trash cans are full. The garbage men are coming early tomorrow morning, so it's important to _____ them _____ to the street right now.

6. Your sister shouldn't sleep so late on such a beautiful day. Would you go _____ her _____?

7. I'll _____ the basket with enough food for a picnic. What can we _____ it _____ with?

8. You need a roommate? Why don't you _____ an ad on the bulletin board in the supermarket? Or I can _____ it _____ for you.

9. We should _____ our neighborhood. There's litter everywhere! Who can help me _____ it _____?

10. "Why are you looking at the entertainment section of that newspaper?" "I want to _____ this week's movies _____."

11. Please _____ your radio. It's disturbing everyone in the park. _____ the volume _____ to low.

12. Can you please _____ my dress at the dry cleaner's? It's ready now. The store closes at 5:00, so please _____ it _____ before then.

13. Does a bookkeeper do math and _____ forms all day long? Does she _____ charts _____, too? That sounds boring to me.

14. You have to _____ some of your community activities! You won't have time for your family if you don't _____ them _____.

15. "What's the plumber's phone number?" "I don't know. You can _____ the number _____ in the phone book." "Can't you _____ it _____ for me?"

6 **Practice** Substitute a phrasal verb from the lists on pages 111 and 112 for the underlined word(s) in each of these sentences. Be careful to put the verb and its particle in the right places.

Example <u>Relax</u>! The policeman isn't giving your car a ticket. *Calm down.*

1. Where can I <u>get</u> a local newspaper?
2. Would you <u>take care of</u> my dog this weekend while I'm away?
3. I'm going to <u>remove</u> my advertisement from the newspaper.
4. Are you going to <u>return</u> to school next year?
5. The city is going to <u>demolish</u> the old community center. Then it's going to <u>construct</u> a new shopping mall in the center of town.
6. Do you want to <u>assist</u> with the preparations for the parade?
7. We can <u>find</u> the phone number of the bank in the phone book.
8. Don't <u>exercise</u> too much at the gym today. It might <u>exhaust</u> you, and you have to give a speech tonight.
9. Let's go for a walk. We can <u>return</u> home for lunch after that.
10. You can <u>leave</u> your bag at my house before we go to the park. And on the way, we can <u>make a quick stop</u> at the market and get some fruit.
11. Please <u>enter</u> the bus in the front and <u>exit</u> the bus at the back.
12. Let's <u>review</u> the directions to my house to make sure you understand them.

Using What You've Learned

 7 **Making Conversations** Work with a partner. Write a conversation for one of these situations and/or a real or imaginary situation of your own. Use as many phrasal verbs as you can for each conversation. (You can begin with the given phrasal verbs.) When you finish, practice your conversation. Then you can perform it for the class.

1. You are roommates. You're studying in your dormitory room. One of you wants to listen to a CD or DVD. The other can't study with music. Include these phrasal verbs in your conversation:

   turn on = start (a machine)
   turn off = stop (a machine)
   turn down = lower the volume
   turn up = increase the volume

   Example A: *Please don't turn on the stereo. I'm trying to study.*
   B: *Music helps me study.*
   A: *Well, I can't study with loud music. Could you turn it down?*
   B: *Sure. Is that better?*
   A: *No, I can still hear it. Would you turn it off?*

2. You are a customer and a salesperson in a clothing store. The customer wants to buy a new sweater and wants to know about styles and colors. Include these phrasal verbs in your conversation:

   put on = dress in
   take off = remove
   try on = put on a piece of clothing to check for fit
   pick out = choose

3. You are a student and a librarian. The student wants to find information about a famous writer, artist, or scientist (you choose the person). The student asks the librarian for help in finding information. Include these phrasal verbs in your conversation:

   find out = discover or learn information about
   look up = look for information in a reference book
   check out = borrow from the library
   fill out = complete a form

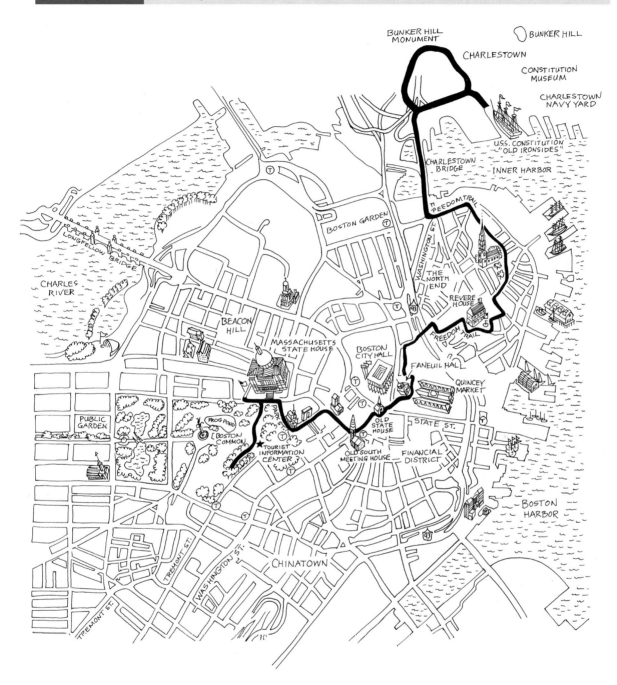

Setting the Context

Prereading Questions Discuss these questions with a small group.

Would you like to visit a city with many historical places? Why or why not?

Reading Read the passage.

Boston's Historic Freedom Trail

A great way to see old downtown Boston, Massachusetts, **during** the day is to walk the Freedom Trail. The trail is three miles long, and it takes you by many famous, historic places **from** the time of the American Revolution (1775–1783). The trail starts **at** an information booth **on** Boston Common, a large park **next to** Boston's Public Gardens. The booth is **on** 5
Tremont Street **between** the Park Street and Tremont Street subway stations. You can get tour information and a trail map **at** the booth. There are many interesting stops **on** the trail.

One important stop is the Old State House **at** Washington and State Streets. Built **in** 1712, it now has a museum with exhibits about Boston's 10
history. **From** the Old State House, you can walk **through** Faneuil Hall and Quincy Market. These old, historic buildings are now a busy center for shopping, dining, and entertainment. Many stores **in** Quincy Market stay open **until** 9:00 P.M., making them a perfect place to come back **to in** the evening, **after** dinner. 15

After Quincy Market, you can walk **toward** the North End. This part of Boston has many wonderful Italian shops, cafés, and restaurants. Also **in** the North End is Revere House, another important stop **on** the Freedom Trail. It is the home of Paul Revere (1735–1818), patriot **during** the American Revolution. Built **in** 1676, it is the oldest standing building **in** Boston. 20

The *U.S.S. Constitution*, a famous warship built **in** 1797, is **across** the Inner Harbor **in** the Charlestown Navy Yard. You can walk **over** the Charlestown Bridge to get there. The *U.S.S. Constitution* is the oldest American warship afloat today. The *U.S.S. Constitution* Museum is **near** the ship. You can visit the ship for free, but you have to pay to visit the museum. 25

Near the Charlestown Navy Yard is the Bunker Hill Monument, the last stop **on** the Freedom Trail. The monument commemorates the Battle of Bunker Hill, an important battle of the American Revolution, fought **on** June 17, 1775. **After** you finish the trail, you will probably be ready for a rest. You may wish to relax **in** one of Boston's beautiful parks, or get a cof- 30
fee **at** one of the many cafés **in** the North End.

Discussion Questions Discuss these questions with a partner.

1. What kinds of places can you visit along the Freedom Trail?
2. Where is the information booth on Boston Common?
3. How can you get from Quincy Market to the North End?
4. What can you do in the North End?

5. How can you get from the North End to the Charlestown Navy Yard?

6. Would you like to visit Boston? Why or why not?

Grammar Structures and Practice

A. Prepositions of Place and Time

Prepositions are words to show relationships between nouns and pronouns and other words in the same phrase.

- Some examples of common prepositions are *with*, *for*, and *of*.
- With examples and explanations of meaning, here are some common prepositions of place (location and direction) and time.

4.13	Prepositions of Place	
Prepositions	**Explanations**	**Examples**
in	Use *in* before buildings, towns, cities, regions, provinces, countries, and continents.	Eduardo is **in** the library. Palermo is a city **in** Italy.
on	Use *on* before streets and bodies of water.	I live **on** a beautiful street. The boat is sailing **on** the river.
at	Use *at* with street addresses and many specific locations.	Jen lives **at** 17 Bow Street. I will meet you **at** the corner of Main Street and Elm Street.
between	*Between* is for a location in the middle of or inside two points.	The video store is **between** the bank and the post office. The house is **between** two big trees.
near	*Near* means "close to."	I hope there is a cash machine **near** the movie theater. The professor's office is **near** the chemistry laboratory.
far from	*Far from* means "separated by distance."	Your house is very **far (away) from** school. The hospital is **far from** town.
next to	*Next to* means "beside."	My friend's house is **next to** yours. The restaurant is **next to** the movie theater.
across from	*Across from* means "opposite" or "on the other side of."	The post office is **across from** the police station. Their house is **across from** a bookstore.
under	*Under* means "below."	Boats pass **under** the bridge. There's parking **under** the shops and stores.
over	*Over* means "above."	Airplanes don't fly **over** the harbor. Isn't your office **over** a café?
to	*To* means "in the direction of in order to reach." As a preposition, it's different from the *to* before verbs in infinitives.	Would you like to go **to** Boston? Let's take the trolley **to** the North End.
toward	*Toward* means "in the direction of."	Are we driving **toward** the river? Let's go **toward** the park.
through	*Through* means "in one side and out the other."	Let's walk **through** Faneuil Hall. Does the train go **through** a tunnel?

4.14 Prepositions of Time

Prepositions	Explanations	Examples
in	Use *in* before years, seasons, months, and parts of the day.	The new post office will open **in** January. Paris is beautiful **in** the springtime.
on	Use *on* before days of the week and dates.	Some stores are closed **on** Sunday. We'll have a St. Patrick's Day parade **on** March 17.
at	Use *at* before a specific time of day and with the nouns *noon*, *night*, and *midnight*.	The laundromat opens **at** 9:00. I love to walk around the city **at** night.
from . . . to	Use *from . . . to* with beginning and ending times.	The library is open **from** 9:30 A.M. **to** 5:00 P.M. The parade will last **from** late morning **to** early afternoon.
during	Use *during* with periods of time.	The supermarket is open late **during** the week. My town is usually covered in snow **during** the winter.
until	Use *until* with ending times.	The coffee shop is open **until** 9:00 P.M. I am going to live here **until** graduation.
before	*Before* means "earlier than."	I want to go to the mountains **before** summer. Run to the store **before** closing time.
after	*After* means "later than."	Let's get a bite to eat **after** the movie. I like to meet my friends in town **after** class.

---

1 **Practice** Circle the prepositions of place and time in the reading on page 118. Then put a *P* above each preposition of place. Put a *T* above each preposition of time.

Example A great way to see old downtown Boston (during) the day is to walk the
$\quad\quad\quad$ Freedom Trail.

2 **Practice** Complete the sentences with prepositions from this list. You can use each word more than once. In some cases, more than one word may be correct.

at	in	on	from . . . to	until	during
after	near	to	toward	through	

1. Boston is _____*in*_____ Massachusetts, a state

_____ the northeastern part of the United States. The

Freedom Trail is _____ Boston.

2. Do you want information about the trail? Go _____ the

information booth. The Freedom Trail starts _____ the booth

_____ Tremont Street.

3. The Old State House is open _____ 9:30 A.M. _____ 5:00 P.M. _____ the summer. It was built _____ 1712.

4. Harvard University, _____ Cambridge, Massachusetts, is the oldest university _____ the United States. Many visitors like to walk _____ its campus.

5. The Bunker Hill Monument is _____ the Charlestown Navy Yard. You can easily get _____ the Monument _____ the Navy Yard.

6. Paul Revere House is located _____ 19 North Street _____ the North End. Paul Revere was a patriot _____ the American Revolution.

7. The Boston Children's Museum is _____ Congress Street. _____ Friday evenings, it's open _____ 9:00 P.M.

8. Many fine stores _____ Boston are _____ Newbury Street. The street stretches _____ the Public Garden _____ Massachusetts Avenue.

9. Quincy Market is open _____ 9:00 P.M. _____ night. It's a good place to shop _____ dinner _____ the evening.

10. _____ summer there are many fireworks displays in Boston. The biggest one is _____ the 4th of July.

3 Practice Look at the picture of a city street on page 122. Answer these questions with the prepositions of place: *in, on, at, between, near, next to, across from, under, over, to, toward, through, down, up,* and *across.* Can you answer each question in more than one way? You may add your own prepositions and other vocabulary.

Example Where is the video store? *The video store is above the health food store. It is next to the bank and across from the florist.*

1. Where is the movie theater?

2. Is there a dentist's office across from the health food store? If not, where is the dentist's office?

3. Where's the ballet school? Do you go through the café to get there?

4. Where is the pet shop? How do you get there from the café?

5. Is there a bank on this street? If so, where is it?

6. Where is the subway? How do you get to the subway train?

7. Where's the bookstore? From the grocery store, do you go across the street?

8. Where is the café?

9. Where's the health food store? Is it in the grocery store?

10. Where is the grocery store in this scene?

11. Is there a flower shop or florist on this street?

12. Where can you go to work out? Where is the gym?

4 **Practice** Look again at the city map of Boston on page 117. With a partner, ask and answer more location and direction questions like the ones in Activity 3.

Example A: *Where's the Tourist Information Center, please?*
B: *It's on Boston Common.*
A: *Is it near the Frog Pond?*
B: *Not really. It's across the park, almost on Tremont Street.*

5 Practice Here is the Community Center schedule for this week. Answer these questions about the schedule with prepositions of time: *on, at, from . . . to, during, until, before,* and *after*. You can add your own vocabulary and information, too.

	Pool open (10:00-5:00)	Café open (10:00-5:00)	Aerobics class (1:00-2:00)	Computer class (2:00-3:00)	After-school activities (3:00-5:00)	Special events
Monday	✓	✓			✓	7:00 Lecture: Recycling and the Community
Tuesday	✓	✓	✓	✓	✓	
Wednesday	✓	✓			✓	
Thursday	✓	✓	✓	✓	✓	7:30: Poetry reading by local author
Friday	✓	✓			✓	
Saturday	✓					
Sunday	Community Center closed					

1. What time does the café open? *The café opens at 10:00.*
2. Until what time is it open?
3. What hours is the pool open?
4. What Community Center facility is open during the day on Saturday?
5. When is the lecture on recycling?
6. On what day and at what time is the poetry reading?
7. What days is the aerobics class offered?
8. Is the aerobics class before or after the computer class?
9. Is there a computer class in the morning? What about the afternoon and evening?
10. What day is the Community Center closed? Is it open Monday through Friday only?

Using What You've Learned

6 Describing a Neighborhood Map Draw a simple map of the main streets of your neighborhood. Include public places, shops, and stores. Then find a partner from a different neighborhood. Don't show your map. Instead, describe it with prepositions of place. From your description, your partner draws another map of the same place. Your partner may ask questions about details. Answer as precisely as possible.

Example A: *There's a small bakery between a bank and an Italian*
            restaurant. And there are apartments above all of these
            businesses.
         B: *Is there anything next to the bank or the restaurant?*

When you finish, change roles. Listen carefully to your partner's description, ask questions, and draw a simple map of his or her neighborhood.

Compare your partner's map of the main streets in your neighborhood with your own drawing. Find mistakes and correct them. Ask and answer details about the buildings on each map, including opening and closing times.

7 **Planning Your Weekend** What do you plan to do this week? Make a list of your planned activities. When you finish, exchange lists with a partner. In turn, ask questions about the items. Use as many different prepositions of place and time as possible. Make a week's schedule for your partner like the one on page 123.

Example A: *Are you going to the movies on Friday?*
         B: *No. On Saturday.*
         A: *What time on Saturday?*
         B: *At 7:30 in the evening.*
         A: *Where is the movie playing?*
         B: *At the Multiplex Cinema on Main Street. When are you going to*
            do the laundry?

Part 4   Articles

Setting the Context

Prereading Questions Discuss these questions with a small group.

Do you ever use travel information? Why or why not?

Reading Read the passage.

Boston's Historic Freedom Trail

A great **way** to see old downtown **Boston, Massachusetts,** during **the day** is to walk **the Freedom Trail. The trail** is **three miles** long, and it takes you by many famous, historic **places** from **the time** of **the Ameri-**

can Revolution (1775–1783). **The trail** starts at **an information booth** on **Boston Common, a** large **park** next to **Boston's Public Gardens. The booth** is on **Tremont Street** between **the Park Street** and **Tremont Street subway stations.** You can get **tour information** and **a trail map** at **the booth.** There are many interesting **stops** on **the trail.**

One important stop is **the Old State House** at **Washington** and **State Streets.** Built in 1712, it now has **a museum** with **exhibits** about Boston's history. From **the Old State House,** you can walk through **Faneuil Hall** and **Quincy Market.** These old, historic **buildings** are now **a** busy **center** for **shopping, dining,** and **entertainment.** Many **stores** in **Quincy Market** stay open until 9:00 P.M., making them **a** perfect **place** to come back to in **the evening,** after **dinner.**

After **Quincy Market,** you can walk toward **the North End. This part of Boston** has many wonderful Italian **shops, cafés,** and **restaurants.** Also in **the North End** is **Revere House,** another important stop on **the Freedom Trail.** It is **the home** of **Paul Revere** (1735–1818), **patriot** during **the American Revolution.** Built in 1676, it is **the** oldest standing **building** in **Boston.**

The *U.S.S. Constitution*, **a** famous **warship** built in 1797, is across **the Inner Harbor** in **the Charlestown Navy Yard.** You can walk over **the Charlestown Bridge** to get there. **The** *U.S.S. Constitution* is **the** oldest American **warship** afloat today. **The** *U.S.S. Constitution* Museum is near **the ship.** You can visit **the ship** for free, but you have to pay to visit **the museum.**

Near **the Charlestown Navy Yard** is **the Bunker Hill Monument, the** last **stop** on **the Freedom Trail. The monument** commemorates **the Battle of Bunker Hill, an** important **battle** of **the American Revolution,** fought on June 17, 1775. After you finish **the trail,** you will probably be ready for **a rest.** You may wish to relax in one of Boston's beautiful **parks,** or get **a coffee** at one of **the** many **cafés** in **the North End.**

 Discussion Questions Discuss these questions with a partner.

1. Where does the trail start?
2. What does the Old State House have?
3. What part of Boston has many Italian restaurants?
4. What is the oldest building in Boston?
5. Where is the *U.S.S. Constitution?*
6. What battle was fought on June 17, 1775?

Grammar Structures and Practice

A. Articles

The Indefinite Article

General nouns and nouns not yet identified in the context are called *nonspecific* or *indefinite*.

- General, nonspecific plural nouns need no article.
- The indefinite article, *a/an*, is for singular nouns.

4.15	Indefinite Articles	
	Explanations	**Examples**
a/an	Use *a/an* before a singular noun to mention it for the first time.	My town has **an** aquarium.
	You can use *a/an* for a generic (general) noun to talk about one of a group of items.	**A** park is **a** nice place for **a** picnic.
(Ø)	Don't use *a/an* before plural nouns.	There are **skyscrapers** in the downtown area. How many **subway lines** are there in your city?

Note: Use *a* before words that begin with consonant sounds. Use *an* before words that begin with vowel sounds. Examples: **a** city, **a** European market, **a** unique experience; **an** hour, **an** important step, **an** elegant hotel.

The Definite Article

The definite article, *the*, is for both count (singular and plural) and noncount nouns. It shows that the nouns are identified, specific, special, or unique.

4.16	The Definite Article	
	Explanations	**Examples**
the	*The* is for an identified noun. A noun becomes identified at its second mention in the context.	My town has **an** aquarium. **The** aquarium is on Baker Street.
	The is for something specific, special, or unique.	**The** oldest building in my town is **the** library.
	When the speaker and the listener both know the item or person, use *the*.	Do you want to take **the** subway or **the** bus? We're going to **the** city this weekend.
(Ø)	When a plural noun names a generic (general) item, don't use *the* before it.	**Parks** are an important part of any city.

Notes: Don't use *the* before names of games (such as *soccer*) or abstract nouns (such as *happiness*). Also, don't use *the* with possessive adjectives like *my* or *his* or the words *this, that, these,* or *those.*

Using *the* with Names

There are many different rules for the use of *the* with names. Here are a few.

4.17 *The* with Names

	Explanations	Examples
People	Use *the* with titles.	**the** president of the United States **the** queen of England
	Don't use *the* with the capitalized titles + names of specific people.	President Kennedy Queen Elizabeth
Places	Don't use *the* with names of streets, cities, states, provinces, and most countries, except plural place names (like **the** *United States,* **the** *Netherlands,* **the** *Philippines*).	Japan Kobe Argentina Buenos Aires
Buildings	*The* is usually used with names of buildings.	**the** Eiffel Tower **the** Leaning Tower of Pisa **the** Taj Mahal
Historical Events	*The* is common with names of historical events.	**the** storming of the Bastille **the** French Revolution **the** fall of the Berlin Wall

1 Practice In the reading on pages 124 and 125, underline the indefinite articles (*a/an*) with the nouns they correspond to, and double underline the definite articles along with the nouns they correspond to.

Example A great way to see old downtown Boston during the day is to walk the Freedom Trail.

2 Practice Fill in the blanks with *a, an, the,* or *X* (for no article). In some cases, more than one answer may be correct.

A. Where can we stay in _____*the*_____ city of _____*X*_____

Boston? _____1_____ Four Seasons Hotel is expensive, but maybe

we can find _____2_____ smaller hotel in _____3_____

part of town farther from _____4_____ downtown area.

B. President John F. Kennedy was from _____1_____ Massachusetts.

There's _____2_____ important building in Boston with his name—

_____ JFK Building—on _____ New
         3   4
Sudbury Street.

C. I like _____ aquariums. There's _____
              1   2
interesting aquarium at _____ Boston Harbor. If we go there,
                             3
we can learn about _____ sea animals and
                        4
_____ plant life.
     5

D. Only a few cities in _____ United States have
                              1
_____ subway systems. Boston has _____
     2   3
subway system and also _____ trolley.
                            4
_____ tourists can get on and off _____
     5   6
trolley at _____ twelve different places.
                7

E. Do you like _____ historic ships and _____
                    1   2
monuments? *The U.S.S. Constitution* was _____ warship
                                               3
during _____ War of 1812. You can learn about
            4
_____ Battle of Bunker Hill at _____
     5   6
Bunker Hill Pavilion, which has _____ multimedia program
                                     7
about this famous battle.

3 Practice Rewrite the following sentences. Correct any mistakes in the underlined words. If there are no mistakes in a sentence, write *Correct* next to the sentence.

Example Let's play the soccer on a Boston Common.
Let's play soccer on Boston Common.

1. Is there <u>the</u> ice cream store on <u>a</u> corner of Mason Street and Avery?

2. A baker lives next door to me. <u>A</u> baker sometimes gives me <u>fresh bread</u>. I like his <u>the</u> cakes and <u>a</u> pies, too.

3. I go to <u>the same</u> café every morning and order a big breakfast. It's <u>Beacon Hill Bistro</u>. It has <u>French</u> and <u>American</u> food.

4. My best friend isn't from <u>a</u> Massachusetts. He doesn't even live in <u>United States</u>. He lives in <u>the</u> Sidney, <u>the</u> Australia.

5. Where is there <u>the</u> beautiful garden in <u>a</u> Boston? <u>A</u> Public Garden is across from <u>a</u> Boston Common.

6. What's <u>Beacon</u> Hill? It's <u>a</u> nineteenth-century Boston neighborhood. It's more like a friendly village than a big-city area.

7. I have to go to <u>a</u> North End next week. I have <u>appointment</u> with my <u>the</u> dentist on <u>the</u> Congress Street.

8. "Where can I buy <u>a</u> watch?" "You can buy <u>a</u> watch on Newbury Street. It's in town."

9. "There is <u>the</u> town council meeting tonight in <u>a</u> library." "Which library do you mean?" "It's <u>the</u> library on <u>Boylston Street</u>, near <u>the</u> Prudential Center."

10. "I'll meet you in <u>a</u> post office in five minutes. I have <u>the</u> package to mail." "But where's <u>library</u>?"

Using What You've Learned

4 **Telling About Your Favorite Place** What is your favorite place in your community? Write for 15 minutes on one of the topics below. Be sure to explain why the place is your favorite. Pay special attention to your use of articles.

- your favorite restaurant or eating place
- your favorite shopping area or store
- your favorite cultural place (such as a museum, a concert hall, or a theater)
- your favorite recreational place (such as an amusement park, a sports arena, or a park)

When you finish, exchange papers with another student. Read each other's descriptions. Underline any mistakes in article use. Which points in your partner's paper are most interesting? For each of these, write a question to get more information. Return your papers. Read and discuss your partner's corrections, questions, and comments—and vice versa. Finally, rewrite your description; make necessary corrections and helpful changes.

You may want to make a class book about your city. Then you can visit some of your classmates' favorite places.

5 **Planning a Local Tour** Form groups of three or four. Get a tourist map of your city or town or another familiar city or town. Plan a three- or four-day tour of the place. Agree on at least ten places to visit. Each group member writes a plan for one day of the trip. Plans for each tourist place should include answers to these questions:

- Where's the place?
- Why are we going there?
- When and how do we get to it?
- What are we going to see?
- What will we do there?

Self-Assessment Log

Each of the following sentences describes the grammar you learned in this chapter. Read the sentences and then check the best box for how well you understand each structure.

	Needs Improvement	Good	Great
I can use *be going to* and the simple future tense to describe and ask about events in the future.	❑	❑	❑
I can use the present continuous and simple present tenses to express future time.	❑	❑	❑
I can use separable and inseparable phrasal verbs to describe actions and activities.	❑	❑	❑
I can use prepositions of place to describe location.	❑	❑	❑
I can use prepositions of time to describe relationships in time.	❑	❑	❑
I can use definite and indefinite articles to modify nouns.	❑	❑	❑

Home

In This Chapter

The Past Tense, Connecting Words

"Home is not where you live but where they understand you.**"**

—Christian Morgenstern
German author and poet (1871–1914)

Connecting to the Topic

1 When did you move into your current home?

2 What do you like about it?

3 What do you not like about it?

Part 1

The Simple Past Tense (Regular Verbs); *Used to*

Setting the Context

Prereading Questions Discuss these questions with a small group.

Do you ever talk with members of an older generation about the "good old days"? Do you talk with members of younger generations about the "good old days"? How are these conversations similar—or different?

Reading Read the conversation.

Grandfather:	**Did** I ever **talk** to you kids about the good old days?
Jason:	The good old days?
Grandfather:	Yes . . . when your grandmother and I **were** your age. We **worked** hard, but we **enjoyed** life. We **didn't need** a lot in the 1950s.
Jason:	You **didn't have** many machines then, right? Your family **didn't have** a computer, or a VCR, or a compact disk player, or . . . .
Jessica:	What? You mean TV **didn't exist**?
Grandfather:	Oh, television **existed**, but there **was** only black and white TV. Anyway, we **didn't own** a TV. My father **decided** we **didn't need** television.
Jessica:	What **did** you **do** for fun? **Did** you **go** to the movies every night?

Grandfather:	No, we **didn't**. We usually **stayed** home and **entertained** ourselves.
Jason:	How **did** you **live** without a TV, and video games, and CDs, and DVDs, and iPods, and . . . ? **Didn't** you **get** bored in the evening?
Grandfather:	No, we **didn't**. The children **played** games—like checkers and chess. My sister **used to play** rock and roll records on her record player, and we **used to dance**. We **listened** to the radio and **discussed** current events. My mother and father **used to talk** a lot.
Grandmother:	Not my family. My parents **didn't use to talk** much. My father **liked to read** the paper. My mother **knitted** and **sewed**. She also **cooked** every day. I usually **helped** in the kitchen.
Jessica:	Really? Why **did** you **cook** so often? Why **didn't** you **order** pizza?
Grandmother:	Because my father **wanted** home-cooked meals. Of course, we **didn't have** a microwave or a food processor or a dishwasher or . . .
Jessica:	What? No dishwasher? Who **used to wash** the dishes?
Grandmother:	I **used to wash** them, and my sister **used to dry** them.
Jessica:	**Didn't** your brother **do** any housework? **Didn't** your father **help?**
Grandmother:	No, I'm afraid not. Only the women **worked** in the house in those days.
Grandfather:	Yes, those *were* the good old days.
Grandmother:	Well that's all changed now. Which reminds me—I hope you **cleaned** the kitchen.
Grandfather:	Yes, dear. I **did.**

 Discussion Questions Discuss these questions with a partner.

1. What are the children talking about with their grandparents?

2. What did the grandfather's family use to do for fun in the evening?

3. How was the grandmother's family different from the grandfather's family?

4. Who did the housework in the grandmother's family? Why?

5. Do you think family life is probably better or worse now than it was in the past? Why?

Grammar Structures and Practice

A. Statements with Past Tense Verbs

Use the simple past tense to talk about completed past events and activities.

5.1 Statements with Past Tense Verbs

	Explanations	Examples
Affirmative	For all regular verbs, add an *-ed* ending in the past tense. This form is used for all subjects, both singular and plural.	Our kids **helped** us paint our kitchen. I **stayed** up late last night. We **listened** to music after dinner. The children **played** games in the living room.
Negative	For negative past verbs, use *did not* before the simple form of the base verb. The contraction for *did not* is *didn't*.	My roommate **didn't like** that restaurant. We **didn't order** pizza last night. Our family **didn't own** a computer until recently. I **didn't live** in a dorm last year.

Spelling Rules for the Past Tense of Regular Verbs

The spelling of a past tense regular verb depends on the ending of the verb—whether it ends with a consonant (C) or vowel (V).

Spelling Rules

Ending of the Simple Form of the Verb	Spelling Rule	Examples
-y after a consonant	Change the *-y* to *i* and add *-ed*.	try/tried carry/carried dry/dried
C + V + C for a one-syllable verb	Double the final consonant and add *-ed*.	plan/planned stop/stopped plug/plugged Exception: Do not double final *w*, *x*, or *y*.
C + V + C for a two-syllable verb	Double the final consonant only if the last syllable is stressed.	permit/permitted prefer/preferred occur/occurred
-e	Add only *-d*.	tie/tied change/changed live/lived
other	Add *-ed* to the simple form of all other regular verbs.	want/wanted ask/asked belong/belonged

The *-ed* ending is pronounced three ways. Its pronunciation depends on the last sound of the simple verb. Pronounce the ending:

- /ɪd/ after the *d* and *t* sounds
  Examples: exist**ed**, need**ed**, want**ed**, trad**ed**

- /t/ after the voiceless sounds *s, k, p, f, sh, ch,* and *x*
  Examples: cook**ed**, help**ed**, wash**ed**, watch**ed**

- /d/ after the voiced sounds *b, g, l, m, n, r, v, z,* and all vowels
  Examples: rob**bed**, listen**ed**, liv**ed**, sew**ed**

Expressions of Past Time

Simple past tense sentences may include expressions of past time like these:

yesterday	last year	next
the day before yesterday	in 1998	the next day
yesterday morning	in April 1992	after that
yesterday afternoon	on November 15	at 3:00
yesterday evening	on Tuesday	a week later
last night	a year ago	then
last Monday	a long time ago	
last week	a few minutes ago	

1 **Practice** In the conversation on pages 134 and 135, circle the regular past tense verbs in affirmative statements. Put a box around the negative past tense verbs.

Examples We (worked) hard, but we (enjoyed) life. We [didn't need] a lot in the 1950s.

2 Practice Fill in the blanks with the correct simple past tense forms of the verbs in parentheses.

When I was a child, we ___*didn't stay*___ (not stay) inside watching TV in

hot weather. We _____ (not own) an air conditioner, so on warm
                              1

summer evenings, we _____ (stay) outside on the porch for
                              2

hours. We children _____ (play) games or
                              3

_____ (look) at comic books. My dad _____ (re-
          4   5

lax) in his chair and _____ (smoke) his pipe. Sometimes he
                              6

_____ (try) to do a crossword puzzle in the newspaper. Occasion-
          7

ally some neighbors _____ (visit) us on the porch. Then my dad
                              8

_____ (stop) reading the newspaper and _____
          9   10

(discuss) current events with them. They _____ (argue) about
                                                      11

politics or the economy.

After my mom _____ (wash) the dinner dishes, she usually
                    12

_____ (join) us on the porch. She and my father
        13

_____ (talk) about the house, the neighborhood, and us kids.
        14

Sometimes she _____ (peel) apples. My dad usually
               15

_____ (help) my mom. When they _____ (fin-
        16   17

ish), they _____ (hand) each of us kids an apple. My family al-
            18

ways _____ (enjoy) those summer evenings on the porch.
        19

3 **Practice** Think about your childhood. Write an affirmative or a negative past tense statement about that time with each of these verb phrases. You can tell about yourself and other family members.

Examples live in an apartment   *We lived in an apartment.*
             share a bedroom   *I shared a bedroom with my sister.*

1. work hard
2. clean the house
3. order in food
4. cook or bake
5. own a computer
6. rent videos
7. use a microwave

8. watch a lot of TV
9. play games
10. talk on the telephone a lot
11. plant a garden
12. wash and dry dishes
13. visit neighbors or friends
14. enjoy being together

B. Yes/No Questions and Short Answers

For simple past tense yes/no questions with main verbs other than *be*, include *did(n't)* before the subject.

- The main verb is in the simple form.
- There is no final *-ed* ending in the question form.

5.2	Yes/No Questions and Short Answers with Main Verbs			
	Explanations	**Examples**	**Possible Answers**	
			Affirmative	**Negative**
Affirmative Questions	The "helping verb" in affirmative simple past questions is *did*. Use *did* before the subject in a yes/no question and after the subject in a short answer.	**Did** your mother **cook** last night? **Did** you **move** to a new apartment? **Did** the neighbors **visit** last week?	Yes, she **did**. Yes, I **did**. Yes, they **did**.	No, she **didn't**. No, we **didn't**. No, they **didn't**.
Negative Questions	The "helping verb" in negative simple past questions is *didn't*. Use *didn't* before the subject in a yes/no question and after the subject in a short answer.	**Didn't** your girlfriend **rent** a video last night? **Didn't** your father **call** you at home?	Yes, she **did**. Yes, he **did**.	No, she **didn't**. No, he **didn't**.
		Didn't the neighbors **paint** their house a few years ago?	Yes, they **did**.	No, they **didn't**.

4 **Practice** Underline the past tense verb forms in yes/no questions in the conversation on pages 134 and 135.

Example Did I ever talk to you kids about the good old days?

 5 **Practice** What did you do last weekend? First, Student A asks simple past tense questions with the phrases on page 141. Student B gives a short answer. Then Student B asks the questions, and Student A gives short answers. After each affirmative short answer, give additional information with a simple past tense sentence.

Examples A: *Did you clean your room last weekend?*
　　　　　　B: *No, I didn't.*
　　　　　　A: *Did you play any sports last weekend?*
　　　　　　B: *Yes, I did. I played tennis on Saturday afternoon.*

1. clean your room?
2. play any sports?
3. listen to the radio?
4. watch TV?
5. cook?
6. telephone anyone?
7. visit your friends?
8. wash your clothes?
9. study at home?
10. finish your homework?
11. receive any letters or packages?
12. mail any letters or packages?
13. use a computer?
14. surf the Internet?
15. stay up late?
16. enjoy yourself?

When you finish, join with another pair of students. What did or didn't your partner do last weekend? Take turns and tell the class five things.

C. Information Questions

Information questions are questions with the words *who*, *what*, *where*, *when*, *why*, and *how*.

■ *Who(m)* and *what* can be the object of the verb (the "receiver" of the action) in a question.

■ Other question words are adverbs. In these cases, simple past tense information questions have *did* before the sentence subject.

■ *Didn't* is common between *why* and the subject.

■ When *who* or *what* is the subject of the sentence (the "doer" of the action), the main verb is in the simple past tense; *did* is not used before the subject.

5.3 Information Questions with Main Verbs

Explanations	Question Words	Examples	Possible Answers
In information questions with *did* or *didn't*, the main verb is in the simple form. It has no *-ed* ending.	Who	**Who did** you **call?**	I **called** my sister.
	What	**What did** you **do** yesterday?	I **cleaned** my house.
	Where	**Where did** your relatives **stay?**	They **stayed** in the upstairs bedroom.
	When	**When did** your relatives **visit?**	They **visited** last month.
	How	**How did** she **find** her apartment?	She **looked** in the paper.
	Why	**Why didn't** you **order** pizza?	I **wanted** a home-cooked meal.
Is *who* or *what* the subject of the sentence? Then the question word order is the same as in a statement.	Who and What as subject	**Who argued** a lot? **What happened** last night?	My sister and I (**argued** a lot). We **rented** a video.

6 Practice Put two lines under the information question verb forms in the conversation on pages 134 and 135.

Example What <u><u>did</u></u> you <u><u>do</u></u> for fun?

7 Practice Fill in the blanks with question words from the list below. In some cases, more than one question word will fit. Try to use each question word at least once. Then interview a classmate about his or her childhood with these questions. He or she will answer in the simple past tense. Write your classmate's answers on the lines below the questions.

What	Where	When	Who	How	Why

1. _____ did you live?

   _____

2. _____ cooked food for your family?

   _____

3. _____ shopped for food?

   _____

4. _____ machines or electronic equipment did your family own?

   _____

5. _____ did you play with?

   _____

6. _____ games or sports did you play?

   _____

7. _____ did you start school?

   _____

8. _____ did you like school?

   _____

9. _____ did you want to study English?

   _____

10. _____ television programs did you watch?

   _____

D. *Used to*

Used to + the simple form of a verb describes a past habit or activity. The action(s) existed in the past, but they are no longer happening in the present.

5.4	*Used to*	
	Explanations	**Examples**
Affirmative Statements	For the affirmative form of statements, add the simple form of the verb to *used to*.	I **used to live** in Brazil. We **used to cook** every day.
Negative Statements	For the negative statements, there is no *-d* ending on *use* with *didn't*.	My parents **didn't use to talk** much.
Questions	Unless the question word *who* or *what* is the grammatical subject of a question, there is no *-d* ending on *use* after *did(n't)*.	Did your parents **use to argue** often? Didn't your best friend **use to live** in New York? Who **used to help** you with your homework?

8 Practice Put three lines under the verb phrases with *use(d) to* in the conversation on pages 134 and 135.

Example My sister <u>used to play</u> rock and roll records on her record player, and we <u>used to dance</u>.

9 Practice Joseph is very different now from ten years ago. Look at these pictures of him and read the information on page 144. Then use the cue words with *use(d) to* to make questions about Joseph ten years ago. Answer each question with either an affirmative or a negative sentence; use *used to* for affirmative statements and *use to* for negative statements. Add information and ideas of your own, too.

Ten years ago

I'm Joe. I'm a teacher because I'm not good at sales. I don't make much money, of course. I live in a small apartment in the city. I'm single. In fact, I don't even date because I don't want to. I like poetry, heavy metal music, and spending time alone. On weekends, I sometimes hang out with single friends; most of them are musicians. I smoke and I like fast food.

Now

I'm Joseph. I'm a very successful salesperson. I live in a big house in the suburbs with my wife and two kids. I like detective novels, jazz, and spending time with married friends and relatives. I don't smoke. My wife and I always prepare home-cooked meals. She doesn't work outside the home, but she enjoys gardening, parenting, and volunteer work. We don't go to the city very often.

Examples (have, long hair) *Did Joseph use to have long hair? Yes, he did. (He used to have long hair.)*

(wear, tie) *Did he use to wear a tie? No, he didn't (use to wear a tie).*

1. have, beard
2. wear, glasses
3. be, single
4. be, salesperson
5. be, teacher
6. smoke
7. live, apartment
8. live, suburbs
9. live, city
10. have, children

11. like, poetry
12. read, detective novels
13. listen, jazz
14. listen, heavy metal
15. like, spending time alone
16. like, spending time with friends
17. prepare, home-cooked meals
18. eat, fast food
19. call himself Joe
20. call himself Joseph

Using What You've Learned

10 **Describing the Past from Photos** Find photos of home and family scenes from the past in books, newspapers, magazines, or other sources. Each group selects one photo to describe in the past. Use sentences with *use(d) to* (when appropriate) and answer this question: *What does the photo show about past events, typical activities, and family habits?*

Examples

▪ *Did young people in those days use to have long hair? Yes, the teenagers used to have long hair, and their parents used to complain about it.*

■ *Did working people use to wear ties? I don't think so. Except for executives, office workers didn't generally use to get dressed up for work.*

One group member writes down the group's best ideas. Another person tells the class about their picture.

 11 **Researching Family Life in the Past** Learn more about the "typical" family and home life of a period in the past such as the 19th century, the 1920s, the 1960s, and so on. (It may or may not be the time period in your photo from Activity 10.) Use the Internet or useful reference books. You may want to focus on one or more of these topics:

■ the role of each family member
■ a typical day in the life of each family member
■ the household technology available at the time
■ the ways in which families entertained themselves at that time

When you are ready, give your class an oral report on what you learned. Use regular past tense verbs or regular and irregular verbs with *use(d) to.*

Part 2	The Simple Past Tense (Irregular Verbs); The Past Tense of the Verb *Be*

Setting the Context

 Prereading Questions Discuss these questions with a small group.

When was your last move from one home to another? Did it go smoothly? If not, why not?

Reading Read the conversation.

Antony: Hi, Lorenz. What's up?

Lorenz: Hi, Antony. I **moved** into my new apartment last week.

Antony: Why **didn't** you **call** me? I **told** you I **was** happy to help you move.

Lorenz: It **wasn't** necessary. My old roommate, Arlo, **was** there to help.

Antony: Well, how **did** it **go?**

Lorenz: It **was** a disaster. Everything **went** wrong.

Antony: What **happened?**

Lorenz: Well, the first problem **was** . . . see, I **bought** a new couch, but it **didn't fit** up the stairs.

Antony: So what **did** you **do** with it?

Lorenz: I **left** it with Arlo. He **took** it back to the old apartment temporarily. Anyway, after we **brought** in all of the other furniture, we **began** to unpack. I **got** up on a ladder to hang some pictures, and I **lost** my balance and **fell**. I **cut** my arm on the ladder as I **fell.**

Antony: What **did** you **do** then?

Lorenz: Well, I really **hurt** my arm. And the cut **bled** a lot, so Arlo **took** me to the hospital to get stitches. That **took** about two hours. Then when we finally **got** back to the apartment, I couldn't find my new house key.

Antony: **Did** you **lose** it?

Lorenz: I **thought** so, but then Arlo **said** he **saw** it on a table at the hospital. Evidently, I **took** it out of my pocket with some other stuff and **forgot** it. So we **drove** all the way back to the hospital to get it.

Antony: **Was** it there? Where **was** it?

Lorenz: Yes, it **was**—in the same place. So when we **got** back to the apartment, we **unpacked** a little more. Arlo **went** home at about 10:00, but I **kept** unpacking. When I finally **quit**, I **felt** exhausted. I **fell** asleep as soon as I **lay** down. I **slept** through most of the next day.

Antony: Wow. It sounds like you **had** a really bad move.

Lorenz: Yeah, I'm really glad it's over. So, anyway, . . . what's up with you?

Antony: Actually, I **came** to tell you some news.

Lorenz: What?

Antony: I just **got** a new apartment. And I . . . um . . . **wanted** to ask you a favor. Um . . . could you please . . . uh . . . help me move in?

Discussion Questions Discuss these questions with a partner.

1. What happened to Lorenz's arm?
2. How did he get to the hospital?
3. What did he forget at the hospital? Where was it?
4. How did he feel when he stopped unpacking?
5. What news did Antony tell Lorenz?
6. Did you ever move or help a friend move into a new home? Did the move go well? Why or why not?

Grammar Structures and Practice

A. Irregular Past Tense Verbs

Many common, useful verbs have irregular past tense forms. These verbs do not take an -ed ending in the past form.

5.5 Irregular Past Tense Verbs				
Explanations	**Examples**			
	Simple Form	**Past Tense Form**	**Simple Form**	**Past Tense Form**
The simple and the past forms of some verbs are the same.	cost cut hit hurt	cost cut hit hurt	let put quit shut	let put quit shut
With some verbs, the simple form ends in -d and the past form ends in -t.	bend build lend	bent built lent	send spend	sent spent
Some verbs have other consonant changes or add a consonant in the past tense.	have hear	had heard	lose make	lost made
Many verbs have vowel changes in the past tense.	begin bleed come choose drink drive eat fall find get give	began bled came chose drank drove ate fell found got gave	grow know ride ring run sing take tear throw win write	grew knew rode rang ran sang took tore threw won wrote

(Continued)

5.5　Irregular Past Tense Verbs

Many verbs have consonant and vowel changes in the past tense.	be*	was / were	leave	left
	bring	brought	lie	lay
	buy	bought	pay	paid
	catch	caught	say	said
	creep	crept	sell	sold
	do	did	sleep	slept
	fly	flew	teach	taught
	go	went	tell	told
	keep	kept	think	thought

Note: Verbs with irregular past tense forms follow the same patterns as regular verbs in affirmative statements, negative statements, yes/no questions, and information questions. See the charts on pages 136, 140, and 141.
*Be is the one exception to the above note. See the following chart for more information on the use of the past form of the verb *be*.

B. Past of *Be*

Be is an irregular verb. The simple past tense form of the verb is *was/were*. This irregular verb is used differently from other irregular verbs in statements, yes/no questions and answers, and information questions.

5.6　The Past Tense of *Be*

	Explanations	Examples
Affirmative	Use *was* with singular nouns and with the pronouns *I, he, she, it, this*, and *that*. Use *were* with plural nouns and with the pronouns *you, we, these*, and *those*.	Mario **was** at home last night. Our children **were** born in Osaka.
Negative	Use *not* after the verb *be* in negative sentences. The contraction for *was not* is *wasn't*; the contraction for *were not* is *weren't*.	I **was not** on the Internet last night. We **weren't** hungry for dinner yesterday.

5.7　Yes/No Questions with the Past Tense of *Be*

| | Explanations | Examples | Possible Answers | |
			Affirmative	Negative
Affirmative	In affirmative yes/no questions, *was/were* comes at the beginning of the question. The subject comes after *was/were*.	**Was** your mother in Colombia last week? **Were** you asleep at 11:00 last night?	Yes, she **was**. Yes, I **was**.	No, she **wasn't**. No, I **wasn't**.
Negative	In negative yes/no questions, *wasn't/weren't* comes at the beginning of the question. The subject comes after *wasn't/weren't*.	**Wasn't** the dog inside this afternoon? **Weren't** those sofas expensive?	Yes, she **was**. Yes, they **were**.	No, she **wasn't**. No, they **weren't**.

5.8 Information Questions with the Past Tense of *Be*

	Explanations	Examples	Possible Answers
Affirmative	In affirmative information questions with *be*, the question word comes first, followed by *was/were*.	**Who was** at your house last week? **Where were** you last week?	My aunt and uncle were there. I was on vacation in Spain.
Negative	In negative information questions with *be*, the question word comes first, followed by *wasn't/weren't*.	**Why wasn't** your sister home for dinner? **Who wasn't** happy with the new apartment?	She was at the library. My mother wasn't happy.

1 Practice Circle the past form of the verb *be* and put a box around the other irregular past tense verbs in the conversation on page 146.

Example I told you I was happy to help you move.

2 Practice Yukata is Japanese. He's going to be a student at Cambridge University in England. The story below is in Yukata's words. In the story, he leaves his home in Japan and finds a new home in England. Fill in each blank with the past form of the verb in parentheses.

Cambridge University _____*sent*_____ me the letter of acceptance on
(send)

May 10. I _____ my father read the letter first. Then he
1 (let)

_____ it aloud to the whole family. I know he and my mother
2 (read)

_____ proud. I _____ really excited. I
3 (be)   4 (be)

_____ badly that night. The next day I _____ my
5 (sleep)   6 (take)

parents downtown. We _____ dinner in a nice restaurant. Two days
7 (have)

later, I _____ shopping for some new clothes with my mother.
8 (go)

The clothes _____ a lot of money, but my mother proudly
9 (cost)

_____ the money. The day before I _____, my
10 (spend)   11 (leave)

friends _____ me a going away party. It _____ a great
12 (throw)   13 (be)

party.

The next morning, my alarm clock _____, but I didn't hear
14 (ring)

it. We had to hurry. I _____ ready quickly and my parents
15 (get)

_____ me to the airport. I _____ the plane just
16 (drive)   17 (catch)

in time.

On the airplane, I _____ about my home and my wonderful
18 (think)

family and friends. I _____ to get a little homesick. We
19 (begin)

_____ to Heathrow Airport in London 12 hours later. After going
20 (get)

through immigration and customs, I _____ a train to Cambridge.
21 (take)

Then I _____ a newspaper and a map of the city at a shop near
22 (buy)

my hotel. I _____ I _____ only a week for apart-
23 (know)   24 (have)

ment hunting before school _____, so I _____
25 (begin)   26 (read)

the classified ads.

I _____ a lot of telephone calls the first few days, but I didn't
27 (make)

have any luck. Someone _____ me to go to an apartment rental
28 (tell)

agency. I _____ to the agency and _____ them a
29 (go)   30 (pay)

fee. They _____ me a list of available apartments. A week later, I
31 (give)

_____ a one-bedroom apartment in a really nice building. I
32 (find)

_____ some nice neighbors on my first day in my new apartment. I
33 (meet)

still miss home, but I think I _____ the right decision to come here.
34 (make)

3 Read these sentences. If there are any mistakes in the underlined words, correct the mistakes. If there are no mistakes, write *Correct* next to the sentence.

Examples They <u>payd</u> their rent late last month. *paid*

The mail <u>didn't come</u> yesterday. *correct*

1. We <u>grow</u> our own vegetables last year.

2. I <u>losed</u> the key to my house yesterday.

3. Why <u>didn't</u> he <u>told</u> me about the new tenant?

4. Yukata <u>buyed</u> some plants for his house.

5. Who <u>made</u> the phone call?

6. <u>Was</u> you with your family last night?

7. My parents <u>builded</u> a new room onto their house.

8. Erlin <u>didn't went</u> back home after class yesterday.

9. When you <u>choose</u> that wallpaper?

10. She <u>haved</u> a computer in her old apartment.

11. My friends <u>threw</u> me a housewarming party.

12. Why Luisa <u>wasn't</u> more excited about her new apartment?

13. She <u>find</u> a roommate last week.

14. She <u>be</u> tired after she cleaned the house.

15. I <u>was do</u> three loads of laundry last night.

Using What You've Learned

4 **Continuing a Past-Time Story** Continue the story in Activity 2 on pages 149 and 150. What do you think happened to Yukata next? Each student can add one past tense statement to the story. When possible, use irregular verbs.

Example A: *Yukata met another Cambridge student in his building.*

B: *The student was a woman.*

C: *Yukata and the woman became friends.*

D: *He asked her out on a date.*

E: *She said yes.*

F: *They went to the movies a week later.*

5 **Talking About the Past in Your Life** Choose a topic from the list below. Prepare a short speech on the topic. Include as many irregular past tense verbs as you can.

- My favorite childhood memory
- Life with my roommate(s)
- My parents
- (your own topic about your home/family)

When you are ready, give your speech to the class. After your speech, your classmates will ask you questions. They will also help you with any mistakes with irregular past tense verbs.

Part 3 | Connecting Words

Setting the Context

 Prereading Questions Discuss these questions with a small group.

Do you have a roommate now—or did you have a roommate in the past? How well do (or did) you get along? If there were conflicts, how did you solve them?

Reading Read the conversation.

Atsuko: This kitchen is a mess!

Erika: I had to leave without cleaning it last night **because** I was late for a concert.

Atsuko: Why didn't you clean it **after** you cooked dinner?

Erika: I meant to clean it **when** I got back. I even thought about it at the concert **because** I thought you might be mad. **When** I got home, it was really late **and** I was exhausted. I fell asleep **as soon as** I lay down. I meant to wake up early this morning to clean the kitchen, **but** my alarm didn't go off.

Atsuko: You always have an excuse! You need to help out in the apartment, **or** you're going to have to move out. I do almost all the cleaning, **and** I do most of the shopping, too. **If** the situation doesn't change, I could get sick from lack of sleep.

Erika: You're right, Atsuko. I don't mean to be so lazy. **But** you know, I'm busy all day at school and at work, **so** I'm usually exhausted **when** I get home. I promise I'll take more responsibility in the future. What do you want me to do? I have some time now, **so** I can start right away.

Atsuko: Well, why don't you do the mid-week grocery shopping?

Erika: I can't **because** the shops are closed **when** I get out of work.

Atsuko: Can't you do it **before** you go to work?

Erika: No, **because** I don't have enough time to come home between school and work. I'll be late to work **if** I try to do other things. Why don't I do it on Saturday or Sunday?

Atsuko: That sounds good, **but** you need to be neater in the apartment as well. **As soon as** I clean a room, you mess it up. Also, help me clean the kitchen.

Erika: Let's make a schedule. You straighten and clean the apartment the first and third weeks of the month, **and** I'll do it the second and fourth weeks. OK? Now I have to leave, **or** I'll be late for my first class.

Atsuko: Erika?

Erika: Yes?

Atsuko: When are you going to clean the kitchen?

Erika: Oh, right! I'll clean it **as soon as** I get back. Bye!

 Discussion Questions Discuss these questions with a partner.

1. Why didn't Erika clean the kitchen last night?

2. Why didn't she clean it this morning?

3. What does Atsuko want Erika to do?

4. Why can't Erika do the shopping during the week?

5. What cleaning schedule does Erika suggest?

6. Do you think it is difficult to live with a roommate? Why or why not?

Grammar Structures and Practice

A. Compound Sentences with *And, But, Or,* and *So*

An independent clause is a group of words with at least one sentence subject and one main verb. A compound sentence combines two or more independent clauses with connecting words.

- The main connectors for compound sentences are *and*, *but*, *or*, and *so*.
- A comma separates the clauses.
- A short two-clause sentence with *and* may not need a comma, especially if the subjects of the two clauses is the same.

5.9	Compound Sentences with *And, But, Or,* and *So*	
	Explanations	**Examples**
and	*And* adds information and connects similar ideas.	I do the shopping in my family. + My wife does the laundry. = I do the shopping in my family, **and** my wife does the laundry.
but	*But* shows contrast and connects opposing ideas.	I don't really like my neighborhood. + I live there because the rent is cheap. = I don't really like my neighborhood, **but** I live there because the rent is cheap.
or	*Or* expresses an alternative or choice.	Do you live alone? + Do you live with a roommate? = Do you live alone, **or** do you live with a roommate?
so	*So* introduces a result.	She doesn't like to cook. + She often eats fast food. = She doesn't like to cook, **so** she often eats fast food.

Note: If the subject (and the verb) of two independent clauses is the same, words can be joined in a compound *phrase* instead of a compound sentence.

---

1 **Practice** Circle the connecting words in the conversation on pages 152 and 153.

Example When I got home, it was really late (and) I was exhausted.

2 **Practice** Combine these sentences with *and, but, or,* or *so*. In some cases, there may be more than one correct answer.

Example We stayed home last night. We watched a video.
We stayed home and (we) watched a video last night.

1. I like the country. I live in the city.

2. Tony shares an apartment with four other people. It's crowded.

3. We bought a microwave. We bought a coffeemaker.

4. I went to bed early last night. I couldn't sleep.

5. Do you want to eat at home tonight? Do you want to go to a restaurant?

6. My husband can make eggs and pasta. He can't make anything more complicated.

7. The rent was too expensive. We found another apartment.

8. Our oven broke last week. Our dishwasher broke this week.

9. Are you going to paint this room? Are you going to put up wallpaper?

10. Their apartment is only 700 square feet. It feels much bigger.

11. Do you live in a house? Do you live in an apartment?

12. I looked for my keys. I couldn't find them.

13. The neighbors were making too much noise. We asked them to be more quiet.

14. He baked a chocolate cake. He gave everyone a slice.

15. I cleaned my whole apartment. It will be clean when my mother visits.

B. Complex Sentences with *Because, Before, After, As soon as, When,* and *If*

A complex sentence consists of two or more clauses: an independent clause and one or more dependent clauses.

- Dependent clauses begin with words such as *because, before, after, as soon as, when,* or *if.*
- When the dependent clause comes first, put a comma after it to separate it from the independent clause.
- Don't use a comma when a dependent clause comes after an independent clause.

5.10	Complex Sentences with *Because, Before, After, As soon as, When,* and *If*	
	Explanations	**Examples**
because	*Because* shows cause and effect.	I felt homesick **because I missed my family.** **Because I missed my family,** I felt homesick.
before	*Before* shows that something happened earlier in time.	My sister lived at home **before she started college.** **Before she started college,** my sister lived at home.
after	*After* shows that something happened later in time.	I found a roommate **after I rented the apartment.** **After I rented the apartment,** I found a roommate.
as soon as	*As soon as* means "immediately following."	We became friends **as soon as he moved in.** **As soon as he moved in,** we became friends.
when	*When* means "at the time that."	Did you have a curfew **when you lived at home?** **When you lived at home,** did you have a curfew?
if	*If* means "in the event that."	What can you do **if your neighbors bother you?** **If your neighbors bother you,** what can you do?

3 Practice Underline the dependent clauses in the conversation on pages 152 and 153.

Example I had to leave without cleaning last night <u>because I was late for a concert.</u>

4 Practice Fill in the blanks with *because, before, after, as soon as, when,* or *if.* In some cases, more than one word may be possible.

I moved to a new apartment _____*because*_____ the neighbors in my old apartment were really inconsiderate. They always had loud parties _____1_____ the weekend started. I don't mind parties _____2_____ they start at eight or nine o'clock, but most of their parties started _____3_____ the 11:00 news ended! It often seemed like _____4_____ I turned off my light and got into bed, the party began. _____5_____ I called my landlord to complain about the parties, he seemed surprised. He promised to call my neighbors _____6_____ we hung up. _____7_____ I spoke with the landlord, I felt better. I was relieved _____8_____ I really thought the problem was solved. But that very night _____9_____ I turned off my light to go to bed, the loud music started up again. _____10_____ I calmed down a little, I called up a friend and asked for an invitation to sleep at her house _____11_____ I couldn't stand even one more sleepless night. I moved out of that apartment the very next day. What can you do _____12_____ you can't get along with your next-door neighbors?

5 Practice Add a dependent clause (with *because, before, after, as soon as, when,* or *if*) to each of the following independent clauses.

Example I get nervous . . . *before I take exams.*

1. I get nervous . . .
2. I feel most energetic . . .
3. I feel confident . . .
4. I get frustrated . . .
5. I study English . . .
6. I feel happy . . .
7. I get bored . . .
8. I learn best . . .
9. I feel embarrassed . . .
10. I feel tired . . .

Using What You've Learned

6 Telling How to Do Something Choose an activity that you do at home. You can use one of the following suggestions or think of one of your own. In a present or past-time paragraph, write directions for the steps in the activity. Include compound and complex sentences with the connecting words *and, but, or, so, because, before, after, as soon as, when,* and *if.*

- How to cook a food
- How to do a craft (such as knitting, sewing, model making, building a piece of furniture, etc.)
- How to tend a garden
- How to program or work a household appliance (such as a VCR or DVD player, a coffee machine, or a microwave)

Example (Present Tense)

How to Make Scrambled Eggs
You need eggs and butter to make scrambled eggs. You also need a pan or a griddle. First crack open as many eggs as you want and scramble them in a bowl. Before you put the eggs in the pan, melt the butter in the pan. (I do this, so the eggs don't stick to the pan.) After all of the butter is melted, pour the eggs into the pan. When the eggs are cooked, remove them from the heat. Don't let them overcook because they will become hard. I serve them as soon as they are ready, so they don't get cold. Before you eat the eggs, you may want to add salt and pepper.

Example (Past Tense)

How I Fixed a Leaky Faucet
As soon as I got up last Saturday, I decided to fix the leak in our bathroom sink. Before I started, I printed out step-by-step instructions from the Internet. After I read them quickly, I turned off the water. If I wanted the correct part from the hardware store, I thought, I'd better take the old part with me. So first, I tried to remove the handle. It didn't move easily, so as soon as my husband got up, I asked him for help. Then . . . .

Self-Assessment Log

Each of the following sentences describes the grammar you learned in this chapter. Read the sentences and then check the best box for how well you understand each structure.

	Needs Improvement	Good	Great
I can use regular and irregular past tense verbs to talk about completed events.	❏	❏	❏
I can use *used to* to describe past habits and activities.	❏	❏	❏
I can use the past tense of *be* to talk and ask about the past.	❏	❏	❏
I can use connecting words like *and*, *but*, *or*, and *so* to combine two independent clauses.	❏	❏	❏
I can use connecting words like *because* and *if* to join an independent and dependent clause together.	❏	❏	❏

Cultures of the World

❝Culture is the widening of the mind and of the spirit.❞

—Jawaharlal Nehru
First Indian prime minister (1889–1964)

Connecting to the Topic

1 Do you enjoy traveling?

2 What have you learned about other cultures when you have traveled?

Setting the Context

Prereading Questions Discuss these questions with a small group.

When you go to other places, do you ever converse with other travelers? If so, what do you usually talk about?

Reading Read the conversation.

Alex: Is anyone sitting here?

Janet: No. Please have a seat. My name's Janet. I'm from the United States.

Koto: I'm Koto. I'm from Japan.

Alex: Nice to meet you both. I'm Alex. I'm from Brazil.

Asim: And my name's Asim. I'm from Egypt. Alex and I **have** just **arrived** in London. Actually, we just met at the airport.

Janet: London is a great city. I think you'll like it.

Asim: What **have** you **done** here so far?

Koto: We**'ve gone** to the Tower of London, Buckingham Palace, Westminster Abbey, and we**'ve** already **been** to the British Museum twice. That's where Janet and I met.

Alex: (*To Janet*) **Have** you ever **been** to England before? Does it feel familiar to you because you're from the United States?

Janet: Well, there are a lot of similarities between the two countries, but the U.S. **hasn't been** a British colony for more than two centuries, you know. Actually, **I've been** surprised at the number of differences. **I've noticed** differences in traditions, foods, lifestyle, . . . even language!

Asim: What **has surprised** you the most?

Janet: Probably the people. I **haven't met** a lot of English people yet, but my first impression is that they're very kind. Even so, they seem much more reserved than I'm used to.

Koto: Actually, I**'ve been** to England twice before and I**'ve** always **felt** very comfortable with the people. I think that's because Japanese people are a bit reserved, too.

Asim: That's interesting. (*Looking at a menu*) Hmmm. **Have** you ever **heard** of shepherd's pie?

Janet: Yes. It's a traditional English dish made with layers of meat, potato, and cheese. I**'ve had** it once or twice recently. It's not bad. But I think English food is a little bland.

Koto: Not the desserts. **Have** you **tried** any traditional English puddings yet? They're delicious!

Alex: I**'ve** never **had** any traditional English foods. I**'ve** only **had** fast food here so far.

Koto: How does English fast food taste?

Alex: A lot like Brazilian fast food! And like the fast food in every country I**'ve** ever **visited**. Fast food is probably the one thing that's the same all around the world!

 Discussion Questions Discuss these questions with a partner.

1. What have Koto and Janet done in London so far?

2. How many times have they been to the British Museum?

3. What differences has Janet noticed between English culture and American culture?

4. Why has Koto always felt comfortable in England?

5. What has been the same in every country Alex has visited?

6. Have you ever visited another country? If so, what differences did you notice between that country and your own?

Grammar Structures and Practice

A. Past Participles

The past participle is the verb form used in the present perfect tense.

6.1 Past Participles

	Explanations	Examples			
		Simple Form	**Past Participle**	**Simple Form**	**Past Participle**
Regular Verbs	For regular verbs, the past participle is the same as the simple past tense (verb + *-ed*).	like live play	liked lived played	study travel visit	studied traveled visited
Irregular Verbs	For irregular verbs, the past participle often changes spelling and/or punctuation.	be become begin break bring buy choose come cost do eat find fly forget get give go have know	been become begun broken brought bought chosen come cost done eaten found flown forgotten gotten given gone had known	meet pay put read ride ring run say see send sit speak sleep take teach tell think win write	met paid put read rode rung run said seen sent sat spoken slept taken taught told thought won written

Note: For more irregular verbs, see Appendix 3.

---

1 Practice Complete this chart with simple verb forms and past participles. If possible, don't look at the chart above until you finish. Then check your answers.

Simple Form	Past Participle	Simple Form	Past Participle
1. be	been	**11.** meet	_____
2. begin	begun	**12.** pay	_____
3. bring	_____	**13.** read	_____
4. buy	_____	**14.** _____	said
5. _____	cost	**15.** study	_____
6. do	_____	**16.** _____	spoken
7. eat	_____	**17.** take	_____
8. live	_____	**18.** think	_____
9. _____	gone	**19.** _____	written
10. have	_____	**20.** visit	_____

B. The Present Perfect Tense

The present perfect tense consists of *have/has* + the past participle form of the verb.

- A specific time is not usually given in a present perfect statement or question.
- Past time expressions such as *yesterday* or *last week* are for the simple past tense.

6.2 The Present Perfect Tense

Purpose	Explanations	Examples	
		Affirmative	**Negative**
Actions or Situations at an Unspecified Time in the Past	Use the present perfect for an event that happened at an unknown or unspecified time in the past. Some common time expressions for this use are *already, ever, just, recently, still, yet, so far,* and *up to now.*	I've **been** to Canada. My parents **have just returned** from there. I've **already seen** their photos. They've **shot** ten rolls of film **so far**.	I **have not been** to India. I've **never seen** the Taj Mahal. My family **still hasn't had** time for a trip. **Up until now,** we **haven't had** the money, either.
Repeated Actions at Unspecified Times in the Past	The present perfect is common for repeated past action, often with time expressions like *once, twice, several times,* etc.	I've **been** to Canada twice. My parents **have been** there many times.	I **haven't eaten** Indian food more than once or twice. We **haven't traveled** outside our country too many times.

Note: The present perfect tense forms contractions with subject pronouns: *I've, we've, you've, they've, he's, she's,* and *it's.* The negative contractions are *haven't* and *hasn't.*

6.3 Yes/No Questions in the Present Perfect Tense

Explanations		Examples	Possible Answers	
			Affirmative	**Negative**
The adverb *(not) ever* is common in present perfect questions about unspecified times in the past.	**Affirmative**	**Have** you ever **been** to New York?	Yes, I have.	No, I haven't.
		Have you ever **seen** the Empire State Building?	Yes, I have.	No, I haven't.
There are no contractions with subject pronouns in affirmative short answers to present perfect yes/no questions.	**Negative**	**Haven't** you ever **been** to New York?	Yes, I have.	No, I haven't.
		Haven't you ever **seen** the Empire State Building?	Yes, I have.	No, I haven't.

6.4 Information Questions in the Present Perfect Tense

Explanations		Examples	Possible Answers
In present perfect questions with *who* or *what* as the subject, the word order is the same as in a statement. In other questions, *have* or *has* separates the question word from the sentence subject.	**Affirmative**	Who **has lived** abroad?	Juan (has lived abroad).
		Why **have** you **come** here?	I have come to learn about other cultures.
		How many times **have** you **been** here?	I've been here twice.
		How much money **have** you **spent?**	I have spent a lot of money!
	Negative	Who **hasn't taken** any pictures?	No one has.
		Why **haven't** you **brought** a map?	I don't need one.

2 **Practice** Underline the present perfect phrases in the conversation on pages 162 and 163. Identify these sentences as affirmative or negative statements or (yes/no or information) questions.

Example Alex and I <u>have</u> just <u>arrived</u> in London. (affirmative statement)

3 **Practice** Fill in the blanks with the correct form of the verbs in parentheses to form the present perfect tense.

Queridos mamae and papai,

I'm sorry I (not write) _____haven't written_____ sooner, but I (not have)

_____ a free moment! There (be) _____ so
              1   2

much to do here in London. I (meet) _____ some great
                                          3

people, and I am having a wonderful time. There's so much to tell you. I

don't know where to begin. What _____ I
                                        4

_____ (do) here so far? Well, I (be) _____ to
        5   6

Westminster Abbey, the most famous church in England. Also, I (visit)

_____ Buckingham Palace, the Queen's home. I (ride)
        7

_____ double decker buses a few times, and I (eat)
        8

_____ traditional English foods like Yorkshire pudding and
        9

steak and kidney pie. (I'm not crazy about the food, so I (lose)

_____ some weight!)
        10

I (speak) _____ with some English people, and they
                    11

(teach) _____ me a few things about British culture. I
                12

(learn) _____ about pubs—places for people to go to meet
                13

friends and relax. I (go) _____ to pubs a few times, and I
                                14

really like them! In the pubs, I (play) _____ a few games of
                                              15

darts, a popular English bar game. I (watch) _____ a few
                                                    16

soccer matches on TV at the pubs. What _____ I
                                              17

_____ (discover)? Soccer is almost as popular here as it is
        18

back home in Brazil! I (be) _____ amazed at the amount of
                                  19

tea served and drunk. I (try) _____ the coffee, but it's
                                    20

usually very weak. I (not be) _____ able to find really
                                    21

strong coffee like we drink in Brazil. Unfortunately, the weather (not be)

_____ very good. It's often rainy and foggy here. I (not see)
                22

_____ sunshine since I left Brazil. With all of this rain, I
                23

(catch) _____ a little cold.
                24

   I can't wait to tell you more about my trip. I (take)

_____ many, many photos. I _____ also
                25   26

_____ (buy) many souvenirs for everyone at home.
                27

   I really like it here, but I think I'd better leave soon—my friends (tell)

_____ me that I (begun) _____ to speak
                28   29

with a British accent!

   Besos,

   Alex

4 **Practice** Write present perfect questions for these answers. Be careful to use the
correct question form (yes/no questions or information questions) as appropriate.

Example 1. Q: *Has your father eaten Indian food?*
             A: Yes, he has eaten Indian food.
          2. Q: *How many times has he eaten Indian food?*
             A: He's eaten it only once or twice.
          3. Q: *Where has he eaten Indian food?*
             A: He's eaten it in London.

A.

  1. Q: _____?

      A: Yes, she has taken a lot of photographs.

  2. Q: _____?

      A: Probably about 6 or 7 rolls.

  3. Q: _____?

      A: Mostly of churches and castles.

B.

  1. Q: _____?

      A: Yes, I've spent a lot of money on transportation.

2. Q: _____?

  A: About £40.

3. Q: _____?

  A: Double decker buses, the tube, and a few taxi rides.

C.

  1. Q: _____?

  A: Yes, I've drunk a lot of tea during my trip.

  2. Q: _____?

  A: I've had at least five cups of tea each day.

  3. Q: _____?

  A: No, I've never had tea with the queen!

  4. Q: _____?

  A: Because she's never invited me.

C. *Ever, Never, Already, Just, Recently, Still,* and *Yet*

These adverbs are common with the present perfect tense.

6.5 *Ever, Never, Already, Just, Recently, Still,* and *Yet*		
	Explanations	**Examples**
Questions	*Ever* means "at any time." It comes before the past participle. *Already* means "before now." It may come before the past participle or at the end of the question. *Yet* means "up to now." It is usually placed at the end of a question.	Have you **ever** been to the British Museum? Have you **already** been to the British Museum? Have you visited the British Museum **already?** Have you visited the British Museum **yet?**
Affirmative Statements	*Just* refers to the very recent past. *Just* comes before the past participle. *Already* and *recently* usually come before the past participle or at the end of the sentence.	I've **just** visited that museum. I've **already** visited that museum. I've visited that museum **already.** I've **recently** visited that museum. I've visited that museum **recently.**
Negative Statements	*Never* means "not at any time." It must come before the past participle. *Yet* usually comes at the end of a negative statement. *Still* means "up to now." *Still* comes before *has* or *have.*	I have **never** visited that museum. I haven't visited that museum **yet.** I **still** haven't visited that museum.

5 **Practice** Put a circle around the adverbs *ever, never, already, just, recently, still,* and *yet* in present perfect sentences in the conversation on pages 162 and 163. Notice the position of these words in the sentences. Can they appear in other places in the sentences? If so, which positions?

Example We've gone to the Tower of London, Buckingham Palace, Westminster Abbey, and we've (already) been to the British Museum twice.

6 **Practice** Insert the adverbs in parentheses into the sentences after them. In some cases, there may be more than one possible position for the adverb.

Asim: What should we do today?

Alex: (still) Well, we ⌃*still* haven't been to the British Museum.

Koto: (already) Janet and I have been there twice!
1

Janet: (recently) I've seen and done so much. I think I'll stay here and do some
2

laundry. (yet) Besides, I haven't had a chance to write any postcards.
3

Alex: Really? (already) I've sent a couple of postcards home.
4

Koto: I may stay behind, too. (never) I've been so tired in my life!
5

Alex: (still) I can't believe I'm in London! (yet) There's so much I haven't seen.
6   7

Asim: Well, then why don't we split up? You can all do your things, and I can do

mine. We can meet up again tonight and do something together.

Janet: OK. (yet) Hey, we haven't seen a play in the West End theater district. Is
8

anyone interested in the theater tonight?

Koto: That's a great idea. (already) I've gotten information about the shows.
9

Asim: I hear *Romeo and Juliet* is playing. (ever) Have you seen it?
10

Janet: I love that play. (already) I've seen it twice, but I'd be happy to see it again.
11

Alex: (never) I've seen it.
12

Koto: (recently) I read it a couple of times. It would be fun to see it on stage.
13

Asim: (just) Well then, we've made our plan for the day! We'll meet you back here
14

at about 6:00.

7 Practice Find the mistakes in each of these sentences; rewrite the sentences correctly. If there are no mistakes in a sentence, write *Correct*. Make sure all the sentences are in the present perfect tense.

1. Janet have been to already the Houses of Parliament. *Janet has already been to the Houses of Parliament.*

2. I have saw some beautiful English gardens.

3. Have you yet eat fish and chips?

4. We seen a clock as big as Big Ben never.

5. I have already taken the London subway three or four times.

6. Have Asim watched any of the popular British TV soap operas?

7. Many famous tennis players have played at the Wimbledon Tennis Championship in southwest London.

8. I has be surprised by the number of different English accents.

9. How much money have you spend on souvenirs?

10. I had have Yorkshire pudding twice.

11. I have not had the chance to travel to Scotland or Wales.

12. We have learn recently a lot about English culture.

13. We decide to travel to France next.

14. You have made yet the reservations?

Using What You've Learned

8 Learning About Your Classmates' Experiences Play "Find someone who . . . ." First make present perfect questions with the cue words. Begin each question with "Have you ever . . . .?" Then quickly go around the classroom. Ask your classmates one of the questions. When someone answers yes, write down that person's name next to the question. Then move on to the next question.

Example A: *Have you ever been to another country?*
B: *No, I haven't.*
A: *Have you ever been to another country?*
C: *Yes, I have.*
A: *Great!*

1. be / to another country?

2. eat / food from another country?

3. go / to a movie made in another country?

4. know / a person from another country well?

5. write / a letter to a person in another country?

6. receive / a letter from a person in another country?

7. drink / a popular drink from another country?

8. read / a book by an author from another country?

9. make / a recipe from another country?

10. see / an art exhibit from another country?

11. sing / a song from another country?

12. try / learn another language?

The person who finds names for all the questions first wins. The class can check the winner's information with questions like these. Additional questions will begin an interesting class discussion.

Example Student A: *OK. Reiko, who has been to another country?*
Reiko (winning student): *Tomoko has been to another country.*
Student A: *Tomoko, have you been to another country?*
Tomoko: *Yes, I have.*
Student B: *Which country have you been to?*
Tomoko: *I have been to Germany.*

 9 **Interviewing People About Foreign Travel** Do you know a classmate, a teacher, a friend, or a family member who has traveled to one or more foreign countries? Interview this person about his or her experiences. Find out the following:

- What foreign country or countries has this person been to?
- What foods has this person eaten in foreign countries?
- What has this person seen in foreign countries?
- What has this person bought in foreign countries?

What have you learned about this person's experiences? Tell the class. Use the present perfect tense where appropriate.

 10 **Talking About the Influence of Cultures on One Another** Technology and the media are making the world smaller. As a result, almost all cultures have influenced other cultures. In small groups, discuss and list some influences of other cultures on your own. Use the present perfect and the adverbs *never, already, just, recently, still,* and *yet*. Each group shares their completed list with the class.

Examples *Chinese food has become very popular in our country recently.*
French fashion has influenced our way of dressing.
American fast food has already affected our diet.
The attitudes of the older generation haven't really changed yet.

Part 2 Superlatives

Setting the Context

 Prereading Questions Discuss these questions with a small group.

When you travel, do you ever write letters home? Or do you send postcards, emails, or text messages? What do you usually write about?

Reading Read the letter.

Dear Mom and Dad,

My trip is going really well. I met **the nicest** people in London and we all traveled together by ferry to France. My friend Alex made us laugh throughout the whole trip. Alex is **the funniest** person of the group. Tomoko is **the shiest**, Asim is **the most thoughtful**, and I'm afraid I'm **the most talkative!**   5

Paris is **the most beautiful** city I've ever seen. The streets are filled with **the most romantic** cafés, the people dress in **the most fashionable** clothes, and there are **the most impressive** monuments. The food is really wonderful, too. Of course I can't afford to go to **the most expensive**   10 restaurants, but even the bread is great here! **The most common** kind of bread is called a baguette. It's a really long, crusty type of roll. In the morning, people often eat that or croissants. French croissants are **the flakiest and most delicious** bread I've ever had. But **the best** bread of all is pain au chocolate—a kind of croissant with a chocolate filling. I usually   15 have one of them and a cup of coffee for breakfast. (It's probably **the worst** thing for my diet!)

Today we went to the Louvre, one of **the largest** art museums in the world. I read that the Louvre has more than eight miles of galleries! I was **the most interested in** paintings by some of **the most important** French 20 artists like Monet, Degas, and Renoir. I also got to see **the most famous** painting in the world—the Mona Lisa.

After we left the museum, we wandered down the Champs-Elysees, one of **the widest and most glamorous** avenues in Paris. I saw **the most expensive** shops and **the most elegant** people you can imagine.   25

There's so much more to tell you, but this is already **the longest** letter I've ever written you. So I'll end this letter here, but I'll write again soon!

Love,
Janet

Discussion Questions Discuss these questions with a partner.

1. How does Janet describe each of her friends? How does she describe herself?

2. How does Janet describe Paris?

3. What does Janet say about the bread in France?

4. What does Janet say about the Louvre museum?

5. What did Janet see on the Champs-Elysees?

6. How do you think a tourist might describe your city?

Grammar Structures and Practice

A. Superlative Forms

Superlatives compare three or more people or things.

6.6 Superlative Forms		
Types	**Explanations**	**Examples**
One-Syllable Adjectives and Adverbs	Add -*est* to one-syllable adjectives and adverbs. Use *the* before the superlative.	Sydney is **the biggest** city in Australia. I think my roommate works **the hardest.**
Two-Syllable Adjectives	Two-syllable adjectives ending in -*er* or -*y* usually add -*est*. Express the opposite idea with *the least* + adjective. Two-syllable adjectives ending in -*ful* usually follow *the most* and *the least*.	I think my sister is **the friendliest** girl. My next-door neighbor is **the least friendly.** Finding accommodations is **the most stressful** part of travel.
Other Adjectives and Adverbs	Adjectives of three or more syllables and adverbs of two or more syllables follow *the most* or *the least* to form the superlative.	Baseball and football are **the most popular sports** in America. They are **the most frequently watched** sports on TV.
Irregulars	The irregular superlative forms are *good/best, well/best, bad/worst, badly/worst, far/farthest, little/least, many/most*, and *much/most*.	The Prado Museum in Spain has some of **the best** paintings in the world. Cairo has **the worst** traffic in Egypt.
Nouns	Use *the most* or *the fewest* with count nouns. Use *the most* or *the least* with noncount nouns.	Who has been to **the most** museums? I have **the fewest** stamps in my passport. I've spent **the least** money.

Notes: A common superlative phrase is: *one of the* + superlative + plural count noun. For example: *Greece is* **one of the oldest civilizations** *in the world.* Also common is a present perfect phrase after a superlative noun phrase. For example: *The best coffee* **I've ever tasted** *was in Turkey.*

Spelling Rules for Adjective/Adverb + *-est* (Superlatives)

Types	Explanations	Examples
One-Syllable Adjectives and Adverbs	For most one-syllable adjectives and adverbs, add *-est*.	quick / quickest tall / tallest long / longest
	When the last letter is *-e*, add only *-st*.	nice / nicest large / largest rare / rarest
	When the word ends in a single consonant after a single vowel, double the last consonant and add *-est*.	big / biggest hot / hottest thin / thinnest
Two-Syllable Adjectives and Adverbs	For two-syllable words ending in *-y*, change the *-y* to *i* and add *-est*.	crazy / craziest easy / easiest funny / funniest

1 **Practice** Underline the superlatives in the letter on page 174. For each superlative, tell the number of syllables in the simple form of the adjective or adverb as compared to the superlative.

Example Alex is <u>the funniest person</u> of the group. *(funny = two syllables, funniest = three syllables)*

2 **Practice** Give the superlative form of each word.

1. happy _____*happiest*_____

2. famous _____

3. lucky _____

4. good _____

5. strong _____

6. rich _____

7. interesting _____

8. pretty _____

9. brave _____

10. beautiful _____

11. foolish _____

12. far _____

13. quick _____

14. dangerous _____

3 **Practice** Use your opinions and ideas to fill in the blanks. When you are finished, share your ideas with the class.

Example ___*Rio de Janeiro*___ is the most exciting city in the world.

1. _____ is the most beautiful city in the world.

2. _____ is the most beautiful language.

3. _____ cuisine is the most delicious food in the world.

4. _____ is the most expensive city in the world for tourists.

5. _____ is the most famous (the best-known) city in the world.

6. _____ culture is the most interesting culture.

7. _____ has the friendliest people in the world.

8. _____ is the most fashionable city in the world.

9. _____ is the most historic city in the world.

10. _____ is the city with the worst traffic.

11. _____ is the city with the least crime.

12. _____ is the country with the largest cultural influence on the world.

4 **Practice** Fill in the blanks with the superlative form of the words in parentheses.

Ten Interesting Facts about France:

1. France is (big) _the biggest_ country in Western Europe.

2. (high) _____ mountain in France is Mont Blanc. It is 4,807 meters high.

3. Some of (important) _____ painting styles started in France. French Impressionists like Renoir and Cubists like Braque are known all over the world.

4. Some of (respected) _____ literature in the world comes from France. Moliere, Racine, Hugo, Saint-Exupery, and Rimbaud are translated into almost every language.

5. The French Revolution occurred in 1789, making France one of (old) _____ democracies in the world.

6. Many people consider French cuisine to be (good) _____ cuisine in the world.

7. The Eiffel Tower is (popular) _____ attraction in France. More than five million people visit the Tower each year.

8. The Tour de France is a three-week bicycle race that covers more than 2,000 miles. It is (big) _____ annual sporting event in the world.

9. France produces some of (fine) _____ perfumes in the world.

10. France is the second (large) _____ producer of wine in the world.

5 **Practice** Compare these three famous national symbols using the information provided, the cue words, and the superlative forms. Circle the correct choice.

The Eiffel Tower

- Height: 300 meters
- Weight: 7,000 tons
- Built between 1887 and 1889
- Number of steps: 1,652
- Average number of visitors (per year): 5.5 million

The Statue of Liberty

- Height: 93 meters
- Weight: 225 tons
- Built between 1875 and 1884
- Number of steps: 354
- Average number of visitors (per year): 4.2 million

The Leaning Tower of Pisa

- Height: 56 meters
- Weight: 16,204 tons
- Built between 1173 and 1350
- Number of steps: 294
- Currently closed to visitors

1. The Leaning Tower of Pisa is (~~the heaviest~~ / the least heavy).

2. The Statue of Liberty is (the heaviest / the least heavy).

3. The Eiffel Tower is (the lowest / the highest).

4. The Leaning Tower of Pisa is (the lowest / the highest).

5. The Leaning Tower of Pisa is (the oldest / the most modern).

6. The Eiffel Tower is (the oldest / the most modern).

7. The Leaning Tower of Pisa took (the most / the least) time to build.

8. The Eiffel Tower took (the most / the least) time to build.

9. The Eiffel Tower has (the most / the fewest) steps.

10. The Leaning Tower of Pisa has (the most / the fewest) steps.

11. The Leaning Tower of Pisa has (the most / the fewest) annual visitors.

12. The Eiffel Tower has (the most / the fewest) annual visitors.

6 **Practice** Alex, Asim, Koto, and Janet are telling each other some interesting facts about their countries. First fill in the blanks with the superlative forms of the words in parentheses. Which facts do you think come from which speaker? Match the number of each fact to the correct speaker in this picture.

1. My country has some of (impressive) *the most impressive* ancient ruins in the world, such as the Pyramids of Giza.

Speaker: _____

2. My country has (large) _____ remaining tropical rain forest in the world.

Speaker: _____

3. Sumo wrestling in my country is one of (popular) _____ traditional sports I've ever seen.

Speaker: _____

4. (exciting) _____ holiday in my country is the Fourth of July.

Speaker: _____

5. Rice is (important) _____ crop in my country.

Speaker: _____

6. In my country, we usually eat one of (big) _____ meals of the year on Thanksgiving Day.

Speaker: _____

7. Haiku is one of (beautiful) _____ styles of poetry I've ever read or heard. This poetry began in my country.

Speaker: _____

8. Cairo is (crowded) _____ city in my country. Alexandria is _____ second (large) _____ city.

Speaker: _____

9. The city with (great) _____ number of people in my country is São Paulo.

Speaker: _____

10. Samba music is one of (famous) _____ styles of music from my country. It's (well-known) _____ dance during the celebration of Carnaval.

Speaker: _____

11. The Nile River runs through my country. It is (long) _____ river in the world.

Speaker: _____

12. The Amazon River runs through my country. It is _____ second (long) _____ river in the world.

Speaker: _____

13. My native language is one of (difficult) _____ languages in the world. It's also one of (commonly spoken) _____.

Speaker: _____

14. Camels are one of (common) _____ forms of transportation in the desert areas of my country. Of course, it may be one of (uncommon) _____ forms in the world.

Speaker: _____

15. Alaska is one of (cold) _____ states in my country. Arizona is one of (hot) _____.

Speaker: _____

16. One of (traditional) _____ kinds of clothing in my country is called the kimono.

Speaker: _____

17. Baseball started in my country, and it is still one of (popular)

_____ sports there.

Speaker: _____

18. My country has won the World Cup in soccer (many) _____ times.

Speaker: _____

19. My country has one of (diverse) _____ populations in the world.

Speaker: _____

Using What You've Learned

7 **Testing Your Cultural Knowledge** Work in a small group. Together, write ten questions about other cultures and countries; use superlatives. (You must know the answers to your questions.) To test the other groups on their cultural knowledge, ask them these questions. The group with the most correct answers is the winner.

Example *What is the most famous museum in Russia?* (the Hermitage)
What is the largest country in Central America? (Nicaragua)
What is the most important holiday in Japan? (the New Year)

8 **Learning About Cultures** What culture (other than your own) do you want to learn more about? Use the Internet or resource books in the library to find out about this culture. You might want to research topics like these:

- the most famous author(s), artist(s), and musician(s)
- the most popular sport(s)
- the most common food(s)
- the most important holiday(s) and/or festival(s)
- the most popular site(s) for visitors, kinds of scenery, and other attractions

When you have finished your research, give a report on the most interesting information.

Setting the Context

Prereading Questions Discuss these questions with a small group.

When you travel, are you usually glad or sad at the end of your trip? (Are you in a hurry to get home, or would you prefer to extend your vacation?) Why?

Reading Read the conversation.

Koto: I wish this weren't our last day in Venice.

Janet: I do, **too**. I'm excited to go to Spain tomorrow, **but** I'll miss Italy.

Asim: I haven't seen half the things I wanted to see here.

Alex: **Neither have** I.

Janet: Which was your favorite city in Italy?

Alex: I think, Rome. All the monuments were fascinating, **and so were** the churches and palaces.

Koto: Florence was *my* favorite city. Rome was **too** loud and busy for me, **but** Florence wasn't. The central square in Florence was **so** beautiful, **and so were** the museums.

Asim: Venice is my favorite city. I've never seen a city without a single car before! The narrow streets are magical, and the canals are, **too**.

Janet: I like the pace of everyday life best. Life here seems **so** relaxed and laid back.

Asim: **So is** life in Egypt. I think you'd really like it. Egyptians are never **too** busy to have a cup of tea with a friend.

Alex: **Neither are** Brazilians. We think that enjoyment of life now is more important than hurrying around, overworking, or making money.

Janet: Really? In the United States people always seem to be in a rush. The small towns aren't **so** bad, **but** the big cities are. New York can be a crazy place.

Koto: **So can** Tokyo. The pace of life there is very hectic, **too**.

Asim: I've always wanted to see Japan and the United States.

Alex: **So have** I.

Janet: We should plan to visit each other! We have a spare room in our house.

Koto: We do, **too**!

Asim: After this gondola ride, let's get another café latte in San Marco Square and talk about it.

Janet: We don't have time! We have to catch the 2:00 train. The 3:00 train doesn't have any seats left, **but** the 2:00 train does. And if we miss the 2:00 train, we'll get into Spain **too** late to find a hostel!

Asim: Janet?

Janet: What?

Asim: Relax. Remember? You're not in New York now!

 Discussion Questions Discuss these questions with a partner.

1. How do Koto, Janet, Asim, and Alex feel about leaving Italy? Why?

2. Which was Alex's favorite city? Why?

3. Which was Koto's favorite city? Why?

4. Which is Asim's favorite city? Why?

5. What does Janet like most about Italy? How does she compare it to the United States?

6. Do you prefer the lifestyle in Japan and America, or in Egypt and Brazil? Why?

Grammar Structures and Practice

A. Expressing Similarities with *So, Too, Either,* and *Neither*

Sometimes two sentences of similarity have different subjects but the same verb. Combine them as shown in the charts.

- Use the appropriate form of *be* or an auxiliary verb + *too*, *so*, *either*, or *neither*.
- You can add this shortened sentence to the first sentence as a clause after *and*, or you can use the second sentence as a response to the first.
- Use *so* and *too* for affirmative statements. Use *either* or *neither* for negative statements.

6.7 So and Too

	Explanations	Full Form	Additions	Responses
With *be*	*Too* follows the auxiliary verb or *be* in an added clause or a response sentence.	I'm Australian. Erik is Australian.	I'm Australian, **and Erik is, too.** I'm Australian, **and so is** Erik.	I'm Australian. Erik **is, too.** I'm Australian. **So is** Erik.
With Auxiliary Verbs	The auxiliary verb or *be* follows *so* in an added clause or a response sentence.	I love salsa music. Erik loves salsa music.	I love salsa music, **and Erik does, too.** I love salsa music, **and so does** Erik.	I love salsa music. Erik **does, too.** I love salsa music. **So does** Erik.

6.8 Either and Neither

	Explanations	Full Form	Additions	Responses
With *be*	*Either* follows the auxiliary verb or *be* in an added clause or a response sentence.	I'm not Australian. Erik isn't Australian.	I'm not Australian, **and Erik isn't either.** I'm not Australian, **and neither is** Erik.	I'm not Australian. Erik **isn't either.** I'm not Australian. **Neither is** Erik.
With Auxiliary Verbs	The auxiliary verb or *be* follows *neither* in an added clause or a response sentence.	I don't like salsa music. Erik doesn't like salsa music.	I don't like salsa music, **and Erik doesn't either.** I don't like salsa music, **and neither does** Erik.	I don't like salsa music. **Neither does** Erik. I don't like salsa music. Erik **doesn't either.**

Note: Do(n't), does(n't), and *did(n't)* are "pro-forms." They can replace a verb or verb phrase in an added clause or response with *so, too, either,* and *neither.* **Examples:** *Koto likes sushi, and so **does** Janet. I don't want to leave, and neither **do** my friends.*

---

1 Practice Underline the additions and responses with *so, too, either,* and *neither* in the conversation on pages 182 and 183.

Example Koto: I wish this weren't our last day in Venice.
Janet: I <u>do, too</u>.

2 Practice In each of these short conversations, change the sentence in parentheses to a short response; use *so*, *too*, *either*, or *neither*. For each sentence, two answers are possible. Write both possible answers on the lines.

Example: Koto: Tokyo is a very crowded city.

      Asim: (Cairo is a very crowded city.)

      _____ So is Cairo. _____ OR

      _____ Cairo is, too. _____

1. **Koto:** Most Japanese people live in cities.

    Alex: (Most Brazilian people live in cities.)

    _____ OR _____

2. **Alex:** Brazil doesn't have a royal family.

    Janet: (The United States doesn't have a royal family.)

    _____ OR _____

3. **Janet:** New York has a very diverse population.

    Alex: (São Paulo has a very diverse population.)

    _____ OR _____

4. **Alex:** Baseball isn't very popular in Brazil.

    Asim: (Baseball isn't very popular in Egypt.)

    _____ OR _____

5. **Alex:** Brazilians aren't usually shy.

    Janet: (Americans aren't usually shy.)

    _____ OR _____

6. **Janet:** Americans celebrate Labor Day.

    Alex: (Brazilians celebrate Labor Day.)

    _____ OR _____

7. **Koto:** Janet bought a map yesterday.

    Janet: (Alex bought a map yesterday.)

    _____ OR _____

8. **Asim:** I will call home today.

    Koto: (I will call home today.)

    _____ OR _____

B. Expressing Contrasts with *But*

Use *but* to join statements of contrast.

6.9	Expressing Contrasts with *But*		
Explanations		**Full Form**	**Additions**
But appears between the two contrasting ideas and follows a comma.	**With *be***	Spanish food is spicy. Irish food isn't spicy.	Spanish food is spicy, **but** Irish food **isn't.**
	With Auxiliary Verbs	Colombians speak Spanish. Brazilians don't speak Spanish.	Colombians speak Spanish, **but** Brazilians don't.

3 **Practice** Circle the additions with *but* in the conversation on pages 182 and 183.

Example I'm excited to go to Spain tomorrow, (but I'll miss Italy.)

4 **Practice** Finish each sentence with the correct auxiliary verb or form of *be*.

Example Asim has a map, but Koto _____ *doesn't* _____.

1. The United States is a multicultural nation, but Japan _____.

2. The United States isn't an ancient civilization, but Egypt

   _____.

3. Japanese people remove their shoes when they enter a house, but Egyptians

   _____.

4. The Brazilian flag isn't red, white, and blue, but the American flag

   _____.

5. European workers get at least three weeks of vacation time each year, but American and Japanese workers _____.

6. Alex went to the tourist office, but I _____.

7. I have read a few books by Italian authors, but Asim _____.

8. My food wasn't spicy, but his _____.

9. This hostel is very nice, but the last one _____.

10. Koto and Janet are traveling to Spain tomorrow, but Alex and Asim

    _____.

5 **Practice** Use the information in the pictures to complete the sentences. Add clauses of similarity or contrast with *so, too, neither, either,* and *but*.

Japan

America

1. Japanese people traditionally bow when they meet, *but Americans don't* .

America

Japan

2. Americans like baseball, _____.

Japan

America

3. Japanese people eat with chopsticks, _____.

4. Men and women don't usually show affection in public in Egypt,

_____.

Egypt

America

5. Egyptian women sometimes wear veils when they leave their house,

_____.

Brazil

America

6. Brazilians often greet their friends with a kiss on each cheek,

_____.

Brazil

America

7. Brazilians celebrate Carnaval, _____.

Japan

America

8. Japanese brides often change into three or four different dresses during their

wedding ceremony and celebration, _____.

6 Practice Use the information in this chart to complete the sentences. Add clauses of similarity or contrast with *so, too, either, neither,* or *but*.

	Koto	Janet
Age	20	20
Height	5' (5 feet)	5' 9" (5 feet, 9 inches)
Weight	110 lbs.	130 lbs.
Color hair	black	brown
Color eyes	brown	brown
Brothers/Sisters	none	none
Lives with	mother, father, grandparents	mother (parents are divorced)
Hobbies	shopping, surfing the Internet	shopping, surfing the Internet
Favorite food	pizza	gumbo
Favorite sport	soccer	soccer
Favorite holiday	New Year's	4th of July

1. Koto is 20, _____*and so is Janet*_____.
2. Koto is 5', _____.
3. Koto weighs 110 pounds, _____.
4. Koto has black hair, _____.
5. Koto has brown eyes, _____.
6. Koto doesn't have brothers or sisters, _____.
7. Koto lives with her mother, father, and grandparents, _____.
8. Koto likes shopping and surfing the Internet, _____.
9. Koto's favorite food is pizza, _____.
10. Koto's favorite sport is soccer, _____.
11. Koto's favorite holiday is New Year's, _____.

Using What You've Learned

7 Comparing Cultures You Know Choose one or two countries from this chapter (the United States, Japan, Brazil, Egypt) or one or two other countries or cultures. In a group, tell what you know about the food, arts, entertainment, and lifestyle of these cultures. Then with your group, compare each of these cultures to your own culture.

Discuss and list both the similarities and the differences. Use *so, too, either, neither,* and *but*. When you are finished, present your list to the class.

8 Learning More About Cultures What two countries or cultures would you like to learn more about? Use the Internet or reference books to find out about the lifestyle of the people of these cultures. Compare one or more of these aspects of the cultures:

- the importance of family
- the pace of life
- the attitudes toward work
- the attitudes toward vacations and leisure time
- the most popular sports, foods, and leisure activities
- the style of dress

When you are finished, give an oral report. Compare the two cultures with *so, too, either, neither,* and *but* when appropriate.

Self-Assessment Log

Each of the following sentences describes the grammar you learned in this chapter. Read the sentences and then check the best box for how well you understand each structure.

	Needs Improvement	Good	Great
I can use the present perfect tense to describe unspecified actions in the past.	❏	❏	❏
I can use adverbs like *ever / never* and *already* to describe present perfect tenses.	❏	❏	❏
I can use superlatives to describe three or more people or things.	❏	❏	❏
I can use *so, too, either,* and *neither* to express similarities.	❏	❏	❏
I can use *but* to express contrasts.	❏	❏	❏

Health

"A good laugh and a long sleep are the best cures in the doctor's book."

—Irish proverb

Connecting to the Topic

1 What do you do to stay healthy?

2 How often do you visit the doctor?

3 How often do you exercise?

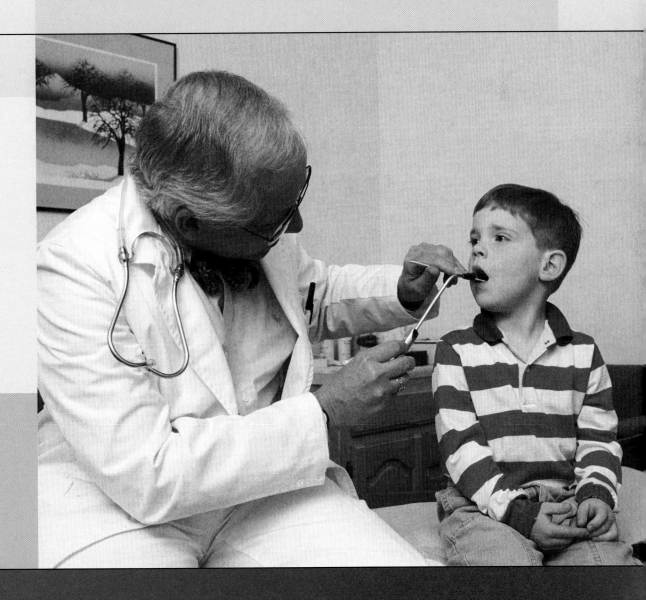

Part 1 — Verb + Object + Infinitive; Modal Verbs: *Should, Had better, Have to,* and *Must*

Setting the Context

Prereading Questions Discuss these questions with a small group.

Do you ever get advice for a health complaint? Do you follow the advice? Why or why not?

Reading Read the conversation.

Husband: How was your day, honey?

Wife: Well, I woke up with a bad headache this morning, so I thought I **should see** Dr. Krank. She **advised me to take** some pills. She also **told me to drink** a lot of water with the pills.

Husband: **Should** I **get** you some water for your pills?

Wife: No, thanks. I didn't **want to take** all those drugs, so I **decided to go** to a nutritionist.

Husband: A nutritionist?

Wife: Yes. He said I**'d better change** my eating habits, and he **persuaded me to buy** a lot of special foods and supplements at the health food store.

Husband:	Oh. That's good.
Wife:	Not really. I **tried to eat** some, but it tasted terrible. So then I went to a therapist.
Husband:	Oh? And what did the therapist **want you to do**?
Wife:	He gave me a lot of books to read. He **advised me to read** every one of them. He also said that I **must learn to relax**. So I went to a yoga class. The instructor **taught me to stand** on my head. She said I **have to learn how to breathe** correctly.
Husband:	Well, how are you feeling now?
Wife:	After all that advice, my headache is worse!

 Discussion Questions Discuss these questions with a partner.

1. Why did the wife go to a doctor, a nutritionist, a therapist, and a yoga class?

2. What did each expert advise her to do?

3. In your opinion, which of these experts should she listen to?

4. What do you do when you don't feel well?

Grammar Structures and Practice

A. Verb + Object + Infinitive

Infinitives commonly follow certain verbs, such as *want, have, try, decide,* and *learn.*

- Some examples are *want to get well, have to stop smoking,* and *learn to relax.*
- Another common sentence pattern is verb + object + infinitive.
- Only certain verbs can appear before an object + infinitive. Here's a partial list of these verbs:

7.1 Verb + Object + Infinitive

Verbs			Examples
advise	expect	remind	The doctor **wants her patient to have** a healthier lifestyle.
allow	force	teach	What did she **ask the patient to do?**
ask	instruct	tell	She **advised the patient to lose** weight.
convince	invite	train	She did**n't tell her to exercise.**
enable	order	want	She **ordered her not to smoke.**
encourage	persuade	warn	She **encouraged her not to eat** junk food.

Note: The word *not* can come before the main verb or before the infinitive, depending on the meaning of the sentence.

1 **Practice** Underline the verb + object + infinitive patterns in the conversation on pages 196 and 197. For each phrase, identify the parts: the main verb, the noun or pronoun object, and the infinitive.

main + object + infinitive

Example She <u>advised me to take</u> some pills.

2 **Practice** The parts of the following sentences are not in order. Unscramble them, and write them on the lines. The verb + object + infinitive pattern should appear in each sentence.

1. want / sweets and junk food / to buy them / Kids often / their parents

   Kids often want their parents to buy them sweets and junk food.

2. encourage / fruit and vegetables / their children / Most parents / to eat

   _____

3. foods with lots of sugar / kids / tell / not to eat / Teachers and dentists

   _____

4. themselves / have to force / low-fat or nonfat foods / Many adults / to eat

   _____

5. their patients / Many doctors / advise / foods high in sugar or fat / to avoid

   _____

6. to exercise / Fitness experts / us / at least three times a week / remind

   _____

7. Many people / to prescribe / diet pills / their doctors / ask

   _____

8. to fix / People / all of their problems / pills / often expect

   _____

9. tell / their patients / not to get addicted to pills / Many doctors

   _____

10. are helping to convince / The media / people / to make healthier lifestyle choices

   _____

3 Practice Use the cue words under each picture and write two sentences about it. Include the pattern verb + object + infinitive with the best verb tense.

1.

not allow / park for free
ask / pay $5 for parking

The parking attendant won't allow

the woman to park for free. He

asked her to pay $5 for parking.

2.

order / not park by the fire hydrant
convince / not give her a ticket

_____

_____

_____

3.

invite / take a seat and wait
remind / not smoke

_____

_____

_____

4.

encourage / lose some weight
advise / start exercising

_____

_____

_____

5.

ask / say "ahh"
tell / breathe deeply

_____

_____

_____

6.

instruct / take some medicine
advise / drink a lot of water with

_____

_____

_____

B. Modal Verbs: *Should, Had better, Have to*, and *Must*

Several modal verbs are used to give advice and express obligation.

7.2	Modal Verbs	
	Explanations	**Examples**
should	In affirmative and negative statements and questions, *should* is for advice. *Should* forms a contraction with *not: shouldn't.*	You **should** see a doctor. What **should** I do? You **shouldn't** eat so much.
had better	In affirmative and negative statements and questions, *had better* is for strong advice or warning. *Had* forms contractions with subject pronouns: *I'd better, you'd better, he'd better, she'd better, we'd better, they'd better.* Questions are usually in the negative form.	That woman **had better** get some help right away. **I'd better** call an ambulance. **Hadn't** we **better** leave?
have to	In affirmative and negative statements and questions, *have to* is for personal obligation. Use *have to* with *I, you, we,* and *they.* Use *has to* with *he, she,* and *it.* *Note:* The negative form (*does/doesn't have to*) has a different meaning. *Does/doesn't have to* = *it is not necessary.*	I **have to** pick my grandmother up at the hospital today. Did you **have to** wear a cast when you broke your leg?
must	In affirmative and negative statements and questions, *must* is for necessity and great urgency. *Must* is often for legal obligations. *Must* forms a contraction with *not: mustn't.*	You **must** bring your passport to the airport. **Must** I take a test to get a driver's license? You **mustn't** drink and drive.

4 Practice Circle the modal verb phrases in the conversation on pages 196 and 197. Identify the parts of each phrase: the modal and the base verb.

modal base

Example Well, I woke up with a bad headache this morning, so I thought I (should see) Dr. Krank.

5 Practice How should you care for a burn victim? Here are some instructions. Replace the underlined part of each sentence with *you should, you shouldn't, you must,* or *you mustn't.*

You must

1. ~~It is extremely important to~~ treat the burn as soon as possible to prevent infection.

2. It is a good idea to make the victim as comfortable as possible.

3. It is recommended that you pour water on the injury for ten minutes.

4. It is helpful to remove any clothing or jewelry from the area of the burn.

5. It is harmful to apply lotions, ointments, or fat to the burn.

6. Be careful not to remove anything sticking to the burn.

7. It is necessary to cover the burn with a sterile dressing or a clean piece of cloth.

8. Be sure not to panic.

9. It is helpful to reassure the victim.

10. Don't forget to record details of the victim's injuries.

11. Make sure you don't delay taking the victim to the hospital.

12. If no vehicle is available, you'll have to call an ambulance.

6 Practice Fill in the blanks with *should (not), must (not), have to,* or *had better (not).* In many cases, more than one answer may be possible, so try to choose the best modal(s) for each sentence.

A. I have a headache.

   1. You _____*should*_____ lie down.

   2. You _____ go out tonight.

   3. You _____ take more than two aspirins at once, or you'll get sick.

B. I want to visit my friend in the hospital.

   1. You _____ visit between the official visiting hours of 10:00 A.M. and 9:00 P.M.

   2. I think you _____ register at the reception desk before you go to your friend's room.

   3. You _____ bring you friend some flowers.

C. My child swallowed some of my medication.

   1. You _____ take her to the hospital immediately!

   2. She will probably _____ stay in the hospital overnight.

   3. You _____ put your medication away more safely, or it could happen again.

Using What You've Learned

7 Giving Expert Advice Work in groups of four. Each student takes the role of one of the experts in the picture on page 196 and gives advice for each of the three situations below. Use *should, have to, had better,* and *must.*

Example

Nutritionist: *The businessman should drink herbal tea to help him relax.*
Doctor: *I disagree. I advise him to get a complete physical exam.*

   1. A successful middle-aged businessman is under a lot of stress. He isn't sleeping well because he has insomnia.

   2. A teenage girl doesn't want to eat. She is very thin, but she thinks she is still too fat.

   3. A college student is tired all the time. He never exercises. He eats a lot of junk food and drinks a lot of coffee.

What advice did each person give for each situation? Each group tells the class. Use the pattern verb + object + infinitive.

Example *Keiko was the nutritionist. She told the businessman to drink herbal tea instead of coffee.*

8 **Discussing Solutions to Problems** Work in small groups. Each student describes a health problem (real or imaginary). The group discusses the problem and agrees on a solution. When you finish, one member from each group reports the problems and solutions to the class.

9 **Researching Emergency Procedures** Use the Internet or first-aid manuals to learn how to help someone in a medical emergency such as:

- choking
- heart attack
- severe bleeding
- drug overdose
- electric shock

Now the class can write a first-aid booklet. For each situation, one student or group explains the steps to help the victim. These steps should include the modals *should (not), had better (not), must / mustn't*, and *have / has to*. Illustrate your manual with drawings or with photos cut out of magazines or downloaded from the Internet.

Setting the Context

Prereading Questions Discuss these questions with a small group.

Have you ever worked out at a gym or health club? If so, what were your experiences like?

Reading Read the conversation.

Nadia:	You look tired. This isn't your first time at a gym, **is it**, Ahmed?
Ahmed:	Yes it is.
Nadia:	Really? Well, you should be proud of **yourself** for finally coming. It's great, **isn't it**?
Ahmed:	Actually, I'm not sure. Some of the people here are annoying. Look at those weight lifters! They're admiring **themselves** in the mirror. That man is practically kissing **himself**. And that woman over there keeps weighing **herself**. She doesn't really think she's going to lose weight after each exercise, **does she**? These people are all in love with **themselves, aren't they**?
Nadia:	Yeah, they are. At least some of them, anyway. But we can just keep to **ourselves**. (Ahmed stops cycling.)
Nadia:	You're not stopping already, **are you**?
Ahmed:	Yes, I am.
Nadia:	Aren't you enjoying **yourself**?
Ahmed:	Actually, no, I'm not. I'm afraid I'm going to hurt **myself** if I do too much on my first day.

Nadia: You aren't going home already, **are you**?

Ahmed: Yes, I am.

Nadia: But you want to lose weight and improve your health, **don't you**?

Ahmed: Yes, I do. But not as much as I want a cheeseburger. Yup, I'm going to make **myself** a nice, juicy double cheeseburger for lunch, and then I may treat **myself** to an ice cream sundae for dessert. You aren't interested in joining me, **are you**?

Nadia: Well, actually I am, but on the other hand, no thanks. My body won't get in shape by **itself**! Also, after I finish exercising, I'm going to town to buy **myself** some new exercise clothes.

Ahmed: See you later, Nadia.

Nadia: Take care of **yourself**, Ahmed.

 Discussion Questions Discuss these questions with a partner.

1. Why does Nadia tell Ahmed that he should be proud of himself?

2. Why does Ahmed think some of the people in the gym are annoying?

3. Why does Ahmed stop exercising?

4. What is Ahmed going to do?

5. Why doesn't Nadia join him?

6. Do you think physical fitness is important? Why or why not?

Grammar Structures and Practice

A. Reflexive Pronouns

If the subject and the (direct or indirect) object of a sentence are the same, the object should be a reflexive pronoun.

7.3 Reflexive Pronouns

	Explanations	Pronouns	Examples
Singular	Singular reflexive pronouns end in -self.	**myself**	I don't want to exhaust **myself.**
		yourself	Help **yourself** to as much fruit as you want.
		himself	Ahmed doesn't like to exercise by **himself**.
		herself	Nadia weighs **herself** every week.
		itself	The problem will take care of **itself.**
Plural	Plural reflexive pronouns end in -selves.	**ourselves**	Let's buy **ourselves** yogurt shakes.
		yourselves	Don't hurt **yourselves** with those weights.
		themselves	They bought **themselves** new gym clothes.

Notes: A reflexive pronoun is often the *indirect* object of the main verb, as in *Will you get yourself some lunch? Let's tell ourselves the truth. By* + a reflexive pronoun means "alone" or "without any help."

---

1 **Practice** Underline the reflexive pronouns (direct or indirect objects) in the conversation on pages 204 and 205. Which noun or personal pronoun subject does the reflexive refer to? Draw an arrow to it.

Example Well, you should be proud of yourself for finally coming.

2 **Practice** Fill in the blanks with reflexive pronouns: *myself, yourself, herself, himself, itself, ourselves, yourselves,* or *themselves.*

Myra Myers looked at _____*herself*_____ in the mirror and decided that she

wanted to buy _____ a new dress. "But I'll have to lose some
                        1

weight first," she said to _____. I'm going to get
                                    2

_____ a membership in the Grunt 'n Groan Health Club. "We all
          3

have to take care of _____." The next morning Myra found
                              4

_____ in a big room with weights and other exercise equipment.
5

A big sign said, "Do something special for _____ today." One
6

muscular man was measuring _____ with a tape measure. Two
7

other handsome men were looking at _____ in the mirror. "I think
8

I'm going to enjoy _____ here," thought Myra.
9

3 **Practice** Write a sentence describing each of these pictures. Use a reflexive pronoun and one of the verbs in this list.

buy	enjoy	introduce	promise
encourage	hurt	look at	weigh

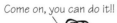

Come on, you can do it!!

1. _The woman is encouraging herself._

_____

One carrot juice, please.

2. _____

_____

3. _____

_____

Hi, I'm Mona.   Hi, I'm Kurt.

4. _____

_____

5. _____

_____

6. _____

_____

7. _____

_____

8. _____

_____

B. Tag Questions

A tag question is a statement with a short question attached at the end.

- People usually use tag questions to ask for clarification or to confirm information they think is true.
- The subject of a tag is always a pronoun.
- Tag questions use the same auxiliary verbs as yes/no questions.

7.4	Tag Questions		
	Explanations	**Examples**	**Expected Answers**
Affirmative Statement (Negative Tag)	Affirmative statements usually have negative tags. With affirmative statements and negative tags, the speaker expects an affirmative answer.	You're a member of this gym, **aren't you?**	Yes, I am.
		Chen is exercising, **isn't he?**	Yes, he is.
		I have a fever, **don't I?**	Yes, you do.
		She lifts weights, **doesn't she?**	Yes, she does.
		You saw a doctor, **didn't you?**	Yes, I did.
		You'll take the medicine, **won't you?**	Yes, I will.
Negative Statement (Affirmative Tag)	Negative statements have affirmative tags. With negative statements and affirmative tags, the speaker expects a negative answer.	You're not getting sick, **are you?**	No, I'm not.
		She isn't here now, **is she?**	No, she isn't.
		They don't like carrot juice, **do they?**	No, they don't.
		She doesn't smoke, **does she?**	No, she doesn't.
		You didn't bring an extra towel, **did you?**	No, I didn't.
		They can't lift weights, **can they?**	No, they can't.

4 **Practice** Circle each tag question in the conversation on pages 204 and 205. Which verb and subject of the main part of the sentence is the tag related to?

Example This isn't your first time at a gym, (is it) Ahmed?

5 **Practice** Answer each tag question with the expected answer.

Example This health club is great, isn't it? _____Yes it is._____

1. You don't have any aspirin, do you? _____

2. This yoga class is getting really crowded, isn't it? _____

3. Those runners are incredibly fast, aren't they? _____

4. Your father smokes two packs of cigarettes a day, doesn't he?

_____

5. We're not too late for the aerobics class, are we? _____

6. You were out sick for over a week, weren't you? _____

7. We met you at a softball game last summer, didn't we? _____

8. You really like all that healthy food, don't you? _____

9. Nadia will join us later, won't she? _____

10. Your roommate plays soccer, doesn't he? _____

6 **Practice** Write the missing pronouns in the blanks.

It's a beautiful day, isn't _____ *it* _____? We couldn't ask for a better

day, could _____? This is great exercise, isn't _____?
                        1   2

Look at that man! He's running fast, isn't _____? All the people
                                            3

here are in great shape, aren't _____? You don't talk much when
                                        4

you run, do _____?
                5

7 **Practice** Write the missing auxiliary verbs in the blanks. Remember to make the tag affirmative or negative, as appropriate.

You ran in this race last year, _____ *didn't* _____ you? The weather was

great then, too, _____ it? You finished that race,
                        1

_____ you? But you didn't win, _____ you?
        2   3

We're going to do well this year, _____ we? You're not getting
                                            4

tired, _____ you? I'm not boring you, _____ I?
            5   6

8 **Practice** Write the missing tag questions in the blanks.

You were in better shape last year, _____ *weren't you* _____? You also tried

harder last year, _____? But you'll finish this year, too,
                        1

_____? We should run faster, _____? We only
    2   3

have a few more kilometers to run, _____?
You can run faster,
4

_____? You're not talking much, _____? You're
5   6

out of breath, _____? I'm not annoying you,
7

_____? This race is fun, _____?
8   9

Using What You've Learned

 9 **Asking and Answering Tag Questions About Health** Write five negative
tag questions you expect your partner to answer affirmatively and five affirmative tag
questions you expect your partner to answer negatively. If possible, these questions
should be about health-related activities and habits.

Example **Negative tag questions:**

You get enough sleep, don't you?
You're a vegetarian, aren't you?

Affirmative tag questions:

You don't smoke, do you?
You can't run five miles, can you?

After you have prepared your questions, interview your partner. Take notes on your
partner's answers. How many questions did your partner answer the way you
expected? How many didn't your partner answer like you expected? What did you learn
about your partner? Tell the class.

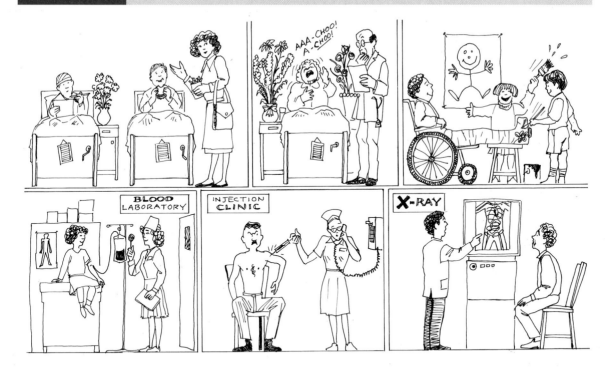

Setting the Context

Prereading Questions Discuss these questions with a small group.

Do you ever write letters to relatives? If so, where do you write the letters from?

Reading Read the letter.

Dear Grandmother,

Thanks for the book **you sent me**. The boy **who shares my room** read the same book last year. He said it's one of his favorite books. The card **you sent with the book** was really nice, too.

This hospital isn't so bad. All the people **that work** here are friendly. I especially like the nurse **who brings our lunch trays** every day. But the food **she brings us** is terrible!

I'm feeling pretty good. My head feels better, and the ribs **which I broke** are healing well. The doctor **who examined me** said I can go home soon. (The stethoscope **that he used** was cold!)

I'm really looking forward to having the special roast chicken **that you**

5

10

cook whenever I come over. Can you make those mashed potatoes *that I love*, too?

Love,
Timmy

15

 Discussion Questions Discuss these questions with a partner.

1. What does Timmy thank his grandmother for?
2. What does Timmy think of the people who work in the hospital?
3. What does he think of the food at the hospital?
4. Who told Timmy that he can go home soon?
5. What is Timmy looking forward to?
6. Have you ever been in the hospital? If so, tell about the experience.

Grammar Structures and Practice

A. *Who*, *That*, and *Which* as Subjects of Relative Clauses

Relative clauses describe, identify, or give more information about the nouns they follow.
- They have a subject and a verb.
- *Who*, *that*, or *which* can be the subject of a relative clause.
   - *Who* is for people.
   - *Which* is for things.
   - *That* is for people or things.
- You can use a relative clause to combine two simple sentences into one complex sentence.

Example I like the nurse. + **She** brings the food. = I like the nurse **who** brings the food.

7.5 Subject Pronouns	
Explanations	**Examples**
who/that = the nurse *which/that* = the bed	I like the nurse **who (that) brings the food.** The bed **that (which) I sleep in** is comfortable.

Note: In formal, written English, some people prefer *that* as the subject of essential relative clauses that are necessary for the meaning of the sentence. Use *who* or *which* (after a comma) as the subject of nonessential clauses, which give additional information not necessary for the sentence meaning. **Examples:** *The doctor **that** is handling my case wrote the reports **that** describe his procedures. Our family doctor, **who** isn't handling this case, wrote the necessary reports, **which** describe the surgeon's procedures.*

1 **Practice** Underline the relative clauses with *who, that,* or *which* as subjects in the letter on pages 213 and 214. Is each of these clauses essential or nonessential? Remember that this is an informal letter.

Example The boy <u>who shares my room</u> read the same book last year.

This is an essential relative clause, and it uses the word "who" without commas.

2 **Practice** Combine each of the following pairs of sentences with a relative clause that has *who, that,* or *which* as its subject. Think about the meaning to choose the best combination.

Example The nurse takes blood. She is nice.

The nurse who takes blood is nice.
NOT
The nurse who is nice takes blood.

1. The man has a lot of visitors. He is sharing my room.

   _____

2. The flowers are beautiful. They are on the table next to my bed.

   _____

3. The doctor examined me. He told me I was getting better.

   _____

4. The patient is allergic to flowers. She has a bunch of flowers in her room.

   _____

5. The book is very boring. It's on the desk.

   _____

6. The boy is in serious condition. He hurt his head.

   _____

7. The man broke his legs. He is sitting in a wheelchair.

   _____

8. The children are painting the man's casts. They are having fun.

   _____

9. The television is broken. It's in my room.

   _____

10. The janitor cleans the rooms. He is going to college part time.

    _____

B. Reduction of Relative Clauses to Relative Phrases

A relative phrase can also modify a noun. However, unlike a relative clause, it does not contain a subject and a verb.

- To reduce (shorten) some relative clauses to relative phrases, leave out the subject pronoun *who, that,* or *which,* along with other unnecessary words.

7.6 Reduction of Relative Clauses to Relative Phrases

	Explanations	Examples	
		Relative Clause	**Relative Phrase**
With a *be* form	To make a relative phrase from a relative clause with a *be* form of a verb, leave out the subject pronoun (*who, that,* or *which*) and the *be* form of the verb.	The man **who is sharing** my room hates the food. The flowers **that are on the table** are beautiful.	The man **sharing my room** hates the food. The flowers **on the table** are beautiful.
Without a *be* form	If there is no *be* form of a verb in the relative clause, sometimes you can leave out the subject pronoun and change the verb to its *-ing* form.	All the people **who work here** are friendly.	All the people **working here** are friendly.

---

3 **Practice** Combine each of the following pairs of sentences. Use relative phrases.

Example The children are staying in this hospital. They are funny.
The children staying in this hospital are funny.

1. The man is in room 202. He is having an operation tomorrow.

2. The nurse takes blood from patients. She wears gloves.

3. The magazines are on the table. They belong to the hospital.

4. The doctor is responsible for all the patients on this floor. He likes to tell jokes.

5. The mountains surround the hospital. They're beautiful.

6. The nurse is giving the man a shot. She is talking on the phone at the same time.

7. The man is waiting for the nurse to get off the phone. He is angry.

8. The receptionist is on duty. She speaks Japanese and English.

9. The doctor takes care of me. He is from Cambodia.

10. The man is in the bed next to mine. He is snoring.

4 Practice Study the pictures at the beginning of Part 3 on page 213. Then complete these sentences about the pictures with relative clauses or phrases. There are many possible answers.

1. The boy _____*who is writing a letter*_____ has a bandage on his head.

2. The boy _____ is eating a hamburger.

3. The doctor _____ is looking at the chart.

4. The patient _____ has casts on his legs.

5. The woman _____ has flowers in her room.

6. The nurse _____ is taking blood from a child.

7. The man _____ is getting an injection from the nurse.

8. The doctor _____ is explaining the results to a patient.

C. *Who(m)*, *That*, and *Which* as Objects of Relative Clauses

Who(m), *that*, or *which* may also be the object of a relative clause. You can use these relative clause object pronouns to combine two simple sentences into a complex sentence.

Examples The nurse is Ms. Alvarez. + He likes **her**. = The nurse **whom** he likes is Ms. Alvarez.

The food was terrible. + We ate **it** in the hospital. = The food **that** we ate in the hospital was terrible.

7.7	Object Pronouns	
	Explanations	**Examples**
who(m)	*Who* is used more often than *whom*, especially in speaking. *Whom* is used only in very formal English.	The people **who/whom we met** in the hospital were nice.
that	*That* is used for both people and things. In the example, *that* refers to *the cough*. *I* is the subject of the relative clause.	The cough **that I had** was annoying.
which	*Which* is used for things.	The injection **which the doctor gave me** was painful.
Ø	The object pronouns *who(m)*, *that*, and *which* are often left out of relative clauses.	The injection **the doctor gave me** was painful.

5 **Practice** Combine each of the following pairs of sentences. Use relative clauses with *who(m), that,* or *which* as objects.

Example The doctors were running to the emergency room. I saw them.
The doctors who(m) I saw were running to the emergency room.

1. The noises at night were scary. I heard them.
2. The work was very hard and tiring. The nurses did the work.
3. The ambulance was shiny and white. The paramedics drove the ambulance.
4. The patients were in a lot of pain. The nurses checked on them frequently.
5. The food is terrible. The patients in the hospital have to eat the food.
6. The flowers were very expensive. The patient's friends sent the flowers.
7. The movie on TV was boring. I watched it.
8. The pills made me tired. I had to take them.

Using What You've Learned

6 **Describing People with Relative Clauses** Write one sentence each about ten people in your class. Use relative clauses or phrases to describe, identify, or give information about each person. When you finish, share your ideas with the class. Can your listeners identify the subject of each sentence?

Examples *The woman who (that) is sitting in front of me is also in my economics class.*
The man on her right is always joking with the teacher.
The woman, who(m) I just met today, is a new student.

7 **Identifying People from Their Descriptions** In small groups, select a picture with only one person from a magazine or a newspaper. Together, think of as many relative clauses and phrases as possible to describe the person in the photo. Write these in sentence form. Then give your photo to your teacher, who will tape the photos up at the front of the classroom, visible to everyone. In turn, each group reads their sentences aloud to the rest of the class. Listeners should try to identify the corresponding photo.

Examples First member of Group A: *The woman that is wearing a polka dot dress is beautiful.*
Second member of Group A: *The woman who has long hair looks angry.*

Third member of Group A: *The woman sitting in the chair is speaking on the phone.*

Member of Group B: (Pointing to a picture at the front of the room) *That's your picture!*

Focus on Testing

Verb + Object + Infinitive; Modal Verbs: *Should, Had better, Have to,* and *Must;* **Reflexive Pronouns; Tag Questions; Relative Clauses**

Testing is a major feature of academic life. Two basic types of tests exist: subjective and objective. Subjective questions can have a variety of answers, but objective questions have only one correct answer. In this book, you will have short practice exams to help prepare you for tests about grammar. Use these practice exam questions to help you learn which structures or ideas you don't understand well and need to study more.

Remember that . . .

✔ A common sentence pattern is verb + object + infinitive.

✔ Certain verbs can appear before objects and infinitives.

✔ Affirmative statements usually have negative tags; negative statements have affirmative tags.

Part 1. Fill in the bubble for the correct completion for the following sentences.

Example   Nora seems _____ happy with her new job in the hospital.

Ⓐ be   Ⓑ being   Ⓒ to be   Ⓓ been

1. My mother treats _____ to only the finest things in life.

Ⓐ myself   Ⓑ herself   Ⓒ ourselves   Ⓓ themselves

2. The beach community wasn't very well prepared for the tornado, _____?

Ⓐ was they   Ⓑ wasn't they   Ⓒ was it   Ⓓ wasn't it

3. The doctor wants her patient _____ a healthier lifestyle.

Ⓐ to have   Ⓑ have   Ⓒ has   Ⓓ had

4. Let's buy _____ a fruit juice.

Ⓐ themselves   Ⓑ yourself   Ⓒ ourselves   Ⓓ ourself

Part 2. Circle the letter below the underlined word(s) containing the error.

Example   I <u>should</u> <u>knowing</u> <u>better than</u> <u>to approach</u> a strange dog.
                 A   (B)   C   D

1. The men <u>whose</u> <u>I saw running</u> from the convenience store <u>were</u> all <u>wearing</u> ski
              A   B   C   D
masks.

2. I <u>was surprised</u> <u>to hear</u> that his friends <u>persuaded</u> him to <u>buying</u> a dog.
         A   B   C   D

3. You <u>had better not to wait</u> <u>to</u> <u>make</u> an appointment <u>with your doctor.</u>
              A   B   C   D

4. This isn't <u>your</u> <u>first time</u> <u>playing</u> soccer, <u>isn't it?</u>
                 A   B   C   D

Self-Assessment Log

Each of the following sentences describes the grammar you learned in this chapter. Read the sentences and then check the best box for how well you understand each structure.

	Needs Improvement	Good	Great
I can use verb + object + infinitive and modals to give medical advice.	❑	❑	❑
I can use reflexive pronouns to talk about personal health.	❑	❑	❑
I can use tag questions to talk about health and exercise.	❑	❑	❑
I can use relative clauses to talk about doctors and hospitals.	❑	❑	❑
I practiced taking a test about verbs, modal verbs, reflexive pronouns, tag questions, and relative clauses.	❑	❑	❑

Chapter

8

Entertainment and the Media

> **❝**Nothing is so intolerable to man as being fully at rest, without a passion, without business, without entertainment, without care.**❞**
>
> —Blaise Pascal
> French mathematician, physicist, and philosopher (1623–1662)

Connecting to the Topic

1 How often do you watch movies or television?

2 What types of movies do you enjoy?

3 What are your favorite television shows?

Setting the Context

Prereading Questions Discuss these questions with a small group.

Have you ever experienced a robbery or other crime? If so, can you describe what happened?

Reading Read the passage.

"Good evening and welcome to the Channel 12 six o'clock news. In our top story tonight, there **was** an attempted robbery at the Bartle Bank in Bakerstown at 3:55 this afternoon. The bank **was closing** for the day when the three robbers **burst** in. According to eyewitnesses, all three **were wearing** masks, and two **were carrying** guns. When they **demanded** money, a quick-thinking bank teller **pushed** a silent alarm that signals the local police. The police **arrived** just as the robbers **were making** their getaway. The suspects **were racing** down Barker Street when the police **caught** up with them and **arrested** them.

"In other news, a fire **burned** down a private home in Clayton Corner last night. The fire **started** when a woman **fell** asleep in bed while **smoking** a cigarette and **watching** TV. Firefighters **believe** the lit cigarette **fell** from the woman's hand while she **was sleeping**. By the time the woman and her roommates **escaped** from the house, the fire **was burning** out of control. Firefighters **arrived** at

5

10

15

the scene within minutes. Two firefighters **were injured** while **battling** the flames. They are in good condition at Adderbrook Hospital.

"On the lighter side, a local man is the winner of this week's Lucky Pick lottery. Alberto Fiorentino **bought** the winning ticket at the Valu-Mart market in Glendale yesterday afternoon while he **was doing** his weekly shopping. Mr. Fiorentino **was working** at his job in the Bakerstown post office when he **heard** the news. His wife **wasn't watching** the news, and she **didn't know.** He immediately **quit** his job and **went** home to celebrate with his family. When our reporters **contacted** Mr. Fiorentino this afternoon, he **was planning** a trip around the world with his family. Join us for more news after this commercial break."

 Discussion Questions Discuss these questions with a partner.

1. What happened at the Bartle Bank at 3:55?
2. When did the police arrive?
3. What happened in Clayton Corner?
4. What was Mr. Fiorentino doing at the Valu-Mart market?
5. What are other "typical" news stories?
6. Do you watch the news? Why or why not?

Grammar Structures and Practice

A. The Past Continuous Tense

The past continuous tense describes activities happening or in progress at a specific time or during a period of time in the past.

8.1 Statements		
	Explanations	**Examples**
Affirmative	Past continuous statements consist of a past form of *be* before the *-ing* form of a verb.	I **was watching** the news at 6:00. The anchorman **was telling** about a robbery.
Negative	Negative statements include *not* after the *be* verb.	He **wasn't telling** about a murder. The bank tellers **weren't screaming.**

8.2 Yes/No Questions with the Past Continuous Tense

Explanation		Examples	Possible Answers	
			Affirmative	**Negative**
The form of yes/no questions and short answers in the past continuous parallels their form in the present continuous—except that *was* or *were* replaces *am*, *is*, or *are*.	**Affirmative**	**Was** the manager **working?**	Yes, he was.	No, he wasn't.
		Were the police **investigating** the robbery?	Yes, they were.	No, they weren't.
	Negative	**Wasn't** the policeman **running** after the suspect?	Yes, he was.	No, he wasn't.
		Weren't the customers **screaming?**	Yes, they were.	No, they weren't.

8.3 Information Questions with the Past Continuous Tense

Explanations		Examples	Possible Answers
The form of information questions and full-sentence answers in the past continuous parallels their form in the present continuous—except that *was* or *were* replaces *am*, *is*, or *are*.	**Affirmative**	What **were** the suspects **wearing?**	They were wearing masks.
		Who **was carrying** weapons?	Two of them were carrying weapons.
	Negative	Why **weren't** the tellers **screaming?**	They weren't scared.
		Who **wasn't paying** attention?	The guard wasn't paying attention.

1 **Practice** Underline the past continuous verb phrases in the reading on pages 224 and 225. Identify each of the sentences as affirmative or negative, singular or plural.

Example According to eyewitnesses, all three <u>were wearing</u> masks, and two <u>were carrying</u> guns. *(affirmative plural)*

2 **Practice** Fill in the blanks in the interviews with the verbs in parentheses. Use past continuous verb phrases.

Interview 1

Reporter: What (do)_____*were*_____ you _____*doing*_____ when the robbery happened?

Manager: I (speak) _____*was speaking*_____ to customers about opening an account.

Guard: I (sit) _____ by the safe.
1

Teller #1: I (cash) _____ a check for a customer.
2

Customers: We (fill out) _____ forms to open an account.
3

Interview 2

Reporter: What (do) _____ you _____
1   2

when the fire began?

Person #1: I (sleep) _____!
3

Person #2: I (read) _____ a book in bed.
4

Person #3: I (get) _____ ready to go to
5

bed.

Couple: We (eat) _____ a late-night
6

snack.

Interview 3

Reporter: What (do) _____ you _____
    1   2
when you found out that you won the lottery?

Father and We (watch) _____ TV.
Grandfather: 3

Mother: I (work) _____ on the computer. (*Pointing to*
    4
her children) They (do) _____ their
    5
homework.

Grandmother: I (knit) _____ a sweater.
    6

 3 Practice Study the pictures in Activity 2. Then one partner closes his or her book and the other asks questions about one of the pictures in the past continuous tense. The first partner tries to answer from memory. Change roles for each picture.

Example A: *Was the guard wearing a hat?*
B: *Yes, he was wearing a hat.*
A: *Was anyone screaming?*
B: *I think the teller was screaming.*

B. The Simple Past Tense Versus the Past Continuous Tense

In contrast to the present tenses (simple vs. continuous), past tenses are for actions and events that don't exist anymore.

8.4 The Simple Past Versus the Past Continuous

Tense	Explanations	Examples
Simple Past	Use the simple past tense to talk about events and activities that began and ended in the past.	I **read** the newspaper. She **didn't use** the computer last night. **Did** you **see** the movie?
Past Continuous	Use the past continuous tense to describe activities that were happening or in progress at a specific time or during a period of time in the past.	I **was reading** the newspaper when I fell asleep. She **wasn't using** the computer at 8:00 last night. **Were** you **watching** the movie when I called?

Note: Some verbs are not normally used in the continuous tense. These verbs, called nonaction verbs, include verbs that express feeling and thought, verbs that express possession, and verbs that express sensory perception. For more information on nonaction verbs, see Charts 2.8–2.10 (*Nonaction Verbs*) on pages 52–53 in Chapter 2.

---

4 Practice Choose between the simple past and the past continuous form of the verb in each set of parentheses. Circle the better form.

Ana: What (did you do / were you doing) yesterday?

Brian: Let's see. I (woke up / was waking up) at around 10:00 yesterday. It

1
(rained / was raining), so I (stayed / was staying) home and

2   3
(read / was reading) the newspaper.

4

Ana: I called you at around 11:00. (Did you read / Were you reading) the

5
newspaper then?

Brian: Yes, I (did / was).

6

Ana: We only spoke for a few minutes. What (did you do / were you doing)

7
after we hung up?

Brian: I (watched / was watching) TV for a while.

8

Ana: (Didn't you go / Weren't you going) outside at all yesterday?

9

Brian: Sure I did. I wasn't home between 5:00 and 6:00.

Ana: Why not? What (did you do / were you doing) during that hour?

10

Brian: I (returned / was returning) the video I (watched / was watching) last

11   12
night.

Ana: So, what (did you do / were you doing) last night?

13

Brian: I (played / was playing) video games. I called to ask you to come over,

14

but you weren't home. What (did you do / were you doing)?

15

(Did you go / were you going) out?

16

Ana: What time (did you call / were you calling)?

17

Brian: About 8:00.

Ana: At 8:00 I (walked / was walking) my dog in the park. I

18

(didn't want / wasn't wanting) to stay home on such a beautiful night.

19

C. *When* and *While* with the Simple Past and Past Continuous Tenses

When and *while* introduce time clauses.

- They can show the relationship between two events or activities that happened (simple past) or were happening (past continuous) at the same time in the past.
- *When* can also show the relationship between events that happened in a sequence (time order).

8.5 *When* and *While*

Structures	Explanations	Examples
when	Clauses with *when* are most often in the simple past tense. The action in the *when* clause happened first.	**When** the movie **ended**, we **went** home.
while	Clauses with *while* are most often in the past continuous tense. If both verbs are in the past continuous, this means the two actions were going on at the same time. In these sentences, the *while* clause can come before or after the main clause.	Alberta **was watching** TV **while** her husband **was using** the computer. **While** Alberta **was watching** TV, her husband **was using** the computer.
when or while	The simple past and the past continuous can appear in the same sentence. In these cases, *while* begins clauses with the past continuous. *When* begins clauses with the simple past. One event began before the other one and was in progress when the second interrupted it. The time clause can appear at the beginning or at the end of the sentence.	My mother **was listening** to the radio **when** she got the call. = **When** my mother got the call, she **was listening** to the radio. My mother **got** the call **while** she **was listening** to the radio. = **While** (she was) **listening** to the radio, my mother **got** the call.

Note: If both clauses have the same subject, a *while* clause in the past continuous may be "reduced." Its subject and *was* or *were* may be omitted, as in *While (I was) working on the computer, I was also watching TV. A woman fell asleep while (she was) smoking a cigarette.*

5 **Practice** Circle the clauses beginning with *when* and *while* in the reading on pages 224 and 225. Tell the tenses of the verbs after *when* and *while*.

Example The bank was closing for the day (when the three robbers burst in.)
(verb tense = simple past)

6 **Practice** Fill in the blanks with either *when* or *while*.

1. I was reading a magazine _____*when*_____ my friends arrived.

2. _____ it was time for the movie to start, we turned on the TV.

3. My roommate was listening to some CDs on headphones

   _____ my relatives and I were watching a movie.

4. _____ a commercial came on, we ordered a pizza.

5. The pizza came _____ we were watching an exciting action scene.

6. The telephone rang _____ we were watching the last scene of the movie.

7. I tried to listen to the movie _____ I was speaking with my mother.

8. _____ I got off the phone, the movie was over. Next time, we should rent a video so we can stop it in the middle.

7 Practice Circle the correct choice in each set of parentheses in this newspaper article. In a few cases, both choices may be possible. When this is the case, circle both choices.

The Hungry Burglar

We watched a different kind of detective drama on TV last night—or was it really a comedy? Anyway, here's the plot:

The would-be victim (slept /(was sleeping)) (while / when) she (heard / was hearing)
                                                                  1   2
a noise. The strange sound (woke / was waking) her up. She quietly (went / was going)
                                                3   4
downstairs and was shocked at what she saw: a burglar (robbed / was robbing)
                                                                              5
her house. But what she saw next was even more surprising: the burglar
(opened / was opening) her refrigerator and (started / was starting) to make himself
              6   7
a snack. She called the police (while / when) he (ate / was eating) a big chocolate
                                              8   9
cake. (While / When) he (heard / was hearing) her on the phone, he
                    10   11
(ran / was running) out the back door without taking anything. The woman
        12
(put / was putting) her possessions away (while / when) the police arrived.
        13   14
They (asked / were asking) her some questions then (went / were going) to look for
          15   16
the suspect. Fifteen minutes later, the woman (fixed / was fixing) the lock on her
                                                                17
door (while / when) the police (called / were calling). What (did / were) they
          18   19   20
they (tell / telling) her? They told her they (had / were having) the burglar. When she
        21   22
(asked / was asking), "How (did / were) you (catch / catching) the burglar so fast?"
        23   24   25
she (got / was getting) a surprise.
        26

232   Chapter 8 ■■■

The police officer told her, "It was easy ma'am. The suspect (ate / was eating)
                                                                                    27
while he (ran / was running) down the street. (While / When) we
             28   29
(stopped / were stopping) him, he (had / was having) big chocolate stains all over
     30   31
his shirt. We (knew / were knowing) then that we (had / were having) our man."
                    32   33

Using What You've Learned

8 **Watching and Remembering the Details of Actions** Play a video of a
news segment or a commercial. Watch the video carefully and take notes on what you
see and hear. Then form small groups. Prepare five to ten past continuous questions
about the video. How much do the members of other groups remember about the
situations and events in the video? Use your questions to find out.

Examples *1. What color tie was the man wearing?*
2. Was he looking straight at the camera?
3. What was he doing with his hands?

9 **Creating Alibis** An alibi is a suspect's explanation about his or her whereabouts
(location) at the time of a crime. In this activity, half the class takes the role of
detectives who are trying to solve a crime, and the other half takes the role of suspects
who must provide alibis.

As a class, decide the details of the crime (such as the type of crime and the time and
place of the crime). Then the suspects pair up with partners to create a detailed alibi.
The purpose of their story is to prove that they did not commit the crime. The suspects
should use the past tense and the past continuous tense in their alibis. Next, the
detectives interview one suspect while the suspect's partner waits outside. The
detectives should ask questions in the past tense and the past continuous tense with
when or while.

Example Detective #1: *What were you doing last night at 7:00 when the*
robbery occurred?
Suspect #1: *I was at the Cineplex movie theater watching a movie.*
Detective #2: *What movie were you watching?*
Suspect #1: *I was watching "Gun Blast 2."*
Detective #3: *Who were you with?*
Suspect #1: *I was with John Simpson.*
Detective #1: *Did anyone see you and John while you were there?*

The detectives take notes on the first suspect's answers. When the second suspect
comes in for questioning, the detectives should notice how well that person's answers
match the first suspect's alibi.

After the detectives interview all the pairs, they decide which suspects had the weakest alibi. They "arrest" that pair for the crime.

Part 2 | Infinitives

Setting the Context

Prereading Questions Discuss these questions with a small group.

Do you watch commercials on TV or listen to commercials on the radio? What products or services are most commercials about?

Reading Read the passage.

"Are you **ashamed to show** your skinny body at the beach? Do the cool guys **seem to laugh** at you? Do the hot babes **seem to ignore** you? Well, **prepare** for all that **to change**. How would you **like to impress** all the gang at the beach this summer with your incredible muscles? You would? Well then—you **need to try** *Insta-Muscle*! 5

"*Insta-Muscle* is **simple to use**. Just rub in a generous amount wherever you **want** muscles **to grow**. *Insta-Muscle* **begins to work** as soon as you put it on. It isn't **unusual to see** results in just one or two weeks. **Continue to use** *Insta-Muscle* each day **to build** even bigger muscles. **Remember to buy** an extra jar or two **to make** sure you never run out. In a 10 few weeks, you won't be **afraid to show** your body anymore. You'll be **able to take** off your shirt with confidence. And when you do, the men are **sure to respect** you and the women are **certain to notice** you. (One warning: **Try not to break** too many hearts!) So **plan to be** the most popular guy at the beach this summer. With *Insta-Muscle*, you're **guaranteed** 15 **to make** a splash.

"It's **easy to order** *Insta-Muscle*. Just dial the toll free number on your screen and say, "I **want to be** an *Insta-Muscle* man."

Discussion Questions Discuss these questions with a partner.

1. What kind of TV viewer is this commercial directed at?
2. What are the directions for using *Insta-Muscle*?
3. Why does Mr. Muscle tell the viewer to buy an extra jar or two?
4. What does Mr. Muscle say will soon happen?
5. How do you feel about commercials like this? Why?

Grammar Structures and Practice

A. Infinitives After Verbs

An infinitive is *to* + the simple form of a verb.
- Infinitives can follow certain verbs.
- All the verbs in this chart can come before infinitives. The verbs with a star (*) can also take infinitives after objects.

8.6 Infinitives After Verbs		
Explanations	**Verbs**	**Examples**
The main verb before the infinitive can be in any tense. Depending on the meaning, in some negative sentences, *not* comes before the first verb. In other sentences, *not* comes between the first verb and the infinitive. Even if it is an object pronoun, the object of the main verb is also the "subject" (the doer of the action) of the infinitive.	ask* need* begin offer continue plan decide prefer expect* prepare* fail pretend forget remember hope seem know how start learn teach* like* try manage want* mean would like*	**Do** you **want me to lower** the volume? Be quiet. **I'm trying to listen** to the news. I **began to read** a new mystery novel last night. I **don't know how to work** this remote control. **Would** you **like to play** a DVD? **Do** you **expect me to set** it up? How **did** you **manage to do** that so fast? We**'re not planning to rent** any violent films. **Try not to watch** too much TV.

Note: Some verbs *must* be followed by an object before the infinitive. These include: *advise, allow, challenge, encourage, order, persuade, require, urge,* and *warn.*

1 Practice Underline the verb + infinitive phrases in the reading on page 234.

Example Do the guys <u>seem to laugh</u> at you?

2 **Practice** Match each of the sentence beginnings to the endings listed in the box to form complete sentences. Write the letters on the lines. Work in sequence from number 1 to number 10 to see a story develop. The matches should be grammatically correct and logical.

_____d_____ **1.** Tom asked

_____ **2.** When I got home, I began

_____ **3.** After I tried on lots of outfits, I finally decided

_____ **4.** My father started

_____ **5.** He asked me what we planned

_____ **6.** My father told me that he expected

_____ **7.** Tom was surprised because he wasn't planning

_____ **8.** My father didn't really try

_____ **9.** Even so, I had fun on the date and I plan

_____ **10.** But next time I'll offer

> a. to ask me a lot of questions about Tom.
> b. me to introduce him to Tom before the date.
> c. to do on the date.
> d. me to go to a movie with him.
> e. to wear my new jeans and a black top.
> f. to meet my father so soon.
> g. to go out with Tom again.
> h. to plan what I wanted to wear on the date.
> i. to meet him at the theater!
> j. to be polite to Tom when they met.

3 **Practice** Complete the sentences with the appropriate forms of the verbs in parentheses. Add *to* and an object, if necessary.

Host: And now it's time to play your favorite game show, *All or Nothing!*

Let's welcome our current champion, Ashraf Zakaria! Ashraf

_____started to play_____ our game just two days ago, and he has
<u>(start, play)</u>

already won $30,000 in prizes! Ashraf tells me that his wife, Gloria,

_____ on our show. So he
1 (persuade, come)

_____ some great prizes for her! And next,
2 (intend, win)

please welcome today's challenger, Nancy Lopez! Nancy is a

schoolteacher who _____ married next month.
3 (plan, get)

Her fiancé _____ *All or Nothing* to win some
4 (encourage, play)

money for their honeymoon. Now, you folks in the audience,

please _____ out the answers. All right, then,
5 (remember, not shout)

Nancy and Ashraf, do you both _____ our game?
6 (know how, play)

Contestants: Yes, Bob!

Host: Great! Let me _____ carefully before you
7 (urge, think)

_____ any questions. Our game
8 (try, answer)

_____ fast. As always, I _____
9 (require, think)   10 (advise, trust)

your intuition. Your first answer is usually right on the money on

All or Nothing!

4 **Practice** Complete the following sentences with your own ideas. When you are finished, share your ideas with the class.

Example The Internet allows people to *find information quickly.*

1. The Internet allows people to _____.
2. Television teaches children to _____.
3. Movies seem to _____.
4. Commercials often try to _____.
5. I have begun to _____.
6. I want to _____.
7. My teacher expects me to _____.
8. I know how to _____.
9. When I was a child, I liked to _____.
10. Now, I prefer to _____.
11. I usually forget to _____.
12. I am going to continue to _____.

B. Infinitives After Adjectives

Some infinitives can follow directly after adjectives.

8.7 Infinitives After Adjectives

Structures	Explanations	Adjectives		Examples
With Subject Nouns and Pronouns	These adjectives are often followed by infinitives in this pattern: Subject + *be* + adjective + infinitive. Adjectives used in this pattern usually describe a person's feelings or attitudes.	afraid ashamed fortunate glad happy lucky	prepared proud ready relieved sad willing	My daughter is **happy to watch** almost anything on TV. My son was **proud to get** an award for his first student film. I was**n't prepared to see** such a violent movie. Are you **afraid to try** to program a DVD player?
With *It*	These adjectives are often followed by infinitives in this pattern: *It* + *be* + adjective + infinitive.	dangerous difficult easy embarrassing expensive fun good important impossible	irresponsible necessary nice pleasant possible rude safe simple wrong	It's **fun to read** the classified ads. It's **important to read** the newspaper every day. It's **not possible to read** every article in the Sunday paper. Isn't it **irresponsible to present** the news as entertainment? Is it **exciting to compete** in a TV reality show?

5 **Practice** Circle the adjective + infinitive phrases in the reading on page 234. Tell what the phrase refers to.

Example Are you ⟨ashamed to show⟩ your skinny body at the beach? *(refers to showing your skinny body)*

6 **Practice** To complete the following soap opera dialogue, put the words in each set of parentheses in the correct order. Write them on the line.

Alexis: I must go. (be / dangerous / It's / to) _____It's dangerous to be_____ here with you.

Chase: No! Stay, my darling!

Alexis: But (to / it's / impossible / go on) _____ this way.
₁

Chase: I know (love / it's / wrong / to) _____ you. But I
₂
can't help myself!

Alexis: Oh, Chase! (difficult / say / to / It's) _____ this, but
₃
. . . I . . . I love you, too!

Chase: (I'm / be / so fortunate / to) _____ the man you
₄
love!

Alexis: But (live / ashamed / I'm / to) _____ this lie! I
₅
must leave you forever!

Chase: (I'm / not willing / give / to) _____ you up! Will
₆
you run away with me?

Alexis: Oh, Chase! (deny / impossible / to / It's) _____
₇
my feelings for you.

Chase: Do you mean . . . ?

Alexis: Yes! Yes! (am / I / to / give up / prepared) _____
₈
everything I have for you! (glad / be / to / I'd / leave)
_____ all of it behind for you.
₉

Chase: My love! (It's / so good / hear / to) _____ that.
₁₀
Let's leave immediately!

7 Practice Complete the following sentences with your own ideas about entertainment and/or the media. When you are finished, share your thoughts with the class.

Example I'm afraid to _____ *watch horror movies by myself* _____.

1. I'm afraid to _____.

2. It's dangerous to _____.

3. I'm prepared to _____.

4. It's irresponsible to _____.

5. It's embarrassing to _____.

6. It's wrong to _____.

7. I am willing to _____.

8. I am sad to _____.

9. It's good to _____.

10. It is important to _____.

11. It is impossible to _____.

12. It's pleasant to _____.

C. Infinitives of Purpose

Infinitives can express the purpose or reason for an action.

8.8	**Infinitives of Purpose**	
	Explanations	**Examples**
Affirmative	In a purpose phrase, *to* = *in order to*.	Let's go outside **to get** some fresh air. Alex turned on the TV **to watch** his favorite game show.
Negative	A negative purpose is expressed with the phrase *in order not to* or *so as not to* + the simple form of a verb.	The sign was removed **in order not to offend** the public. He put his keys in his pocket **so as not to lose** them.

8 Practice Put a box around infinitives of purpose in the reading on page 234.

Example Continue to use *Insta-Muscle* each day to build even bigger muscles.

9 Practice Match each of the sentence beginnings on the left to the infinitive phrases of purpose on the right to form complete and logical sentences.

_____e_____ **1.** I read newspapers

_____ **2.** I have a laptop

_____ **3.** I bought a VCR

_____ **4.** I use the Internet

_____ **5.** I use a cell phone

_____ **6.** I signed up for cable TV

_____ **7.** I have a fax machine

_____ **8.** I have an answering machine

_____ **9.** I use a computerized appointment book

_____ **10.** I need a vacation

a. to record TV programs when I am out.

b. to get more TV channels.

c. to make calls from my car.

d. to get away from it all!

e. to know what is happening in the world

f. to keep track of all of my appointments

g. to do work when I am away from my office

h. to send and receive email.

i. to send and receive important paper documents.

j. in order to take messages when I'm not home.

Using What You've Learned

10 Interviewing Someone About Interests Interview a partner about his or her media interests and habits. Use the words that follow to form questions with infinitives. Then switch roles. (The person who was interviewed now becomes the interviewer.)

Example A: *Do you like to read the newspaper?*
B: *Yes, I do.*
A: *Which one?*
B: *I like to read the Daily Sun.*
A: *Why?*
B: *Because it has a good sports section.*

1. like / read / the newspaper? (If so, which one[s]? Why?)

2. like / listen / music? (If so, what kind? Why?)

3. like / go / to movies? (If so, what kind? Why?)

4. like / watch / sports on TV? (If so, which one[s]? Why?)

5. prefer / watch TV or be outside?

6. need / watch your favorite "reality shows" regularly? (If so, which one[s]?)

7. willing / watch less TV? (If so, why?)

8. happy / watch infomercials? (If so, why?)

9. afraid / go to horror movies by yourself? (Why or why not?)

10. know how / create your own website?

What did you learn about your partner? Tell the class the most interesting things.

11 **Telling Your Opinions About the Media** In small groups, discuss one or more of these statements.

- It is irresponsible for the media to show graphic (strong visual) violence.
- In some situations, it is necessary to censor (to remove parts of) books, movies, and records.
- It is important for the media to provide role models (good examples for young people).
- It is wrong for the media not to respect the privacy of famous people.
- It is silly for ordinary people to compete on TV reality shows.
- It is unnecessary for the news media to replace "real news" with high-profile celebrity court cases.

How many members of your group agree with the statement(s) you discussed? How many disagree? What did you learn from this discussion?

12 **Talking About Newspapers** What are some reasons people still read newspapers? To help you with ideas, you may want to look through a newspaper while you do this activity. In groups, list the reasons.

Examples *People read the newspaper to find out about local news.*
People read newspapers to look up movie schedules.
Nonnative speakers of English may read newspapers in English to practice their reading skills.

Setting the Context

Prereading Questions Discuss these questions with a small group.

When you go to the movies, do you always watch in silence? Do you usually understand the plot, or do you ask your companion to explain things to you?

Reading Read the conversation.

Yukio: This movie is so romantic, **I can** hardly **stand it!** But why doesn't **he kiss her**?

Uma: **He may not know she** loves **him**.

Yukio: I thought **somebody** told **him**.

Uma: No, **nobody could tell him.** Now **will you please watch** the movie?

Yukio: This movie is confusing. **May I ask** . . . isn't that **her** child? Or is **it his**?

Uma: **It's his.** Now please, Yukio. **You'd better not ask** any more questions. **You must be** quiet.

Yukio: There's **something** else I **can't understand** . . .

Uma: Yukio, **nobody can hear** the movie. **Everybody** is looking at **us! They** need **you** to be quiet!

Yukio: Really? **I** didn't hear **anybody** complain. **No one** said **anything**.

Uma: **Would you** please just not say **anything** anymore?

Yukio: **I** don't like **our** seats. **I can't believe** that woman in front of **us** is wearing a hat. How **can** people **be** so rude? **Somebody should tell her** that **she** isn't the only person in this movie theater!

 Discussion Questions Discuss these questions with partner.

1. Where are Yukio and Uma?

2. Why are the people around them annoyed?

3. What does Uma keep asking Yukio to do?

4. What does Yukio say about the woman in front of her?

5. What would you do in this situation if you were Uma?

Grammar Structures and Practice

A. Summary of Modal Verbs

Modals are a special group of words that do not use verb tense endings. They go with verbs to create special meanings.

8.9 Summary of Modal Verbs		
Meanings	**Modals**	**Examples**
Ability	can/can't	I **can** write my own computer programs. I **can't** watch violent movies.
Future possibility	may might	There **may** be a good movie playing tonight. We **might** be too late.
Future plans, predictions	will/won't	What **will** happen next? **Will** he die? No, he **won't**.
Requests	can/can't could/couldn't will/won't would	**Can** you help me? **Could** you change places with me? **Will** you please be quiet? **Would** you hand me the TV schedule?
Permission	may can/can't	**May** I have some popcorn? **Can** I watch another program?
Advice	should/shouldn't had better/had better not	You **should** get an email address. We'**d better not** talk during the movie
Obligations	have to	We **have to** show our ID cards to get into the campus movie theater.
	must/mustn't	You **mustn't** talk in the movie theater.

1 Practice Fill in the missing modals in the following movie dialogues. In some cases, more than one answer is possible. Then answer these questions about the three dialogues: *Which is from a Western? Which is from a romance movie? Which is from a horror film?*

1. **A:** You _____'d better not_____ go in there. People say that old house is

   haunted. If you do, you _____ not come out alive.
   ₁

   B: You _____ scare me with your silly ghost stories. I
   ₂

   _____ go in that house, with you or without you.
   ₃

   A: OK. But you _____ take this knife with you, just in case
   ₄

   you need it.

   Type of movie _____

2. **A:** Don't go. Not yet.

   B: Darling, I _____ go. The taxi's waiting.
   ₁

   A: How _____ you do this to me? You're my reason for
   ₂

   living. I _____ die without you.
   ₃

   B: We _____ be strong, my love. I _____
   ₄   ₅

   never forget you.

   A: I _____ believe we _____ never see
   ₆   ₇

   each other again.

   Type of movie _____

3. **A:** _____ I help you, ma'am?
   ₁

   B: Yes. I _____ find the sheriff immediately.
   ₂

   _____ you tell me where he is?
   ₃

   A: Well now, Sheriff Jackson _____ be at the dry goods
   ₄

   store, or he _____ be over at the stables. Then again, at
   ₅

   this time of night, you _____ find him in the saloon. I
   ₆

   _____ help you find him if you'd like.
   ₇

B: Thank you kindly. I'm sure I _____ find him myself.
8

A: I think I _____ accompany you, ma'am. A young lady
9

_____ be walking around by herself in this town at night.
10

Type of movie _____

2 **Practice** Complete these sentences with the missing modal verbs. In some cases, more than one answer is possible. Then match each sentence to the appropriate speaker or thinker in the pictures. Write the letter of the speaker (from the balloons) in the parentheses.

1. _____ Would _____ you please turn down the volume? It's so loud, I

_____ can't _____ hear myself think! (b)

2. Do you want sparkling teeth and minty fresh breath? Then you

_____ use Glisten Toothpaste! (   )
1

3. And now our reporter in the traffic helicopter _____ tell you
2

freeway drivers about the present conditions. (   )

4. I (not) _____ stand all that noise! I _____
3   4

tell you one last time—turn it down! (   )

5. The president _____ leave on a tour of Asia next month. His
5

plans are not yet certain, but there are reports that he _____
6

visit Tokyo. (   )

6. Because of a major accident, there _____ be heavy traffic on
7

Highway 405. (   )

7. You _____ take another route if possible. (   )
8

8. _____ you like some advice? If you want to be popular, you
9

_____ have a bright smile! (   )
10

9. Tension is increasing on the border. It seems unlikely that negotiators

_____ be able to come to an agreement. (   )
11

10. You (not) _____ watch so much TV, anyway! TV (not)
12

_____ help you improve your grades. (   )
13

B. Summary of Pronouns

Subject and object pronouns replace nouns.
- Possessive adjectives come before nouns; possessive pronouns do not come before nouns.
- Reflexive pronouns refer to the subject of a sentence or sentence part.

8.10 Summary of Pronouns				
Subject Pronouns	**Object Pronouns**	**Possessive Adjectives**	**Possessive Pronouns**	**Reflexive Pronouns**
I	me	my	mine	myself
you	you	your	yours	yourself
he	him	his	his	himself
she	her	her	hers	herself
it	it	its	____	itself
we	us	our	ours	ourselves
you	you	your	yours	yourselves
they	them	their	theirs	themselves

C. Indefinite Pronouns

Indefinite pronouns are for unidentified people or things. They begin with *some-*, *no-*, *any-*, or *every-* and end with *-body, -one,* or *-thing.*

8.11	Indefinite Pronouns		
	Explanations	**Indefinite Pronouns**	**Examples**
some-	A pronoun with *some-* usually appears in an affirmative statement or in a question. A pronoun with *some-* refers to a specific unidentified person or thing.	**someone/somebody** **something**	**Someone** is making noise. Are you looking for **somebody?** I want to tell you **something.**
no- **any-**	A pronoun with *no-* usually appears as the subject. A pronoun with *no-* means "not a" or "not any." *Not +* *any-* is more common as the object. A pronoun with *any-* means "it doesn't matter which."	**no one** **nobody** **nothing** **anything** **anyone/anybody**	Who left early? **No one.** **Nobody** liked the movie. **Nothing** is wrong. There isn't **anything** to watch on TV. Did **anyone** call? There isn't **anybody** in the theater.
every-	A pronoun with *every-* means "all the people" or "all the things."	**everyone/everybody** **everything**	Is **everyone** ready? **Everybody** likes movies. Just pick one movie. We can't see **everything.**

---

3 **Practice** Circle the correct pronouns in each set of parentheses.

Look at these movies. (They're / Their) all full of sex and violence! (I / me / myself)
                                                                                          1

don't want (men / my / mine) children to see (they / them / theirs).
                  2   3

(Anybody / Something / No one) should see garbage like this. When (I / me / myself)
          4   5

was a kid, I used to enjoy (me / mine / myself) at innocent romances and comedies.
6

Kids today don't enjoy (their / them / themselves) at those kinds of movies. But
7

(everyone / any / no one) knows that violence isn't only in the movies. Did
8

(someone / anyone / no one) read the newspaper last night? A crazy man shot
9

(he / him / his) wife and then (he / him / himself) killed (he / himself / herself)!
10   11   12

(Us / Our / Ours) society is too violent. And the media doesn't do
13

(anything / everything / something) to help. Actually, the media is part of the
14

problem because it's always showing (us / our / ours) violence. I think the media
15

should take responsibility for (it / its / itself) effect on society.
16

4 **Practice** Fill in each blank with an appropriate pronoun.

_____ *I* _____ 'm a football widow and _____ hate
1

TV! During football season, _____ don't have a husband because
2

_____'s married to the TV set. When _____'m in
3   4

the room with _____, _____ doesn't say a word
5   6

to me; I often end up talking to _____. For months
7

_____ children forget that _____ have a father.
8   9

During football season, my husband can hardly remember _____
10

names! _____ talked to _____ neighbors about
11   12

this situation and _____ all have the same problem with
13

_____ husbands. Does _____ have a solution?
 14   15

_____ need advice! _____ please help me!
 16   17

_____'m not sure _____ family can survive
 18   19

another football season.

Using What You've Learned

5 **Giving Expert Advice** In most newspapers, there is an "advice column" section. People write to an advice columnist about their problems. They ask this person for advice. The columnist then publishes the letter in the newspaper with his or her answer.

For this activity, play the role of an advice columnist. Read the letters below. Choose one, and respond to it with a letter of advice. Make sure you use modal verbs and pronouns in your response.

Dear Doris,

My 5-year-old son is watching too much TV. Every time I try to turn off the TV, he screams and cries.

Help!

Panicky in Portugal

Dear Doris,

I am a "football widow." My husband completely ignores me when football season starts. It's impossible to get his attention until football season ends.

What should I do?

Widowed in Washington

Dear Doris,

My 10-year-old daughter wants to be just like her favorite rap star. Lately she is dressing like this rap star (in clothes that are much too old for her) and she has started to use bad language.

Can you give me some advice?

Agonizing in Amsterdam

6 **Explaining the Plot of a Show** Work in small groups. Choose a movie or an episode of a TV show that you have seen recently. Explain the plot (the story) to the people in your group. The first time you mention a character, use his or her name. After that, use mostly pronouns for that character.

Focus on Testing

The Past Continuous Tense; The Simple Past Tense; Infinitives; Modal Verbs; Pronouns; Indefinite Pronouns

Standardized tests of English proficiency often have sections on grammar, including the past continuous tense, the simple past tense, infinitives, modal verbs, and pronouns. Review what you studied in this chapter. Check your understanding of the grammar points by completing the sample questions below.

Remember that . . .

✔ The past continuous tense describes activities in progress during a period of time in the past.

✔ The simple past tense is used to talk about events and activities that began and ended in the past.

✔ *Can/Can't* are used to express present ability/inability.

✔ Possessive adjectives come before nouns. Possessive pronouns do not come before nouns.

Part 1. Fill in the bubble for the correct completion for the following.

Example I'm afraid she's very worried about _____ teenage son.

Ⓐ she   Ⓑ herself   ⦿ Ⓒ her   Ⓓ hers

1. Sorry I couldn't call you earlier. The phone _____ off the hook all morning.

Ⓐ was ringing   Ⓑ ring   Ⓒ were ringing   Ⓓ rung

2. I _____ usually get through the first time I try calling my family overseas. The lines are all busy.

Ⓐ had better not   Ⓑ can't   Ⓒ wasn't   Ⓓ haven't

3. _____ was using the computer at 8:00 last night.

Ⓐ Anybody   Ⓑ Everything   Ⓒ Someone   Ⓓ Anything

4. I wasn't prepared _____ such a violent movie.

Ⓐ seeing   Ⓑ see   Ⓒ to see   Ⓓ to be seeing

Part 2. Circle the letter below the underlined word(s) containing the error.

Example   The TV <u>seems</u> awfully loud; <u>do you</u> <u>want me</u> <u>lower</u> the volume?
                        A   B   C   Ⓓ

1. Usually I <u>wake up</u> early, but yesterday I <u>was waking up</u> at <u>around</u> 10:30.
   A   B   C   D

2. Instead of <u>going out</u> for dinner, <u>while the movie</u> <u>ended</u>, <u>we went</u> home.
                A   B   C   D

3. He said he <u>wanted</u> <u>to go</u> outside <u>to getting</u> <u>some</u> fresh air.
                A   B   C   D

4. I can't <u>cook</u> pastries very <u>well</u>, but I <u>can't</u> <u>bake</u> good bread.
            A   B   C   D

Self-Assessment Log

Each of the following sentences describes the grammar you learned in this chapter. Read the sentences and then check the best box for how well you understand each structure.

	Needs Improvement	Good	Great
I can use statements and questions in the past continuous and simple past tenses to describe news events.	❏	❏	❏
I can use *when* and *while* to show relationships in time for past events.	❏	❏	❏
I can use infinitives to talk about entertainment and the media.	❏	❏	❏
I can use adjectives and *It* with infinitives to describe people and entertainment.	❏	❏	❏
I can use modal verbs and pronouns to talk about entertainment.	❏	❏	❏
I can use indefinite pronouns to talk about unidentified people and things.	❏	❏	❏
I practiced taking a test about the past continuous tense, the simple past tense, infinitives, modal verbs, pronouns, and indefinite pronouns.	❏	❏	❏

Social Life

> "Friendship is born at that moment when one person says to another: "What! You, too? Thought I was the only one."
>
> —C.S. Lewis
> Irish author and scholar (1898–1963)

Connecting to the Topic

1 Do you enjoy spending time with friends?

2 What do you like to do with them in your free time?

Setting the Context

Prereading Questions Discuss these questions with a small group.

Are you happy with your social life? Why or why not?

Reading Read the conversation.

Rosa: What's wrong, Jess?

Jess: I'm bored. **I've lived** here **for a year,** and I still don't really have a social life. I **haven't gone** to a party **since the summer**. I **haven't even gone** to a movie **in weeks**!

Rosa: Maybe you **haven't met** new people because you **haven't gotten** involved in new activities **for so long**. I joined the soccer team last August, and I**'ve made** lots of new friends on the team **since then.**

Jess: I**'ve meant** to join a club all semester, but I **haven't had** any extra time **since the semester started**. How **have** I **spent** all my time **since September?** Studying and writing papers!

Rosa: I think you also feel bad because you **haven't exercised for months.** To feel good, you need to get some exercise every day.

Jess: You may be right. That may be why I **haven't slept** well **since I stopped going to the gym**.

Rosa: Is something else bothering you?

Jess: Now that you mention it, yes—my love life! I **haven't met** anyone **since I broke up with Jack.**

Rosa: Well that's no surprise. You**'ve barely left** the house **for weeks.** You need to make an effort to get out and meet people. Hey, I have a friend who might be perfect for you. Do you want me to introduce you?

Jess: Oh no. Not a blind date! I**'ve always avoided** them!

Rosa: Trust me. I think you'll really like John.

Jess: **How long have** you **known** him?

Rosa: I**'ve known** him **since August.** He's on the men's soccer team.

Jess: **How long has** he **been** on the team?

Rosa: I think he**'s been** on the team for a year or two. His team **has won** a few trophies **since he joined**. He's really good-looking and really nice.

Jess: I guess he sounds OK.

Rosa: Great! He**'s been** out sick since last week, so I **haven't seen** him **for a few days**. But I'll speak with him as soon as he comes back.

Jess: OK. But you'd better be right about this!

 Discussion Questions Discuss these questions with a partner.

1. Why is Jess bored?

2. What has happened to Rosa since she joined the soccer team?

3. Why hasn't Jess joined any clubs?

4. What does Jess ask about John?

5. Why can't Rosa contact John right away?

6. Since you moved to your present city or neighborhood, how have you tried to meet new people? Have those methods worked for you? Why or why not?

Grammar Structures and Practice

A. The Present Perfect Tense (2)

The present perfect tense consists of *have/has* before the past participle of a verb.

- Actions or situations that began in the past and continue to the present are often in the present perfect.
- This tense tells how long something has lasted up to this point.
- Often, the present perfect tense is for (repeated past) actions or situations that occurred at an unspecified time in the past. See Chapter 6 for this use of the present perfect.

9.1 The Present Perfect Tense

	Explanations	Examples
Affirmative	The present perfect can be contracted with subject pronouns: *I've, we've, you've, they've, he's, she's,* and *it's.*	We **have been** here since February. We**'ve been** here for two weeks. Rosa **has played** tennis for a long time.
Negative	The negative contractions are *haven't* and *hasn't.*	I **have not seen** them since last week. She **hasn't missed** a single class.

9.2 Questions with the Present Perfect Tense

Explanations	Structures	Examples	Possible Answers	
			Affirmative	**Negative**
In present perfect questions, *has* or *have* usually comes before the subject.	**Yes/No Questions**	**Have** you **lived** here since January?	Yes, I have.	No, I haven't.
		Have you **been** married for a long time?	Yes, I have.	No, I haven't.
How long = since when. These are common question phrases.	**Information Questions**	How long **have** you **known** Ruben? = Since when **have** you **known** Ruben?	I've known him since January.	
		How long **has** Jess **been** your girlfriend? = Since when **has** Jess **been** your girlfriend?	She's been my girlfriend for a year.	

---

1 Practice Underline the present perfect verb phrases in the conversation on pages 256 and 257. Identify the participle forms of the main verbs, and tell their base forms.

Example   I've lived here for a year, and I still don't really have a social life.
(*participle = lived; base form = live*)

2 Practice Complete the following sentences with the correct present perfect verb phrases. Use the verb from the first sentence in each line.

Example Kevin's sister is married. She _____*has been*_____ married since she was 22.

1. I know John. I _____ him for a few months.

2. He loves sports. He _____ sports since he was a little boy.

3. He works at the sports center. He _____ at the sports center since Christmas.

4. He lives alone. He _____ alone for six months.

5. He has a beard. He _____ a beard for two years.

6. He is sick right now. He _____ sick for a week.

7. He and his best friend are in a band. They _____ in a band since 2003.

8. John plays the guitar. He _____ the guitar since he was a boy.

9. John doesn't eat meat. He _____ meat since he became a vegetarian.

10. He has a dog. He _____ a dog since October.

B. Time Expressions with the Present Perfect: *For, Since, All, Always*

A present perfect statement or answer often includes a time expression.

- A phrase with *since, for, all*, or *always* can answer the questions *"How long . . . ?" or "Since when . . . ?"*

9.3 Time Expressions with the Present Perfect

	Explanations	Examples
for	Use *for* with an amount of time. Examples: *for* an hour, *for* a week, *for* five years, *for* a long time	I have played soccer **for** five years.
since	Use *since* with a time or point in past time. The phrase tells when an activity or a condition started. Examples: *since* 7:00, *since* Monday, *since* May 15th, *since* my birthday	My best friends have been married **since** January.
all	Use *all* for a complete time period. Examples: *all* day, *all* night, *all* week, *all* my life	Maya has been at her friend's house **all** week.
always	Use *always* for an action or a state that began in the past and continues to the present. *Always* comes between the auxiliary verb and the main verb.	We have **always** wanted to go skydiving.

Note: It is also possible to use the time expression *in* for negative sentences. **For example:** *I haven't been to a concert **in** years.*

---

3 **Practice** Fill in the blanks in the following sentences with *for, since, all,* or *always*.

Example The members of the volleyball team have been at the beach

_____*all*_____ day.

A.

Sara has _____ been my best friend—at least for as long as I
                    1

can remember. I've known her _____ nursery school. I've
                              2

_____ told her all of my secrets. We have lived in this town
        3

_____ our lives. We've _____ wanted to travel,
        4   5

however. We've talked about it _____ years.
                                      6

B.

Susana has been on summer vacation with her family _____ three weeks. She's been gone _____ May. I've been lonely and bored _____ she's been gone.

C.

The weather has been terrible _____ week. It has been gray and rainy _____ last week. I've tried to call my friend Sid _____ afternoon. His line has been busy _____ 12:00. I haven't spoken to him _____ my birthday. I haven't seen him _____ a few weeks. He's been too busy to get together _____ the last week or two. I've known Sid _____ 1993. He's _____ made me laugh.

D.

Maybe we can go out for dinner. I haven't eaten _____ day. I've been hungry _____ this morning. Maybe we can go dancing tonight. I haven't been to a dance club _____ last summer. I have to do something! I've done nothing but sit in the house _____ weeks!

4 **Practice** Form questions with *how long* about each of these statements. Answer them with time expressions that include *for, since, all*, or *always*.

Example I'm a member of the chess club.
How long have you been a member of the chess club?
I've been a member since the first meeting in September.

  1. Hisato lives with his best friend.

_____ ?

_____

2. I know the steps to this dance.

_____?

_____

3. Michael is my soccer coach.

_____?

_____

4. Tomas and Gina are married.

_____?

_____

5. My cousin owns a nightclub.

_____?

_____

6. Carlos and Daria are in love.

_____?

_____

7. Amile plays the guitar.

_____?

_____

8. My parents are on vacation.

_____?

_____

9. This club has a dance floor.

_____?

_____

10. I like foreign movies.

_____?

_____

5 Practice Combine the information in each pair of sentences. Put the main verb in the present perfect tense and include a time phrase with *for* or *since*. There may be more than one possible answer.

Example Darcy joined the soccer team last year. She is still a member of the soccer team.

Darcy has been a member of the soccer team for a year.

1. Juanita liked Daniel three years ago. She still likes him.

2. Adrian moved to Mexico last year. He still lives there.

3. Angela was tired this morning. She's still tired.

4. Jong got a cell phone in 1998. He still has a cell phone.

5. My teammates woke up at 8:00. They are still awake.

6. Someone turned the stereo on an hour ago. The stereo is still on.

7. Leyla stopped talking to me five years ago. She still doesn't talk to me.

8. I wasn't hungry last night. I'm still not hungry.

9. My visitors arrived a week ago. They are still here.

10. Dara got glasses when she was seven years old. She still wears glasses.

C. Time Clauses with *Since* in the Present Perfect

Sentences in the present perfect (or present perfect continuous) tense often have a time clause with *since*.

9.4 Time Clauses with *Since*	
Explanation	**Examples**
The main clause must be in the present perfect (or present perfect continuous) tense. The clause with *since* is usually in the simple past.	Ian and Sara **have been** in love **since** the first time they **saw** each other. They **have been dating** for three years.
A *since* clause can come at the beginning or in the middle of a sentence. Put a comma after the *since* clause at the beginning of the sentence.	**Since I joined the gym, I've had** more energy.

6 Practice Circle the time expressions (phrases) in the conversation on pages 256 and 257. Put a box around time clauses with *since*.

Examples I haven't gone to a party since the summer.

That may be why I haven't slept well since I stopped going to the gym.

7 Practice Combine each pair of sentences into one sentence with *since*. Don't change their order. Remember that *since* can come at the beginning or in the middle of the sentence. Use correct punctuation.

Example Young went on a diet. He has lost a lot of weight.
Since Young went on a diet, he has lost a lot of weight.

1. Hanna has met a lot of new people. She joined the tennis club.
2. Alfonso went to the concert last night. He has had a headache.
3. Taro went on vacation. He has been much more relaxed.
4. I haven't seen Reiko and Yoko. They moved to an apartment off campus.
5. Patrick hasn't been in school. He broke his leg.
6. Saeed took an art history course. He has been interested in art.
7. We haven't gone to the movies very often. We had children.
8. I haven't heard from Juan. We went on a date last week.

 8 Practice Fill in the blanks to make present perfect sentences about yourself. Then read your partner's statements. Tell another pair of students about your partner.

Example A: I've been ____*extremely busy*____ since ____*the semester started*____.
B: *Hamid has been extremely busy since the semester started.*

1. I've been _____ since _____.
2. I haven't been _____ for _____.
3. I've had _____ since _____.
4. I haven't had _____ all _____.
5. I've known _____ for _____.
6. I've studied _____ since _____.
7. I've always wanted _____.
8. I've meant to _____ since _____.

Using What You've Learned

 9 Interviewing Someone About Life Events and Time Periods Interview a classmate about his or her life. Ask simple past tense questions and present perfect questions beginning with *how long*.

Example A: *Where do you live?*
B: *I live in Cobble Hill.*

A: *How long have you lived there?*
B: *About five years.*
A: *Are you married?*
B: *Yes, I am.*
A: *How long have you been married?*

Take notes on your classmate's answers. After the interview, write a list of present perfect statements about him or her. Do not put the person's name on the paper. Exchange your list with another student. Each student reads aloud the list he or she has been given. The class tries to guess the identity of the student from the information in the list.

Example *This student has lived in Cobble Hill for about five years.*
She has been married since she was 21.
She has been a writer for the school newspaper for a year.

 10 **Matching Events to Time Periods** On separate index cards or pieces of paper, each student writes five time expressions commonly used with the present perfect tense (such as *all week, since last winter,* and *since I was a child*). The teacher collects these. The teacher then gives each pair of students ten of the cards, face down. With your partner, take turns turning over the index cards. Then make true present perfect statements with the time expressions.

Example A: (turns over a card that says *all week*) *It has rained all week.*
B: (turns over a card that says *since last winter*) *I haven't gotten sick since last winter.*
A: (turns over a card that says *since I was a child*) *I haven't gone to the circus since I was a child.*

The Present Perfect Continuous Tense; The Present Perfect Continuous Tense Versus the Present Perfect Tense

Setting the Context

Prereading Questions Discuss these questions with a small group.

Have you had any conversations with new friends or acquaintances lately? If so, what did you talk about?

Reading Read the conversation.

John: Jess?

Jess: John?

John: Hi! Sorry I'm late. **Have** you **been waiting** long?

Jess: No. I've only **been waiting** for five or ten minutes. You seem out of breath. **Have** you **been running**?

John: Yes, I **have**. I ran from my house in Chester Heights. The bus I take into town **hasn't been running** on time lately. So after I waited a few minutes, I decided to run here.

Jess: That's really far to run!

John: It's not that bad. And it's good exercise. I've **been training** for a ten-kilometer race anyway.

Jess: Wow. You're on the soccer team and you're training for a race? I bet you're busy.

John: I am! Besides the race, I've also **been learning** karate, and lately I've **been doing** volunteer work at a soup kitchen, too. But I'd rather talk about you! Rosa told me that you're from New York. How long **have** you **been living** here?

Jess: I've **lived** here for a year so far. I've **been studying** law at the university.

John: That sounds difficult. What do you do in your free time?

Jess: I usually read to relax. Of course, I**'ve been** so busy with school work—I**'ve been reading** the same book for a month! Also, to be honest, I**'ve** probably **been watching** too much TV. I**'ve been meaning** to get involved in some new activities. I'm thinking about a photography class.

John: Oh, that sounds great! I**'ve been taking** a photography class for the last month or two. Since I started the class, my photos **have gotten** much better.

Jess: You're taking a photography class, too? How **have** you **found** the time for everything?

John: Well, I**'ve had** some free time lately because I **haven't been playing** guitar with my band. We**'ve been taking** a break because everyone in the band is so busy right now. I**'ve been needing** more time to work on my book. Did I mention that I**'ve been writing** a book . . . ?

 Discussion Questions Discuss these questions with a partner.

1. Why is John out of breath?

2. What has he been doing recently?

3. What has Jess been doing recently?

4. Why has John had some free time recently?

5. What have you been doing recently?

A. The Present Perfect Continuous Tense

The present perfect continuous tense consists of *have/has* + *been* before the *-ing* form of a verb.

■ With time expressions, this tense emphasizes duration or repetition of an action or a situation. It often implies that the action or situation will continue in the future.

■ Time expressions common with the present perfect (continuous) name a period or an amount of time from the past to the present. Here are some examples:

for a short time	**since** yesterday	**all** day	**today, nowadays**
for a few years	**since** the end of the month	**all** week	**recently, lately**
for a week or two	**since** you arrived	**all** my life	**How long?**

9.5 The Present Perfect Continuous Tense

Purpose	Explanations	Examples	
		Affirmative	**Negative**
To Emphasize Duration	Use only action verbs in the present perfect continuous for activities that started in the past and continue to the present.	It**'s been raining** for an hour. Jenny **has been talking** on the phone all evening.	We **haven't been living** here for more than a month. I **haven't been playing** soccer this week.
To Express a General Activity	*Recently* and *lately* are common adverbs for "indefinite time in the recent past."	I**'ve been going** to a lot of parties **recently.** Karim **has been reading** a good book **lately.**	Lara **hasn't been sleeping** well **recently.** I **haven't been doing** much **lately.**

9.6 Questions with the Present Perfect Continuous Tense

Explanations		Examples	Possible Answers	
			Affirmative	**Negative**
In present perfect continuous questions, *has* or *have* comes before the subject—except when *who* or *what* is the sentence subject.	**Yes/No Questions**	**Have** you **been seeing** a lot of movies these days? **Has Jun been living** here long?	Yes, I have. Yes, she has.	No, I haven't. No, she hasn't.
	Information Questions	Where **have** you **been living?** Who**'s been playing** music? What **have you been doing?**	I**'ve been living** in Escondito. My neighbors (**have been playing** music). I**'ve been going** to the beach a lot lately.	

Notes: See Appendix 4 for spelling rules for the *-ing* ending. Some verbs are less common in the continuous tenses than in the simple tenses. These "nonaction" verbs include verbs that express feeling and thought, verbs that express possession, and verbs that express sensory perception. For more information on nonaction verbs, see Part 3, Section B (*Nonaction Verbs*) in Chapter 2, pages 52 and 53.

1 Practice Underline the present perfect continuous verb phrases in the conversation on pages 266 and 267. Notice the past participle *been*. Identify the *-ing* forms of the main verbs, and tell their base forms.

Example <u>Have</u> you <u>been waiting</u> long? *(base form = wait; -ing form = waiting)*

2 Practice Make present perfect continuous sentences with these cue words. Include a time expression (*since, for,* or *all*) in each sentence.

Example I / prepare for the party / 2:00 this afternoon
　　　　　I have been preparing for the party since 2:00 this afternoon.

1. I / look forward to this party / weeks
2. the music / play / night
3. everyone / dance / hours
4. that woman / flirt with that man / the party began
5. that couple / fight / the beginning of the party
6. the DJ / play disco music / long time
7. my head / hurt / about 10:00
8. we / wait for food / a long time
9. I / feel sick / I had a drink
10. I / want to go home / a few hours

3 **Practice** Make present perfect continuous questions with *how long* for each of these sentences.

Example A: Khalid is saving money for a sports car.
B: *How long has Khalid been saving money for a sports car?*

1. A: Oscar and Milena have been arguing a lot.

B: _____?

2. A: She's been flirting with Felipe!

B: _____?

3. A: She dyes her hair.

B: _____?

4. A: He wears a hairpiece.

B: _____?

5. A: He's dieting.

B: _____?

6. A: Felipe lives downtown.

B: _____?

7. A: His parents pay his rent.

B: _____

8. A: He's been saving money to buy a house.

B: _____?

9. A: Felipe and Alicia are dating.

B: _____?

10. A: I've been planning a party.

B: _____?

4 Practice Make sentences with these cue words. Answer the question "What have you been doing recently?" Fill in numbers 9 to 12 with your own recent activities.

Example read a good book *I've been reading a good book* .

1. go out with friends _____ .

2. play a lot of tennis _____ .

3. go to a lot of parties _____ .

4. have friends over for dinner _____ .

5. rent videos _____ .

6. play soccer _____ .

7. shop with friends _____ .

8. spend time in cafes _____ .

9. _____ .

10. _____ .

11. _____ .

12. _____ .

5 Practice Fill in the blanks with the present perfect continuous form of the verbs in parentheses.

Jim: So, Diane. What have you been doing lately?

Diane: I _*'ve been studying*_ a lot this semester. This week, I
                    (study)

_____ a term paper. My roommate _____
        1 (write)   2 (help)

me. But we _____ all the time. We _____
                    3 (not work)   4 (have)

a good time, too. We _____ tennis and _____ .
                              5 (play)   6 (relax)

Jim: I'm glad to hear that you _____ yourselves. I
                                            7 (enjoy)

_____ much. My wife _____ really
        8 (not relax)   9 (work)

hard these days, too. She _____ any time off. She
                                  10 (not take)

_____ late at work for extra money and she
    11 (stay)

_____ an extra project, too. We _____
    12 (manage)   13 (think)

about a vacation.

Diane: Wow! It sounds like you both _____ much too hard. Stop
                                                14 (work)

thinking about a vacation. Just take one!

6 **Practice** What has each person or pair of people in these pictures been doing? Study the pictures for clues. Make a present perfect continuous statement for each picture.

1. _____ *She has been crying.* _____   5. _____

2. _____   6. _____

3. _____   7. _____

4. _____   8. _____

7 Practice Fill in each of the blanks with the appropriate words to form the present perfect continuous of the verbs in parentheses.

Sally: So what _____*have*_____ you _____*been doing*_____ with
(do)

yourself, Ann? _____ you _____
1   2 (not spend)

much time in the library?

Ann: No. Actually, I _____ on my thesis very much this
3 (not work)

semester. I _____ out a lot.
4 (go)

Sally: Really? Who _____ you _____ out
5   6 (go)

with? I heard that you _____ the teaching assistant in
7 (date)

our chemistry class. Is that true?

Ann: Well, I . . .

Sally: _____ he _____ you to fancy
8   9 (take)

restaurants? I bet he has! Where _____ you
10

_____ ?
11 (eat)

Ann: Well, we . . .

Sally: _____ he _____ you flowers?
12   13 (send)

Ann: Well, uh . . .

Sally: Your life sounds so romantic. Married life is completely different. We

_____ out at all lately, have we Carlos?
14 (not go)

Carlos: How can you say that? Just a month ago we went out for a pizza!

Sally: But what _____ we _____ since

                       15   16 (do)

           then?

Carlos: We _____ lots of time alone. What could be more

                   17 (spend)

           romantic than that?

Sally: Oh, Carlos. Watching old horror movies on late night TV isn't exactly

           what I had in mind.

B. The Present Perfect Continuous Tense Versus the Present Perfect Tense

The present perfect continuous and present perfect tenses both describe actions or situations that began in the past and continue to the present.

9.7 The Present Perfect Continuous Versus the Present Perfect Tense		
	Explanations	**Examples**
Present Perfect Continuous	The present perfect continuous emphasizes the duration or repetition of the activity or situation.	We've **been talking** for hours. How long **has** it **been raining?**
Present Perfect	The present perfect emphasizes the length of time of the activity or situation. The present perfect is for nonaction verbs.	Ludmilla **has been** in Mexico all summer. She**'s liked** Meng for years. I **have known** him for six years.
Present Perfect Continuous or Present Perfect	With certain verbs (such as *live*, *work*, and *teach*), there is little difference in meaning between the present perfect and the present perfect continuous when there's a time expression. With action verbs, the continuous form is more common.	I **have lived** here since 2003. = I **have been living** here since 2003. They **have been playing** tennis for two hours.

8 Practice Circle the best verb choice in each set of parentheses.

Example I've (watched /~~been watching~~) you for a while. Has something bad
(~~happened~~/ been happening)?

1.

A: You look worried. Is anything wrong?

B: Well . . . I've (thought / been thinking) about asking out a girl in my English class.
1

A: What's the problem?

B: I don't think she has (noticed / been noticing) me since the class began.
2

2.

A: Hey, wake up.

B: How long have I (slept / been sleeping)?
1

A: You've (snored / been snoring) almost since we started the video. I thought you
2
liked horror movies.

B: I haven't (liked / been liking) them since I was a kid.
3

3.

A: My boyfriend has (acted / been acting) strange lately.
1

B: What has he (done / been doing)?
2

A: Well, he hasn't (had / been having) much time for me for weeks now. He also
3
hasn't (been / been being) home for the last few nights. I have (called / been calling)
45
him, but nobody ever answers.

B: Hasn't he (studied / been studying) for final exams? Maybe he's (been / been being)
6
at the library.

4.

A: Hey, it's time to get ready for the party. We've got to clean up this apartment.

B: But I've (cleaned up / been cleaning up) the apartment all morning! Didn't you
1
notice? Why haven't you two (helped / been helping) me?
2

C: I've (thought / been thinking) about the refreshments for hours.
3

A: And I've (planned / been planning) the music.
4

5.

A: Have you (heard / been hearing) the news about Eliana and Laura?
1

B: No. What happened?

A: They haven't (gotten / been getting) along lately. They haven't (talked / been talking)
23
to each other for days, and now Eliana is moving out of the apartment.

9 **Interviewing Someone About Life Changes** Interview your partner about a significant recent change in his or her life. How has this change affected his or her daily life? Possible changes to focus on include:

- starting high school/college
- getting married
- moving to a new town
- moving to a new apartment
- having children
- starting a new job

Take notes during the interview. Afterwards, tell the class about the changes and their effects on your partner's life. Use the present perfect continuous.

Example

A: *Since she moved to her new apartment, Anna is closer to school, so she's been walking to campus every day. She's also been staying later at the language laboratory.*

B: *Has she been meeting friends after school?*

A: *I think so, but not all the time. Because her new apartment is more expensive than her last place, she hasn't had as much money for recreation and entertainment. She's been going to the movies less often, and she hasn't been eating out as much.*

 10 **Taking the Roles of Famous People** Choose a famous person familiar to your classmates—a modern or a historical figure. In this activity, you're going to pretend to be that person. Imagine that you're all at a party. Ask the other people: *"What have you been doing lately? What's been happening in your life recently?"* Talk about events and activities. Later, the class tries to guess the identities of the "party guests."

A: *What have you been doing lately?*

B: *I have been inventing new computer programs. I've also been selling some of the stock in my company.*

A: *That sounds interesting.*

B: *Yes, it is. I've been enjoying it because I've been making billions of dollars. I've been giving millions to charity. So, what have you been doing lately?*

A: *Oh, you know, just the usual. I've been ruling France, and invading Russia . .*

B: *That sounds tiring!*

(A is Bill Gates. B is Napoleon Bonaparte.)

Setting the Context

Prereading Questions Discuss these questions with a small group.

Do you (still) date—or did you use to go out on dates? If so, what do or did you usually tell your best friend(s) about the dates?

Reading Read the conversation.

Rosa: Well, how was the date?

Jess: It was OK, I guess.

Rosa: Wasn't John **handsome enough**?

Jess: Are you kidding? He's **handsome enough** to be a movie star.

Rosa: Wasn't he **smart enough**?

Jess: I don't think I've ever met **such an intelligent man**. And he's **so funny**. I had **such a great time**.

Rosa: Then what's the problem?

Jess: He's **so busy**. I don't think he has **enough time** for me. He has **too many hobbies and interests**.

Rosa: That's silly. If he likes you, he'll make time for you.

Jess: That's not the real problem, anyway.

Rosa: I'm **so confused**. What *is* the problem?

Jess: I'm sure he doesn't like me. He's **so active** and interesting. I'm just **not exciting enough**. I think I'm **too dull** for him.

Rosa: John asked me not to tell you this but . . .

Jess: You've spoken with him since last night?

Rosa: Yes. He called me early this morning because he was **so excited**. He really liked you. He can't wait to see you again. But he's afraid you may not like him! He thinks he talked **too much**.

Jess: That's funny. I was **so sure** he wasn't interested in me.

Rosa: You've always been **so negative**! You haven't had **enough confidence** in yourself since your last break-up.

Jess: This is **so exciting!** Oh well, I'm sure he'll change his mind on the second date.

Rosa: Jess!

 Discussion Questions Discuss these questions with a partner.

1. How does Jess describe John?

2. What does Jess say about John's hobbies and interests?

3. Why does Jess think that John doesn't like her?

4. Why does John think that Jess may not like him?

5. Do you think Jess and John are a good match? Why or why not?

Grammar Structures and Practice

A. *So* and *Such*

So and *such* make the meaning of an adjective or adverb stronger.

9.8	*So* and *Such*	
	Explanations	**Examples**
so	*So* comes before an adjective or an adverb. *So . . . that* expresses results or consequences.	The movie was **so** good. The movie was **so** good **that** I would see it again.
such	*Such* comes before an adjective + noun. The indefinite article *a/an* appears between *such* and the adjective when the noun is singular (countable). *Such . . . that* expresses results or consequences.	It was **such** a good movie. It was **such** a good movie **that** I want to see it again.

1 Practice Underline the phrases with *so* and *such* in the conversation on pages 277 and 278. Identify (tell) the adjective. Can you think of a phrase or clause to add to any of the sentences?

Example I don't think I ever met <u>such</u> an intelligent man.

(adjective = intelligent - such an intelligent man as John)

2 Practice Fill in the blanks with *so* or *such*. Then match the sentence beginnings with the most logical endings to form complete sentences.

_h_ **1.** I went to ___such___ a good party last night

___ **2.** There was _____ delicious food

___ **3.** The music was _____ good

___ **4.** The people were all _____ friendly

___ **5.** I met a guy who was _____ funny

___ **6.** I was having _____ a good time

___ **7.** The hostess was _____ kind

___ **8.** It was _____ late when I got home

___ **9.** I was _____ tired when I got home

___ **10.** My father was _____ angry this morning

a. that everyone else in my family was sleeping.

b. that almost everyone was dancing.

c. that I made a bunch of new friends.

d. that I fell asleep in just a few minutes.

e. that he told me I can't go to any more parties for a month!

f. that it was all eaten really quickly.

g. that I didn't realize how late it was.

h. that nobody wanted it to end.

i. that she called a taxi for me.

j. that I couldn't stop laughing.

3 Practice Fill in the blanks to make true statements about your own life and experiences. If you wish, you can add a *that* clause to the sentence.

Example My social life is so _____*busy*_____

(*that I'm almost never at home*).

1. My social life is so _____

   (_____).

2. The last movie I saw was so _____

   (_____).

3. The last party I went to was so _____

   (_____).

4. The last restaurant I went to was so _____

   (_____).

5. I have such _____ friends

   (_____).

6. I have such a _____ house/apartment

   (_____).

7. I have such _____ weekends

   (_____).

8. I have such _____ clothes

   (_____).

B. *Enough* and *Too*

Enough and *too* are adverbs used to give extra meaning about the quantity of something.

	Explanations	Examples
enough	*Enough* means "as much or as many as needed." It implies a positive result. *Enough* comes after adjectives and adverbs.	My daughter is old **enough**. (+ She can date.) = My daughter is old **enough** to date.
	Enough usually comes before nouns.	There are **enough** chairs here. (+ We can all sit down.) = There are **enough** chairs here (for us all) to sit on. There are**n't enough** chairs here. (+ Some of us have to stand.) = There aren**'t enough** chairs here (for us) to sit on.
	Not enough implies a negative result.	She doesn**'t** have **enough** experience. (+ She has a boyfriend.) = She doesn**'t** have **enough** experience to have a boyfriend.
too	*Too* indicates a problem. It implies a negative result. It is the opposite of adjective/adverb + *enough*.	She is **too** young. + She can't date. = She's **too** young to date.
	Too comes before an adjective or adverb.	He works **too** slowly.
	Too many comes before countable nouns; *too much* comes before noncount nouns. They express the opposite of *enough* + noun.	There are **too many** chairs here. (They are in the way.) This soup has **too much** salt.
	Too much/many can also be adverbs.	Richard eats **too much**.
	. . . *too* . . . *to* . . . can express negative results.	She is **too** young **to** have a boyfriend.

Note: It is possible to drop the noun after *enough* or *too much/many* if the meaning is clear. **Example:** *I've eaten too much (food).*

---

4 **Practice** Put a circle around the phrases with *enough* and *too* in the conversation on pages 277 and 278. Identify the adjectives. Can you think of a phrase or clause to add to any of the sentences?

Example Wasn't John handsome (enough)? *(handsome enough to please you)*

5 **Practice** Fill in the blanks with *enough* or *too*.

Example Why don't we go swimming? It's warm _____enough_____.

1. Makoto is _____ young to go out with boys alone.

2. The music is _____ loud. I can't hear what you're saying.

3. The movie theater is close _____ (for us) to walk there.

4. Angelina is thin _____ to be a model.

5. Can I call you back later? I'm _____ busy to talk now.

6. You aren't walking fast _____. We're going to be late.

7. You're speaking _____ quietly. I can't hear what you're saying.

8. I'm tired _____ to fall asleep right here!

9. This food isn't hot _____. I'm going to send it back.

10. This dress is _____ expensive. I can't afford it.

6 **Practice** Fill in the blanks with *enough, too, too many,* or *too much*.

Rikki: How did you like that restaurant?

Tamu: It was good, but the food was a little _____*too*_____ spicy for me.

Also, there wasn't _____1_____ food. I'm still hungry.

Tamu: Really? I'm stuffed. I thought there was _____2_____ food!

Tamu: I hope this movie is good. I've seen _____3_____ stupid movies lately.

Rikki: Wow. Look at that price. That's _____4_____ money for a ticket.

Tamu: Do you have _____5_____ money? If you don't, I can lend you some.

Rikki: No, I've got _____6_____.

Tamu: The line is _____7_____ long. Let's get a cup of coffee and come back.

Rikki: Do we have _____8_____ time? The movie starts in 20 minutes.

Tamu: There's a café right next door. It won't take _____9_____ time. Let's go.

7 **Practice** Write a sentence about each of these pictures. Use either *...too...to* or *...enough...to*.

Example   *The women don't have enough money to pay the bill.*

1. _____   2. _____

3. _____   4. _____

5. _____

8 Practice Finish the following sentences with true statements about yourself.

Example I am old enough to _____ *have a driver's license* _____.

1. I am old enough to _____.

2. I am too old to _____.

3. I am young enough to _____.

4. I am too young to _____.

5. I have enough money to _____.

6. I don't have enough money to _____.

7. I have enough time to _____.

8. I don't have enough time to _____.

Using What You've Learned

9 Telling Your Feelings About an Experience Describe a movie or a restaurant that you went to recently. Use the adverbs of intensity: *so, such, too,* and *enough.*

Example *Last week I went to see "Last Exit." It was such a silly movie. There were too many explosions and car crashes. There weren't enough interesting characters. The movie was so long that I fell asleep while I was watching it.*

10 Learning About a Club Find out about an athletic or academic club at your school. You may want to visit the club or speak to a club member. Find out the answers to these questions and others:

- What are the requirements for new members?
- Do you have to pass any tests to join the club?
- Are there any membership fees?
- How much time does the club require?

Now write about the club. Can you join it? Do you want to join it? Why or why not? Use *so, such, too,* and *enough* in your explanation.

The Present Perfect Tense; The Present Perfect Continuous Tense; Adverbs of Degree: *So, Such, Enough,* **and** *Too*

Standardized tests of English proficiency often have sections on grammar, including the present perfect tense, the present perfect continuous tense, and adverbs of degree such as *so, such, enough*, and *too*. Review what you studied in this chapter. Check your understanding of the grammar points by completing the sample items below.

Remember that . . .

✔ The present perfect describes actions or situations that began in the past and continue to the present.

✔ A sentence in the present perfect or present perfect continuous tense often has a clause with *since*.

✔ *For* usually refers to a specific amount of time; *since* means from a past time period until now.

Part 1. Fill in the bubble for the correct completion for the following sentences.

Example   You've been sick a lot this semester, _____ you?

(A) have   (B) haven't   (C) were   (D) weren't

1. Who _____ my soda? It's only half full now, and I've only had one sip!

(A) drinks   (B) has been drinking   (C) has drunk   (D) drunk

2. Is the boy old _____ to drive?

(A) such   (B) too   (C) so   (D) enough

3. I have always _____ to be a famous movie star.

(A) want   (B) been wanted   (C) been wanting   (D) wanted

4. _____ I joined the gym, I've had more energy.

(A) For   (B) After   (C) When   (D) Since

Part 2. Circle the letter below the underlined word(s) containing the error.

Example　My cousin <u>has been</u> <u>living</u> <u>in</u> New York <u>since</u> three months.
　　　　　　　　　　　A　　　　　B　　C　　　　　　　Ⓓ

1. I <u>have</u> <u>been going</u> to Disneyland four times <u>since</u> I <u>came</u> to the United States.
　　　A　　　B　　　　　　　　　　　　　　　　　C　　　D

2. He <u>has</u> <u>been going</u> to graduate school <u>since</u> <u>over</u> ten years.
　　　A　　　B　　　　　　　　　　　　C　　D

3. <u>Since</u> Hanna <u>joined</u> the tennis club, she <u>has</u> <u>been met</u> a lot of new people.
　　　A　　　　　B　　　　　　　　　　　　C　　D

4. We <u>been</u> <u>living</u> <u>in</u> Tokyo <u>for</u> almost three months now.
　　　A　　B　　C　　　D

Self-Assessment Log

Each of the following sentences describes the grammar you learned in this chapter. Read the sentences and then check the best box for how well you understand each structure.

	Needs Improvement	Good	Great
I can use the present perfect tense to talk about friendships and people.	❏	❏	❏
I can use *for, since, all*, and *always* to describe the present perfect tense.	❏	❏	❏
I can use the present perfect continuous tense to describe continuing or repeating actions in the past.	❏	❏	❏
I can use adverbs of degree like *so, such, enough*, and *too* to describe people.	❏	❏	❏
I practiced taking a test about the present perfect tense, the present perfect continuous tense, and adverbs of degree.	❏	❏	❏

Customs, Celebrations, and Holidays

> **❝** If I need a cause for celebration,
> Or a comfort I can use to ease my mind,
> I rely on my imagination,
> And I dream of an imaginary time. **❞**
>
> —Billy Joel
> American singer, songwriter, and pianist (1949–   )

Connecting to the Topic

1 What is your favorite holiday or celebration during the year?

2 What do you for that holiday?

3 Who do you celebrate with?

Setting the Context

 Prereading Questions Discuss these questions with a small group.

Do you usually celebrate your birthday? Do you enjoy other people's birthday celebrations? Why or why not?

Reading Read the conversation.

(A family is celebrating two birthdays at the same time. The grandfather is 70 years old and Jenny is five years old today.)

Mother:	Isn't this fun, Dad? It's so nice **to celebrate** your birthdays together.
Grandpa:	Well, maybe it's fun **to celebrate** Jenny's birthday, but I'm too old **to like** birthdays. Besides, it's silly **to have** a birthday party for such an old man.
Jenny:	But Grandpa, **having** a birthday is very special. You *have* **to enjoy** yourself.
Jimmy:	Come on everybody. It's time for Grandpa and Jenny **to make** a wish and blow out the candles.
Jenny:	Remember, Grandpa, it's important **to make** a wish when you blow out the candles.
Grandpa:	**Blowing** out 70 candles is too hard.
Father:	**Doing** it alone is hard. But you have Jenny **to help.**

Mother: After you blow out the candles, it's your job **to cut** the cake, Dad.

Grandpa: **Eating** cake and ice cream is bad for an old man.

Jenny: But you have **to have** some cake! And after we eat cake, we get **to open** our presents! **Opening** the presents is so much fun. It's hard **to wait.**

Grandpa: **Giving** presents on birthdays isn't necessary.

Jimmy: Grandpa, shhh . . . *(The family sings "Happy Birthday." Then Jenny and her grandfather blow out the candles.)*

Jenny: Hooray! Now all our wishes will come true!

Grandpa: *(smiles)* Well, maybe **having** a birthday isn't so bad after all.

 Discussion Questions Discuss these questions with a partner.

1. What does Jenny think about birthdays? What does the grandfather think? Why?

2. What birthday customs does the reading mention?

3. What are some birthday customs in your culture?

4. Do you like celebrating birthdays? Why or why not?

Grammar Structures and Practice

A. Gerunds and Infinitives as Subjects

Gerunds and infinitives can appear as subjects of sentences. Their meaning is identical.

10.1	**Gerunds and Infinitives as Subjects**	
Structures	**Explanations**	**Examples**
Infinitives	It's uncommon to begin a sentence with an infinitive. Instead, it sounds better to use the impersonal *it*. The infinitive follows the adjective or noun.	**To get** presents is fun. = It's fun **to get** presents. Is it universal **to celebrate** birthdays?
Gerunds	A gerund is the *-ing* form of a verb. It is different from that part of a continuous verb phrase because it is used as a noun in the sentence.	**Getting** presents is fun. Is **celebrating** birthdays universal?

Note: Not is placed in front of a gerund to make the gerund negative.

1 **Practice** Underline the gerund subjects and circle the infinitive subjects in the conversation on pages 290 and 291. (Be careful: Not all the -ing verbs are gerunds, and not all the infinitives are parts of grammatical subjects.) For the sentences with gerund subjects, can you make make infinitive sentences with the same meaning— and vice versa?

Examples It's so nice (to celebrate) your birthdays together. (= Celebrating your birthdays together is so nice.)

But Grandpa, having a birthday is very special. (= It's very special to have a birthday.)

2 **Practice** In two different ways, tell the opinions of these people about celebrating birthdays. Use each of the words or phrases in the balloons to form one sentence with a gerund as the subject and one sentence with an infinitive as the subject.

1.

> **a.** wonderful
> **b.** great

2.

> **a.** important
> **b.** a tradition

a. *Celebrating birthdays is wonderful*.

= *It's wonderful to celebrate birthdays*.

b._____.

=_____.

a._____.

=_____.

b._____.

=_____.

3.

a. silly

b. depressing

a._____.

=_____.

b._____.

=_____.

4.

a. a lot of work

b. a big mess

a._____.

=_____.

b._____.

=_____.

3 **Practice** Make an equivalent sentence with a gerund or an infinitive for each of the following sentences.

Example Guessing what's in the box is hard.

It's hard to guess what's in the box.

1. It's hard to blow up balloons.

_____

2. It's fun to make a birthday cake.

_____

3. Decorating the house with balloons and colored streamers takes time.

_____

4. Singing "Happy Birthday" is traditional.

_____

5. It's not easy to blow out all the candles.

_____

6. Making a wish before you blow out the candles is very important.

_____

7. Opening the presents is exciting.

_____

8. It's great to be with all of your friends.

_____

9. It's sad to say goodbye to your guests.

_____

10. Washing the dishes after the party isn't fun.

_____

Using What You've Learned

4 **Telling Traditions for Special Occasions** Choose a holiday or a celebration. One student tells a tradition that is a part of the holiday or celebration, with a gerund as the subject. Then the second student tells another tradition that is part of the holiday or celebration, again using a gerund as the subject. Keep taking turns until you cannot think of any more traditions. The last person to tell a tradition wins the game—_if_ he or she can repeat the previous traditions using infinitives as subjects. Play the game again with a new holiday or celebration. This time tell the traditions using infinitives as subjects. To win the game, the last person must repeat the same ideas with gerund subjects.

Example A: _Eating cake is a birthday tradition._

B: _Blowing out candles is a birthday tradition._

A: _Making a wish as you blow out the candles is a birthday tradition._

B: _Gettting presents is a birthday tradition._

A: _Getting cards is a birthday tradition._

B: _Singing "Happy Birthday" is a birthday tradition._

A: _I can't think of another birthday tradition!_

China

United States

Brazil

Prereading Questions Discuss these questions with a small group.

Do you enjoy New Year's celebrations? Why or why not? What do you usually do on New Year's Eve and New Year's Day?

Reading Read the passage.

New Year's Around the World

"New Year's is the most important festival of the year in my country. Because it is so important, most Chinese people insist **on doing** everything right to prepare for the celebration. People aren't satisfied **with** just **cleaning** their houses well before the New Year. It's important to clean them perfectly! It's also customary to write 5 good luck wishes on red paper and hang them all over the walls and doors of the house. Decorating our houses with flowers is another common custom. So is putting plates of oranges and tangerines all around (because oranges are symbols of happiness). **After preparing** for many days, finally on New Year's Eve and New Year's Day, 10 families get together and eat feasts of delicious, traditional foods. They get enthusiatic **about wearing** new clothes and **setting** off firecrackers. At midnight on New Year's Eve, we believe **in letting** the old year out **by leaving** every door and window in the house open."

—Yian Chen, China 15

"In my country, people usually get excited **about going** to New Year's Eve parties. Other people are content **with staying** home. At most New Year's Eve parties, people celebrate **by dancing, singing**, and **drinking** a toast to the New Year. At midnight, it's the custom to explode fireworks, blow horns, and hug and kiss. These parties can 20 go on for hours after midnight. I've heard **of** New Year's parties **lasting** until four or five o'clock in the morning! On New Year's Day, some people have to recover **from staying** out all night. **After celebrating** the New Year, many people make New Year's resolutions. (These are promises people make to themselves with the intention 25 **of changing** something about their lives.) For example, someone could decide 'I am tired **of being** overweight. I am going to go on a diet' or 'I'm going to work **at quitting smoking**.' Of course these are difficult promises and many people don't succeed **in keeping** them!"

—Justin Korfine, USA 30

"Everyone looks forward **to celebrating** the New Year in Brazil. In all the cities, we have a big party on New Year's Eve. Many Brazilians are happy **about being** with large groups of friends for the occasion. We have a special tradition for New Year's clothing: we believe **in wearing** white clothes on New Year's Eve because we think this brings good luck and peace for the coming year. After midnight, many people plan **on going** to the beach and **jumping** into the waves. It's customary to light candles in the sand and throw flowers in the sea **while making** a wish for the New Year. We expect fireworks to start at midnight and last for about half an hour. During this time, making wishes for the new year is the most common activity. We dream **of having** love, health, and fortune in the 12 months to come. It's a wonderful evening. I never get tired **of celebrating** New Year's."

— Carlos Huaman, Brazil

 Discussion Questions Discuss these questions with a partner.

1. How is New Year's celebrated in China?

2. How do people in the United States usually celebrate the New Year?

3. How is New Year's celebrated in Brazil?

4. What are some of the similarities and differences in the New Year's celebrations in these three countries?

5. How do people in your native culture or country usually celebrate the New Year?

Grammar Structures and Practice

A. Gerunds as Objects of Prepositions

Gerunds can be the objects of prepositions and can also have objects themselves.

10.2 Gerunds as Objects of Prepositions	
Explanations	**Examples**
Gerunds can be used as the objects of prepositions.	Thanks **for coming** to my party.
A gerund can have an object.	She wrapped the present **before giving it** to me.

1 Practice Fill in each blank with a gerund. Choose from the verbs in the box.

add	dry	serve
bake	eat	sit
buy	look	stand
carve	put	start
clear	save	stuff

Thanksgiving is a holiday celebrated in November in the United States and in October in Canada. People celebrate this holiday by getting together with family or friends to give thanks for their good fortune and to eat a large turkey dinner.

Making Thanksgiving dinner is not an easy job. Only by _____*starting*_____

very early can the cook finish everything. Some cooks save time by

_____ the rolls and pies instead of _____ them
　　　　　1　　　　　　　　　　　　　　　　　　　　　2

themselves. Before _____ the turkey into the oven, the cook
　　　　　　　　　　　3

usually fills it with a bread mixture. By _____ the turkey, he or
　　　　　　　　　　　　　　　　　　　4

she prevents it from _____ out. Three to six hours later, the
　　　　　　　　　　5

turkey is ready. After _____ it with a sharp knife and
　　　　　　　　　　6

_____ it to family and guests, the cook can finally sit down and
　　　7

enjoy the meal.

It seems that only a short time after _____ down at the table,
                                            8

everyone finishes. After _____ all that food, no one feels much
                              9

like getting up. Especially because they know, without even _____,
                                                                    10

that the kitchen is a complete mess. Finally, one brave family member starts by

_____ up and beginning to clear off the plates. After
      11

_____ everything off the table, the family has to put away the
      12

leftover food. Many cooks plan for turkey soup or turkey sandwiches by

_____ all the leftover turkey. Some cooks even save the carcass.
      13

By _____ the bones to soup, cooks make a rich, flavorful broth
       14

their families will enjoy for days.

B. Gerunds After Adjectives with Prepositions

A gerund can follow an adjective-preposition combination.

10.3 Gerunds After Adjectives and Prepositions		
Expressions		**Examples**
afraid of	nervous about	I'm **pleased about spending** the holidays with you.
capable of	pleased about	
content with	responsible for	I'm **responsible for cooking** the holiday dinner.
dedicated to	sad about	
enthusiastic about	satisfied with	Do you get **nervous about entertaining** guests in your home?
excited about	scared of	
famous for	tired of	Which holidays are you most **interested in?**
happy about	worried about	
interested in		

Note: In an infinitive phrase, the word *to* is not a preposition. Compare: *We're dedicated **to following** traditions* versus *It's important **to follow** tradition.*

---

2 Practice Look back at the reading on pages 296 and 297. Then answer the questions below with full sentences. Base your answers on the reading or on your own experiences, as appropriate.

Example What aren't many Chinese people satisfied with doing before the New Year?
Many Chinese people aren't satisfied with just cleaning their houses well before the New Year.

1. What do many Americans get excited about doing on New Year's Eve?

   _____

2. What are other Americans content with doing on New Year's Eve?

   _____

3. What do many Brazilians believe in doing on New Year's Eve?

   _____

4. Are you satisfied with celebrating New Year's Eve the way you usually do?

   _____

5. Are you interested in doing anything different next New Year's Eve?

   _____

3 Practice Underline the gerunds after the prepositions in your answers to Activity 2. Circle the prepositions. Is the word before each preposition a noun, a verb, an adjective, or a preposition?

Example *Many Chinese people aren't satisfied (with) just cleaning their houses well before the New Year.*
(word before preposition = satisfied, adjective)

4 Practice Complete the sentences with the missing prepositions and gerunds. Use *with, to, of,* or *about* with the verbs in parentheses.

El Dia de los Muertos (The Day of the Dead) is one of the most popular

holidays in Mexico. It is a holiday to remember ancestors, family members, and friends who have died. It is believed that the spirits of the dead return to visit with

the living on this day. The people are not scared _____*of visiting*_____ with the
                                                              (visit)

spirits of the dead. Instead, they are happy _____ the dead and
                                                         1 (honor)

they are excited _____in the many activities that are a part of the
                        2 (participate)

holiday.

During the Day of the Dead, families visit cemeteries and gather around the

graves of relatives who have died. People are not sad _____to the
                                                                  3 (go)

graveyards. Instead, they are happy _____ with each other and
                                                4 (be)

with the spirits of their loved ones. Part of this day is dedicated

_____ and decorating the graves of the dead. Local musicians are
        5 (clean)

often hired to come to the cemeteries as well. They are responsible

_____ the favorite songs of the people who have died. People
        6 (play)

stay at the graves together until late at night. They are not nervous

_____ there. They are pleased _____ this time
        7 (be)   8 (spend)

together. During the night, hundreds of candles are lit and gifts of food and flowers

are left for the dead.

Many activities take place in the home during this holiday as well. In homes

across the country, tables full of food and drink are laid out for the dead. People

are not satisfied _____ small offerings. Instead, these tables are
                          9 (prepare)

filled with flowers, candles, fruits, vegetables, and the favorite foods of individual

spirits. Paths of flower petals and burning incense lead spirits to the houses of their

living relatives. After the spirits have had a chance to enjoy the food and drink

prepared for them, the living people are excited _____ the food
                                                              10 (eat)

that is "left over." Of course, since the spirits of the dead aren't capable

_____ very much, this leaves a lot of food for the living!
        11 (eat)

5 Practice Finish each of the following sentences with true statements about people on holidays or special occasions. Use gerunds.

Example Some people are afraid of ___*walking alone at night on Halloween*___.

1. Some people are afraid of _____.
2. Most of them are capable of _____.
3. In my native culture, people get excited about _____

   _____.
4. They're usually good at _____.
5. I'm especially interested in _____.
6. I don't generally get nervous about _____.
7. In my family, I'm responsible for _____.
8. But personally, I'm getting tired of _____.

 6 Practice Take turns sharing your true statements from Activity 5 with a partner. Make comments about your partner's statements.

Examples A: *Some people are afraid of walking alone at night on Halloween.*
B: *In my opinion, they should be. I always ask someone to go with me.*

A: *Most people are capable of eating a lot of candy on Halloween.*
B: *Yeah, I know. People are enthusiastic about eating sweets on most special occasions.*

C. Gerunds and Phrasal Verbs

This section gives examples of gerunds that follow phrasal verbs or verb-preposition combinations.

10.4 Gerunds and Phrasal Verbs		
Explanations	**Expressions**	**Examples**
A gerund can follow a phrasal verb or verb–preposition combination. The preposition can have an object in addition to the gerund.	admit to believe in choose between count on plan on dream of apologize for give up heard of look forward to object to thank (someone) for think of recover from	I **plan on going** home for Christmas. My husband **apologized for forgetting** my birthday

7 **Practice** Look back at the reading on pages 296 and 297. Then answer the questions below with full sentences.

1. What do many Chinese people believe in doing at midnight on New Year's Eve?

_____

2. What do some Americans have to recover from doing on New Year's Day?

_____

3. What don't many Americans succeed in keeping?

_____

4. What do many Brazilians believe in wearing on New Year's Eve?

_____

5. What do many Brazilians dream of having in the New Year?

_____

8 **Practice** Underline the gerunds after the phrasal verbs in your answers to Activity 7.

Example _Many Chinese people believe in leaving all doors and windows open at midnight on New Year's Eve._

9 **Practice** Fill in each of the blanks with the missing preposition and gerund. Use _of, for, on,_ or _between_ and the verb in parentheses.

Valentine's Day is a holiday that celebrates love. It is celebrated in many parts of the world. It is common to send cards, flowers, or gifts to express affection on Valentine's Day. In the following conversation, Michael has just received flowers on Valentine's Day. The card that came with the flowers says only "From a Secret Admirer."

Michael: (to himself) Red roses! They're beautiful! I bet they're from Janet. It's so nice of her to think ___*of sending*___ me flowers on Valentine's
(send)
Day. I'll call her. (He dials Janet's number. The phone rings.)

Janet: Hello?

Michael: Hi, Janet. It's Mike. I just wanted to thank you

_____ so romantic. I've often dreamed
1 (be)

_____ roses from a woman.
2 (get)

Janet: Roses? I . . . uh . . . didn't send you roses. Anyway, haven't you heard?

Phil and I are dating.

Michael: Sorry, Janet! I didn't know! I apologize _____.
3 (call)

Janet: Why don't you try calling Sarah?

Michael: Sarah?

Janet: She told me that she was thinking _____ you
4 (send)

flowers. The last time I spoke with her, she was trying to choose

_____ you a card or flowers.
5 (send)

Michael: Really? I didn't even know that she liked me.

Janet: She's been planning _____ you, but she's so shy!
6 (tell)

Michael: Wow. Thanks _____ me know. I've always had a
7 (let)

crush on her, too! I'm going to call her right now.

Using What You've Learned

10 **Doing Research About a Holiday** As a group, use the Internet or resource books in the library to find out about a holiday from another culture. Prepare a description of the holiday for the class, using as many gerunds as you can.

Example *Germans look forward to celebrating Fasching (Carnival) near the end of every winter. Dancing and participating in parades are common activities, and it's traditional to wear costumes. People look forward to having a great time at Fasching.*

11 **Creating a Special-Occasion Role Play** Write a role play that takes place during a holiday. Perform your role play for the class. You may want to include some of these phrasal verbs:

approve of	feel like	put off
believe in	forget about	rule out
care about	get out of	succeed in
count on	hear of	talk about
decide against	look forward to	work at
dream of	plan on	worry about

12 **Making More Sentences About Celebrations** Take turns reading aloud an example of an adjective-preposition and verb-preposition combination from the lists in the boxes below. Name a holiday or special occasion, too. Your partner must use the combination to make up a sentence about that occasion with a logical gerund.

Example A: *Good at (Christmas).*
B: *Hmmm. My roommate is very good at wrapping presents at Christmas.*
OK, it's your turn: dream about (Halloween).
A: *I dream about running away from monsters on Halloween.*

Common Adjective-Preposition Combinations

adequate for	famous for	preferable to
afraid of	good at/for	proud of
aware of	guilty of	responsible for
capable of	happy about	similar to
careful about	innocent of	sorry for
content with	jealous of	successful in
enough for	necessary for	tired of

Common Verb-Preposition Combinations

approve of	feel like	plan on
ask about	forget about	put off
believe in	get out of	rule out
count on	hear of	succeed in
decide against	look forward to	talk about
dream of/about	object to	worry about

Setting the Context

 Prereading Questions Discuss these questions with a small group.

Do you know what "body language" is? What common gestures and movements of yours come to mind?

Reading Reaad the passage.

Body Language

In addition to holidays and other traditions, many body movements and gestures, sometimes called *body language*, are specific to a particular culture. For example, in some cultures, when two friends **want to greet** each other, they **tend to kiss** on the cheek or hug. In other cultures, women **like to hug** or **kiss** each other, while men **choose to** shake hands. In some cultures, people may

5

prefer standing very close while speaking to each other, while in others, people may **avoid standing** closer than arms' length. In some cultures, people commonly use their hands to gesture **while speaking**. However, in others, people are **taught to speak** quietly **while keeping** their hands still. **Before visiting** another country, a person should **consider learning** about the body language used in that country. Otherwise, the visitor could **risk insulting** others **by** accidentally **using** inappropriate body language.

10

 Discussion Questions Discuss these questions with a partner.

1. In the pictures, how do each pair of people outside the restaurant greet each other?

2. What kinds of body language do you notice inside the restaurant?

3. According to the reading, what are some examples of the ways body language can be different in different cultures?

4. What countries or cultures could each of the examples in the reading refer to?

5. Which forms of "body language" are common in your country?

Grammar Structures and Practice

A. Verbs Followed by Gerunds

Certain verbs must be followed by a gerund.

10.5 Verbs Followed by Gerunds		
Explanation	**Verbs**	**Examples**
If a verb comes after these verbs, it must be the gerund (*-ing*) form.	avoid discuss quit celebrate dislike risk consider enjoy suggest deny keep understand	He **avoids going** to parties. My parents **enjoy cooking** holiday meals.

B. Verbs Often Followed by Gerunds or Infinitives

Certain verbs are often followed by either a gerund or infinitive.

10.6 Verbs Often Followed by Gerunds or Infinitives				
Explanation	**Verbs**			**Examples**
Either a gerund or an infinitive can follow these verbs with little or no difference in meaning.	begin can't stand continue	hate intend like	love prefer start	I **hate celebrating** my birthday. I **start shopping** for Christmas in October.

1 **Practice** Fill in each of the blanks with one of the verbs from the box.

avoid	keep
can't stand	like
consider	quit
continue	risk

1. Why do you _____*keep*_____ interrupting me? In my culture, we never interrupt a speaker!

2. Some people _____ making eye contact with strangers to be rude.

3. Many people _____ to sit next to smokers in restaurants.

4. In many countries, people _____ standing very close to one another.

5. In Mexico City, guests _____ being alone if they arrive on time for a party.

6. _____ pointing! Don't you know that it's rude to point?

7. In Asian cultures, people often _____ smiling, even when they are angry or upset.

8. Wine is a very popular drink in France. In fact, some French children even _____ drinking a little wine with their dinner.

2 **Practice** Fill in each blank with a verb-gerund phrase in the appropriate tense. Use the two verbs in parentheses.

The Dinner Party (Part 1)

Martin was pleased when his American friend, Keith, invited him to a dinner

party on Friday night. Martin immediately _____*began planning*_____ for the party. He

(begin/plan)

_____ gifts to people, so he asked his roommate, Kevin, for
     1 (like / bring)

suggestions. Kevin _____ a bottle of wine. But Martin didn't drink
                      2 (suggest / take)

wine, so he bought Keith a new CD player for his car. Kevin also _____
                                                                   3 (advise / wear)

casual clothes to the party, but Martin _____ his best suit and tie.
                                          4 (prefer / wear)

C. Verbs Before Objects and Gerunds

Certain verbs that take objects can come before gerunds.

10.7	**Verbs Before Objects and Gerunds**		
Explanation	**Verbs**		**Examples**
The object of the main verb performs the action of the *-ing* verb.	feel hear see find notice watch		The waiter **heard the man singing**. Didn't you **notice them waving**?

Note: Certain verbs that are often followed directly by gerunds can also be followed by objects and gerunds. These verbs include: *appreciate, can't stand, (don't) mind, hate,* and *like.*

3 **Practice** Fill in each blank with a verb-gerund phrase in the appropriate tense. Use the two verbs (and the object, if there is one) in parentheses.

The Dinner Party (Part 2)

When Friday night arrived, Martin ___*started getting*___ ready several hours
                                          (start / get)

in advance. The invitation said that the party was going to begin at 7:30. Martin

always _____ late, so he arrived at Keith's house at 7:00. He
          1 (avoid / be)

_____ in the kitchen, and he _____ a shower.
2 (find / Keith's girlfriend / cook)   3 (hear / Keith / take)

After Keith got dressed, he came out to the kitchen to talk to Martin. "Martin, I

didn't know that you were coming early! Would you _____ me
                                                    4 (mind / help)

with some cooking?"

Martin didn't want to _____ mistakes in Keith's kitchen, so he
                        5 (risk / make)

didn't help. Instead, he _____ to Keith while Keith worked.
                          6 (continue / talk)

Martin also gave him the present.

"Martin, I really _____ me this lovely gift, but I can't accept it.
7 (appreciate / your / give)

It's too much," said Keith. Martin felt embarrassed. "Please take it. I

_____ gifts." Then Keith had an idea. "I _____ it
8 (hate / return)   9 (suggest / keep)

for yourself, Martin."

4 **Practice** Combine each pair of ideas into one sentence with a gerund.

1. Keith heard + Martin was talking to his girlfriend in the kitchen.
   Keith heard Martin talking to his girlfriend in the kitchen.

2. Martin saw + Keith's sister was sitting in front of the TV.

   _____

3. He enjoyed + He was watching the show with her.

   _____

4. Finally Martin heard + Other guests were arriving.

   _____

5. He noticed + They were wearing casual clothes.

   _____

6. Martin continued + He was focusing on the program.

   _____

7. Keith saw + Martin was paying attention to the TV.

   _____

8. Keith noticed + He was ignoring the other guests.

   _____

5 Practice Complete each sentence with your own ideas. Use gerunds in each sentence. Then compare sentences with one or two classmates.

Example I can't stand people _____ *talking very loudly in restaurants* _____.

1. I can't stand people _____.
2. I sometimes hear people _____.
3. I sometimes notice other students _____.
4. My teacher doesn't mind me _____.
5. Have you seen anyone _____?
6. I really appreciate friends _____.

D. Verbs Before Objects and Simple Forms of Verbs

The verbs *have, let*, and *make* can all appear as the first verb in the pattern verb + object + verb.

10.8	Verbs Before Objects and Simple Forms of Verbs	
Explanation	**Examples**
In general, verbs of perception that can take the pattern verb + object + verb *-ing* (such as *see, watch, notice,* and *hear*) can also appear in the pattern verb + object + verb. The *-ing* form of the verb emphasizes the continuation of the action.	**Let me introduce** myself. I **watched them cook.** I **watched them cooking.**

6 Practice Fill in each blank with the appropriate tense and form of the two verbs and the object in parentheses.

The Dinner Party (Part 3)

From his chair in front of the TV set, Martin _____ *watched the guests socialize* _____.
                                            (watch / the guests / socialize)

He waited for Keith to introduce him to his friends, but Keith was busy. Finally, a

woman who _____ there spoke to him.
           1 (see / Martin / sit)

"Hi. _____ myself. I'm Susan. I'm Keith's cousin. Don't you
      2 (let / me / introduce)

have anything to drink? I'll _____ you something."
                            3 (have / Keith / fix)

Martin was thirsty, but he wanted to be polite. "No, Susan. I don't want to

_____ me," he answered.
     4 (make / Keith / serve)

     "Okay," said Susan. "Anyway, it's time for dinner. Come on. I'll _____
                                                                          5 (have / you / sit)
next to me."

     "Thank you," said Martin. " _____ you with your chair." "Oh,
                                    6 (let / me / help)
Martin. That's not necessary. You're so old fashioned!"

     As Martin _____ out her own chair, he thought to himself "I
                    7 (watch / Susan / pull)
have a lot to learn about this culture."

Using What You've Learned

7 **Retelling a Story** The goal of this activity is to try to retell all three parts of "The Dinner Party" without looking back at the story. Form a circle with a small group. Going around the circle, each person contributes one sentence to the story, using a gerund, if possible. Continue going around the circle as many times as necessary until the story is complete.

Example: A: *OK. I think the story began when Keith invited Martin to a dinner party.*
B: *Right. Then Martin began planning for the party.*
C: *Then Martin discussed buying a present with his roommate.*

8 **Discussing the Story** In small groups, discuss the story "The Dinner Party." Answer these questions, using gerunds when possible.

1. What social mistakes did Martin make?

2. What mistakes might he make next?

3. What social rules are there for dinner parties in your culture?

Example *Martin insisted on wearing a suit. When he noticed the other guests wearing casual clothes, he felt uncomfortable.*

Summarize your discussion for the class.

Part 2. Circle the letter below the underlined word(s) containing the error.

Example   Many <u>children</u> are afraid <u>of</u> <u>to sleeping</u> <u>in</u> the dark.
                     A   B   ©   D

1. <u>Get married</u> <u>can be</u> one of <u>the biggest</u> events of a <u>person's</u> life.
       A   B   C   D

2. A: <u>I have</u> never <u>liked</u> the taste of alcohol.
          A   B

     B: <u>Neither</u> <u>do</u> I.
        C   D

3. I <u>try</u> <u>to start</u> <u>shop</u> for the holidays <u>in</u> October.
       A   B   C   D

4. The waiter <u>heard</u> the man <u>to call</u>, but he <u>was</u> too busy <u>to answer</u>.
                  A   B   C   D

Self-Assessment Log

Each of the following sentences describes the grammar you learned in this chapter. Read the sentences and then check the best box for how well you understand each structure.

	Needs Improvement	Good	Great
I can use gerunds and infinitives to talk about celebrations.	❑	❑	❑
I can use gerunds with prepositions to talk about holidays.	❑	❑	❑
I can use gerunds after adjectives and prepositions to describe holidays and celebrations.	❑	❑	❑
I can use gerunds with phrasal verbs to talk about customs and holidays.	❑	❑	❑
I can use verbs before objects, gerunds, infinitives, and simple forms of verbs to describe parties and customs.	❑	❑	❑
I practiced taking a test about gerunds, infinitives, and verbs.	❑	❑	❑

Appendix 1

Parts of Speech, Sentence Parts/Word Order Chart, and Grammar Terms

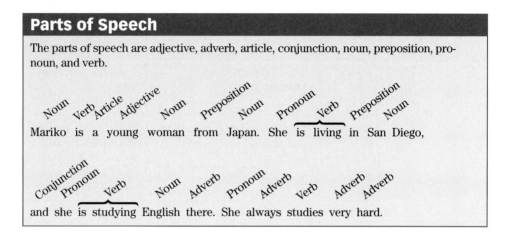

Parts of Speech

The parts of speech are adjective, adverb, article, conjunction, noun, preposition, pronoun, and verb.

Noun Verb Article Adjective Noun Preposition Noun Pronoun Verb Preposition Noun
Mariko is a young woman from Japan. She is living in San Diego,

Conjunction Pronoun Verb Noun Adverb Pronoun Adverb Verb Adverb Adverb
and she is studying English there. She always studies very hard.

Sentence Parts/Word Order Chart

Subject	Verb	Phrase	Subject	Verb	Object
Mariko Mariko	is studies	from Japan. every night.	Mariko She	studies does	English. her homework.

Grammar Terms

Term	Definition	Examples
Singular	= one	a boy one dog
Plural	= two or more	boys three dogs
Subject	= the main person, place, thing or idea in a sentence	**Mariko** came yesterday. **She** is from Japan. **Her mother** is going to visit her soon.
Verb	= an action or situation	Mariko **came** yesterday. She **is** from Japan.
Object	= the receiver of an action	Mariko met **her mother** at the airport. Mariko bought **a present** for her mother.
Phrase	= two or more words together	yesterday afternoon from Japan in the United States
Sentence	= a subject/verb combination that expresses a complete idea	Mariko came yesterday afternoon. She is from Japan. She is living in the United States. (not: She from Japan. 　　　She in the United States.)

Appendix 2

Numbers and Calendar Information

Numbers

This chart gives you both the cardinal and the ordinal numbers. Note that the thirties, forties, and so on, follow the same pattern as the twenties.

Cardinal	Ordinal	Cardinal	Ordinal
zero		twenty	twentieth
one	first	twenty-one	twenty-first
two	second	twenty-two	twenty-second
three	third	twenty-three	twenty-third
four	fourth	twenty-four	twenty-fourth
five	fifth	twenty-five	twenty-fifth
six	sixth	twenty-six	twenty-sixth
seven	seventh	twenty-seven	twenty-seventh
eight	eighth	twenty-eight	twenty-eighth
nine	ninth	twenty-nine	twenty-ninth
ten	tenth	thirty	thirtieth
eleven	eleventh	forty	fortieth
twelve	twelfth	fifty	fiftieth
thirteen	thirteenth	sixty	sixtieth
fourteen	fourteenth	seventy	seventieth
fifteen	fifteenth	eighty	eightieth
sixteen	sixteenth	ninety	ninetieth
seventeen	seventeenth	(one) hundred	(one) hundredth
eighteen	eighteenth	(one) thousand	(one) thousandth
nineteen	nineteenth	(one) million	(one) millionth

Calendar Information

Days of the Week		Months of the Year		Seasons
Sunday	Sun.	January	Jan.	winter
Monday	Mon.	February	Feb.	spring
Tuesday	Tues.	March	Mar.	summer
Wednesday	Wed.	April	Apr.	autumn or fall
Thursday	Thurs.	May		
Friday	Fri.	June		
Saturday	Sat.	July		
		August	Aug.	
		September	Sept.	
		October	Oct.	
		November	Nov.	
		December	Dec.	

Appendix 3

Irregular Verbs

Simple Form	Past	Past Participle	Simple Form	Past	Past Participle
arise	arose	arisen	flee	fled	fled
awake	awoke/awaked	awaked/awoken	fly	flew	flown
be	was/were	been	forbid	forbade	forbidden
bear	bore	borne/born	forget	forgot	forgotten
beat	beat	beat	forsake	forsook	forsaken
become	became	become	freeze	froze	frozen
begin	began	begun	get	got	got/gotten
bend	bent	bent	give	gave	given
bet	bet	bet	go	went	gone
bite	bit	bitten	grind	ground	ground
bleed	bled	bled	grow	grew	grown
blow	blew	blown	hang	hung/hanged	hung/hanged
break	broke	broken	have	had	had
breed	bred	bred	hear	heard	heard
bring	brought	brought	hide	hid	hidden
broadcast	broadcast	broadcast	hit	hit	hit
build	built	built	hold	held	held
burst	burst	burst	hurt	hurt	hurt
buy	bought	bought	keep	kept	kept
cast	cast	cast	know	knew	known
catch	caught	caught	lay	laid	laid
choose	chose	chosen	lead	led	led
cling	clung	clung	leap	leapt	leapt
come	came	come	leave	left	left
cost	cost	cost	lend	lent	lent
creep	crept	crept	let	let	let
cut	cut	cut	lie	lay	lain
deal	dealt	dealt	light	lit/lighted	lit/lighted
dig	dug	dug	lose	lost	lost
do	did	done	make	made	made
draw	drew	drawn	mean	meant	meant
drink	drank	drunk	meet	met	met
drive	drove	driven	overcome	overcame	overcome
eat	ate	eaten	pay	paid	paid
fall	fell	fallen	prove	proved	proved/proven*
feed	fed	fed	put	put	put
feel	felt	felt	quit	quit	quit
fight	fought	fought	read	read	read
find	found	found	ride	rode	ridden

Appendix 3

Irregular Verbs

Simple Form	Past	Past Participle	Simple Form	Past	Past Participle
ring	rang	arisen	stand	stood	stood
rise	rose	awaked/awoken	steal	stole	stolen
run	ran	been	stick	stuck	stuck
say	said	borne/born	sting	stung	stung
see	saw	beat	strike	struck	struck/stricken*
seek	sought	become	strive	strove	striven
sell	sold	begun	swear	swore	sworn
send	sent	bent	sweep	swept	swept
set	set	bet	swim	swam	swum
shake	shook	bitten	swing	swung	swung
shoot	shot	bled	take	took	taken
show	showed	blown	teach	taught	taught
shut	shut	broken	tear	tore	torn
sing	sang	bred	tell	told	told
sink	sank	brought	think	thought	thought
sit	sat	broadcast	throw	threw	thrown
sleep	slept	built	thrust	thrust	thrust
slide	slid	burst	understand	understood	understood
slit	slit	bought	upset	upset	upset
speak	spoke	cast	wake	woke/waked	woken/waked
spend	spent	caught	wear	wore	worn
spin	spun	chosen	weave	wove	woven
split	split	clung	wind	wound	wound
spread	spread	come	withdraw	withdrew	withdrawn
spring	sprang		write	wrote	written

*These participles are often used with the passive voice.

Appendix 4

Spelling Rules and Irregular Noun Plurals

Spelling Rules for *-s, -ed, -er, -est,* and *-ing* Endings

This chart summarizes the basic spelling rules for endings with verbs, nouns, adjectives, and adverbs.

Rule	Word	*-s*	*-ed*	*-er*	*-est*	*-ing*
For most words, simply add *-s, -ed, -er, -est,* or *-ing* without making any other changes.	clean cool	cleans cools	cleaned cooled	cleaner cooler	cleanest coolest	cleaning cooling

Spelling changes occur with the following.

Rule	Word	*-s*	*-ed*	*-er*	*-est*	*-ing*
For words ending in a consonant + *y*, change the *y* to *i* before adding *-s, -ed, -er,* or *-est*. Do *not* change or drop the *y* before adding *-ing*.	carry happy lonely study worry	carries studies worries	carried studied worried	carrier happier lonelier worrier	happiest loneliest	carrying studying worrying
For most words ending in *e*, drop the e before adding *-ed, -er, -est,* or *-ing*. *Exceptions:*	dance late nice save write agree canoe		danced saved	dancer later nicer saver writer	latest nicest	dancing saving writing agreeing canoeing
For many words ending in one vowel and one consonant, double the final consonant before adding *-ed, -er, -est,* or *-ing*. These include one-syllable words and words with stress on the final syllable.	begin hot mad plan occur refer run shop win		planned occurred referred shopped	beginner hotter madder planner runner shopper winner	hottest maddest	beginning planning occurring referring running shopping winning

Spelling changes occur with the following.

Rule	Word	-s	-ed	-er	-est	-ing
In words ending in one vowel and one consonant, do *not* double the final consonant if the last syllable is not stressed. *Exceptions:* including words ending in *w*, *x*, or *y*	enter happen open travel visit bus fix play sew	buses	entered happened opened traveled visited bused fixed played sewed	opener traveler fixer player sewer		entering happening opening traveling visiting busing fixing playing sewing
For most words ending in *f* or *lf*, change the *f* to *v* and add *-es*. *Exceptions:*	half loaf shelf belief chief proof roof safe	halves loaves shelves beliefs chiefs proofs roofs safes	halved shelved	shelver		halving shelving
For words ending in *ch*, *sh*, *s*, *x*, *z*, and sometimes *o*, add *-es*. *Exceptions:*	church wash class fix quiz tomato zero dynamo ghetto monarch piano portfolio radio studio	churches washes classes fixes quizzes tomatoes zeroes dynamos ghettos monarchs pianos portfolios radios studios				

Irregular Noun Plurals

person	people	foot	feet	deer	deer	series	series
child	children	tooth	teeth	fish	fish	species	species
man	men			goose	geese		
woman	women			ox	oxen		

Irregular Noun Plurals with Foreign Origins

alumnus	alumni	analysis	analyses	basis	bases	crisis	crises
criterion	criteria	curriculum	curricula	hypothesis	hypotheses	oasis	oases
memorandum	memoranda	synthesis	syntheses	thesis	theses	radius	radii
phenomenon	phenomena	nucleus	nuclei	stimulus	stimuli		
syllabus	syllabi or syllabuses						
index	indices or indexes						

Appendix 5

Pronunciation Guidelines for -s and -ed Endings

-s Endings: The -s ending of verbs and nouns is pronounced in three different ways: /-s/, /-z/, and /-ɪz/. Practice the words below, paying attention to the pronunciation of the endings.

/-s/	/-z/	/-ɪz/
hops	beings	boxes
picks	goes	buzzes
starts	needs	kisses
	studies	washes
	travels	watches

-ed Endings: The -ed ending of verbs is pronounced in three different ways: -t, -d, and -ɪd. Practice the words below, paying attention to the pronunciation of the endings.

/-t/	/-d/	/-ɪd/
helped	carried	needed
looked	climbed	persisted
watched	robbed	waited
zipped	traveled	wanted

Photo Credits

Skills Index

verbs
- before objects, 13, 56, 311
- gerunds after, 307–309
- infinitives after, 219–220, 235, 308
- irregular, 147–148, 164
- modal, 56–58, 88, 100, 200, 219–220, 245, 252–253
- nonaction, 52–53, 229, 268
- with object and infinitive, 197
- past participles, 163–164, 165
- phrasal, 108, 111–112, 302
- *See also* infinitives; present tense

want, 197
wasn't, 148
weren't, 148
what, 19, 141, 143, 166, 268
when, 20, 97, 141, 155, 230
where, 19, 141
which, 214, 216–217
while, 97, 230
who, 19, 141, 143, 166, 214, 217, 268
whom, 19, 141, 217

whose, 41
why, 20, 141
will, 56–58, 88, 100, 245
with, 119
won't, 245
would, 88, 245
yes/no questions/answers
- alternative words for, 11
- with *be* forms, 8, 148
- with *be going to,* 96
- with modal verbs, 57
- with past continuous tense, 226
- with past tense, 140
- with present continuous tense, 47
- with present perfect continuous tense, 268
- with present perfect tense, 165, 258
- with present tense, 17
- with simple future tense, 100
yet, 169
you, 88